Making Sound Credit Policy Decisions

By
Frederick C. Scherr

National Association of Credit Management
8840 Columbia 100 Parkway
Columbia, MD 21045-2158

Address Inquiries to:
National Association of Credit Management
Attn: Publications Department
8840 Columbia 100 Parkway
Columbia, MD 21045-2158

ISBN 0-934914-99-0

Printed in the United States of America

10 9 8 7 6 5 4 3

Table of Contents

Chapter 4. Negotiating the Conditions of Credit-Granting

Chapter 5. Credit Limits

Chapter 6. Expert and Statistical Scoring Systems

Chapter 7. Terms of Sale and Collection Policy

Chapter 8. Monitoring Credit Performance

Chapter 9. Credit Strategy

Preface

Trade credit, also known as industrial or business credit, is credit granted by a business seller to a business buyer for the purpose of purchasing goods and services. It is a pervasive feature of the business world.

The management of trade credit is about *making decisions*; decisions about how much credit investigation should be performed, who should get credit, how much credit should be granted, and so forth. We can break credit decision-making into two parts: *credit analysis* and *credit policy-making*. Credit analysis is frontline decision-making: decisions about credit investigation, credit-granting, and collection that are made regarding individual customers. Credit analysis is the main function of the average credit employee, and there is a great deal of useful literature available on how to perform this function.

But prior to any credit analysis, a broader and deeper evaluation of the relationship between credit and the selling firm's goals, strengths, and objectives must be performed. The intent of this evaluation is to formulate credit policy—i.e., the guidelines by which credit analysis is to be undertaken and decisions based on credit analysis are to be made. Credit policy specifies these guidelines based on tradeoffs among the various benefits and costs that granting and administering trade credit presents to the selling firm. In the language of the military, credit policy is strategic while credit analysis is tactical, and tactics follow strategy.

Unfortunately, little literature is available which addresses the making of credit policy. This book attempts to fill this gap by presenting the principles inherent in advantageous credit policy.

It is important to understand at the outset that no "cookbook" solutions to the formulation of credit policy are possible; there are no magic formulas for credit policy-making. Advantageous policy-making involves *understanding and making tradeoffs among benefits and costs*. Therefore, this book centers on the benefits and costs associated with various credit policy decisions.

Who Should Read this Book

This book is primarily intended for people who make trade credit policy for business firms. People who perform credit analysis and make frontline decisions regarding customers will also find it useful in understanding the policies they implement and in preparing themselves for their eventual role in policy formation.

Every book must assume something from its readers, and this book is no exception. Readers are assumed to be proficient in the basic methodologies of credit analysis and collections (analysis of the financial statements of debtors and similar topics) and are assumed to have a basic knowledge of the principles of financial management for business firms.

What is in this Book

This text deals with policy decisions which are unique to credit management, rather than decisions which are generic to all managers (such as hiring and firing). Chapter 1 introduces the topic. Chapters 2 through 7 address four basic aspects of credit policy:

1. *Credit Investigation.* What types of credit investigation should the analyst be guided to perform? How much credit investigation should be performed?

2. *Credit-Granting.* Who should get credit? How much credit should be granted? How should mechanisms to enhance credit-granting (guarantees, etc.) affect the credit-granting decision?

3. *Terms of Sale.* What terms of sale should the firm use? When should terms of sale be changed? Should cash discount terms of sale be used to detect changes in customer creditworthiness?

4. *Collections.* What collection strategies should collection personnel be guided to use? How rapid and aggressive should collection policy be?

When decisions are made regarding these aspects of credit policy, the credit manager will have certain expectations about the outcomes of these policy decisions; further, these outcomes will have important effects on the selling firm's profitability. Therefore, the credit manager needs good and reliable tools to accurately monitor the outcomes of credit policy decisions, and Chapter 8 is devoted to discussion of this monitoring task.

Chapter 9 deals with three broader strategic topics: the coordination of credit policy with the firm's overall strategy, alternatives to in-house trade credit management (outsourcing strategies), and credit strategy for smaller firms. Each chapter concludes with a summary of its implications for credit policy-making and with a short case for analysis and discussion. Example responses to this case are provided at the end of the text. The numerical tables presented in the chapters, cases, appendices, and case responses are included as Lotus 123 version 2.0 files on the computer disk which accompanies this text.

Acknowledgments

This book applies the principles of modern financial management to credit policy decisions. Kudos are due to the many financial researchers who contributed to the development of the financial principles on which modern financial management is based. Much of the material presented here was originally developed for the various educational programs and publications administered by the National Association of Credit Management, and the author gratefully acknowledges the support of the NACM in these endeavors. Finally, appreciation is due to the many participants in the author's NACM-sponsored educational sessions; these individuals provided invaluable feedback on many of the topics addressed here.

—FCS

How to Use the Disk

Included with this text is a CD containing files for all the numerical tables from the chapters, cases and appendices as Microsoft Excel files. Each table is a separate file on the CD.

While no text can provide examples of the analysis of every credit policy situation that the credit manager may face, these tables can be customized to help with decision-making in many circumstances. However, some proficiency in spreadsheet analysis is required, and the credit manager should be very careful to be sure that the analysis captures the relevant elements of the decision to be made.

Note that this CD is protected under copyright laws. It is for personal use only.

1 Trade Credit Management and the Goals of the Firm

In this introductory chapter, we describe principles for the analysis of credit policy that are used throughout the remainder of this book. The relationship between the firm's goals, its organizational structure, and trade credit policy-making are addressed first. The maximization of the value of the firm's common stock (its value to its owners) is presented and defended as the most important goal of the firm. We will see that a major problem occurs in many firms because their organizational structure causes conflict in the achievement of this goal. We will explore the approaches to credit policy formulation that flow from various organizational structures. The effects of credit policy decisions on the firm's various costs and revenues are then examined. This is followed by a discussion of two mathematical approaches by which the effects of these costs and revenues on the firm can be evaluated. Concluding this chapter is a summary of the policy implications of the material presented and a case for discussion and analysis.

The Goals of the Firm and Their Implementation

The firm's decisions must revolve around one or more goals. For large firms whose stock is publicly traded, the single most important corporate goal must be to maximize the *long-run value of the firm's stock*. This means that the firm works to enhance its value in the interest of its owners, the shareholders. There are at least two good reasons why this is an overriding goal. First is the moral principle that it is the duty of managers, as employees of the shareholders, to act in shareholders' interests. There is little that managers can do to assist shareholders except to enhance the value of the firm to increase shareholders' wealth. Second, if managers do not act in shareholders' interests, management can be removed. A third party can buy up a controlling interest (a takeover) or shareholders can remove managers via action by the Board of Directors.

Smaller privately-held firms face a somewhat more complex problem in developing their goal structures. For these firms, there are more ways that the firm can affect the well-being of the owner-manager than simply through the maximization of firm value. For example, the firm can undertake charitable actions which entail costs to the firm but which provide psychological or other benefits to the owner. Still, it is the rare business owner who does not prefer that the firm increase in value, so firm value maximization will almost certainly be one of the most important goals for the privately-held firm.

Implementing the Value Maximization Goal

While the maximization of long-term shareholder value is the important long-term goal of the firm, for several reasons it would be unwise to simply instruct employees to "maximize stock value." First, this instruction is too vague; it would leave employees directionless and their actions uncoordinated. Second, this instruction makes it difficult to evaluate the individual performance of each employee, since it is the aggregate performance of all which determines stock price. Finally, stock price is influenced by many factors external to the firm (such as the level of interest rates) which are not under employees' control. Stock price is a "noisy" signal of performance. That is, it is very difficult to determine which changes in stock price are due to employees and which changes are due to external factors.

The upshot is that, while stock value maximization is the key goal, the firm's management faces the problem of finding ways by which this principle can be implemented. The classical strategy for incorporating stock value maximization within the firm is to:

1. **Substitute goals based on drivers of stock price for stock price itself.** Much research on the value of firms has shown that stock price is determined by the risk-adjusted value of the future cash flows that the firm is expected to generate. Cash flow is the firm's profits adjusted for noncash items and cash needs. Since profit is a large part of this picture, is reasonably measurable, and is less influenced by uncontrollable external factors than stock price, firms substitute profit maximization for stock value maximization.

2. **Assign the management of various costs and revenues to different parts of the organization.** Profits are sales minus costs. Rather than giving all employees the general goal of enhancing sales and controlling costs, firms break the task of revenue and cost management into parts and assign various aspects of the task to various departments within the organization. Sales and marketing departments generate revenue and finance departments control costs. Different reward and performance evaluation systems are developed for different departments in recognition of their different roles within the organization.

There are two great advantages of assigning responsibility for different costs and revenues to different parts of the firm. First, in this system the performance of each unit of the firm is judged by its success in managing the revenues or costs for which it has responsibility. Limiting evaluation criteria to these narrow, measurable costs and revenues simplifies performance evaluation considerably. Second, such a splitting of responsibilities allows the hiring of specialists with talents or training in particular areas of expertise: sales, credit, production, etc.

Problems Inherent in a Classical Organizational Strategy

Unfortunately, while dividing up responsibility for management of the firm's various costs and revenues seems a straightforward solution to the problem of structuring the organization to achieve shareholder wealth maximization, substantial difficulties are created by this strategy. One major difficulty that arises from this is goal conflict. Because units are responsible for different costs and revenues, they will have different policy preferences. For example, employees with production responsibilities will want long production runs to minimize step-up costs, regardless of the impact on inventory levels. Sales personnel will want to sell regardless of credit risk.

Note that this goal conflict is a result of specialization and departmentalization. A small firm run by an owner/manager does not experience goal conflict. Since the owner/manager makes all the decisions, he or she can balance the effects of each decision on revenues and costs. Goal conflict is the price the organization pays for the benefits of specialization. It results from the different reward and performance evaluation systems that are a part of a departmentalization of the firm's workforce.

The conflict between the credit and the sales departments in traditionally-organized firms is a classic example of goal conflict. The sales force is typically assigned the task of revenue generation, and sales personnel are evaluated, compensated, and promoted based on their ability to generate sales revenue. Credit personnel are assigned the task of controlling certain costs of these sales (bad debt losses, accounts receivable carrying costs, collection costs, and so forth), and are evaluated based on their efficiency in controlling and reducing these costs. If carried to extreme, the result is irreconcilable conflict within the organization. Sales and credit personnel will respond to the incentives they see in their respective evaluation, compensation, and promotion systems. The sales force will pursue sales volume regardless of the resulting credit costs; the credit department will institute and enforce an overly-restrictive credit policy to keep credit costs at a minimum.

Dealing with Goal Conflict in Credit Departments

Many of the advances in management strategy over the last few decades have been in response to this problem of goal conflict in organizations: maintaining the effectiveness of specialization while structuring the firm to achieve profit maximization. All strategies must to some extent sacrifice simplicity in the firm's evaluation, compensation, and promotion systems in order to align employee incentives with the stock value maximization goal. While no strategy is without difficulty in implementation, here are a few strategy suggestions which have appeared in the literature:

Evaluating of Credit Personnel Relative to Budgeted Expenses Rather than Expense Minimization—Minimizing credit costs does not necessarily maximize profits, because cost minimization requires that the credit manager deny credit to firms based on credit costs when these firms would be profitable customers. Instead of being instructed to "minimize receivables balance and bad debt expense" (a goal which inevitably leads to an overly-restrictive credit policy), each credit manager is instead given targets (budgets) for accounts receivable turnover, for bad debt as a percent of sales volume, and for similar credit-related costs. These budgets are set in keeping with both the riskiness of the types of accounts handled by the credit manager and the profitability of sales to these accounts. When evaluating the credit manager, *budget variances in either direction, too high or too low,* are considered indicators of poor performance because the budget is intended to capture the value-maximizing tradeoff between credit costs and profits from sales. (Budgeting as a way to monitor credit policy outcomes is discussed in much more detail in Chapter 8.)

Like all budgetary solutions to goal-setting, this one contains the potential for abuse. Managers can "game the numbers" in various ways. Also, insight and analysis are necessary to set the budgeted figures in such a way that these represent maximum shareholder wealth enhancement.

Evaluating Sales Personnel to Include Credit Costs; Evaluating Credit Personnel to Include Lost Sales—In this system, the firm requires that credit and sales specialists both be evaluated in a broader context. For example, bad debts from sales to customers who eventually default is one of the performance criteria used by sales management in evaluating their salespeople. In the extreme case, salespeople paid on commission do not receive their commission until the customer's payment is received.

One way of implementing this system in the evaluation of credit personnel is for the sales force to provide lists of sales that were lost because credit was denied. Credit managers must then justify these losses to their supervisors based on anticipated credit-related costs versus lost profits from sales, showing why the granting of credit was unjustified.

The difficulty with this system is that each department can blame the other for its own failings. Sales can blame credit for allowing shipments to firms that default; credit can blame sales for not finding accounts of reasonable credit risk.

Increasing the Portion of Compensation of Credit Personnel that is Based on Shareholder Wealth—This strategy has long been suggested as an important tool for aligning the incentives of employees with those of shareholders. In it, an important portion of the employee's compensation is based on the firm's profitability or its stock price. This performance-based compensation can be in the form of a bonus based on the firm's earnings or in stock options. While many firms use some version of this system, its success has been limited because factors external to the employee's performance affect profitability and/or share price. While the compensation reflects shareholder wealth enhancement, it does not directly reflect an individual employee's performance or provide direct incentives for good performance.

One last note on the structure of the firm and the effects of this structure on employee performance is important. It is frequently said that educating salespeople about credit and educating credit people about sales will enable the two departments to cooperate and to maximize profits. Unfortunately, in the classical organizational structure while education will certainly enable the two to understand each other, it is unlikely to affect the decision-making of either in any major way because it leaves the conflict in incentives (goals) unchanged. The only way to effectively change behavior is to change the incentives that the departments face.

Implications for Credit Policy

The trade-offs inherent in addressing goal conflict within the organization are difficult ones. Firms have used the previously described approaches as well as other methods to restructure the organization so that the incentives facing employees lead to profit maximization. Other firms have decided to stay with the traditional organizational structure and live with the goal conflict that results. The makers of credit policy must formulate guidelines for credit analysts based on the goal structure that organization has chosen. Since all credit policy decisions have implications for both revenues and credit costs, the procedure that the policy-maker uses to evaluate policy alternatives will depend on the organization's goal structure. For purposes of discussion, let us highlight the different cases:

A Firm With a Traditional Organizational Structure—The credit department is assigned the task of minimizing credit-related costs and the sales department is assigned the task of making every sale regardless of these costs. The only effective constraint on the actions of each department is the political pressure within the organization that one department can bring on the other. In this circumstance, it would be counterproductive for the credit manager to institute credit policy which considers the revenue effects of credit decisions. Instead, each credit decision should be based on cost effects only. Evaluation of alternative policies should be based on the estimation of the costliness of policy alternatives, and the politically-acceptable alternative with the least cost should be chosen.

A Firm Evaluates and Rewards Credit Personnel in a Way Which is Linked to Profits—In this circumstance, in addition to estimating the cost effects of each alternative policy, revenue effects should be assessed and included in the analysis.

The policy with the highest expected contribution to the firm's profits should be chosen.

In deciding how to proceed, two points are of particular note. First, the goal structure of most firms will not be either of these polar cases but will lie somewhere on the continuum between the two. In this case, *the first task of the credit manager is to determine where on this continuum the firm is positioned.* If the credit department is seen largely as a cost minimizer, then primary emphasis in evaluating alternative credit policy choices should be on costs, not profits. On the other hand, if the firm is structured so that employees are evaluated and rewarded primarily based on the profit results they produce, then a profit-oriented approach is necessary. *This will vary from firm to firm and it is up to the credit policy-maker to determine this before any analysis of credit policy is undertaken.*

Second, whether the credit department is seen as a cost-minimizer or a profit-maximizer, the cost effects of alternative credit policies need to be considered. The difference between the two situations is that, in the second, revenues from sales are considered as well. In the following portions of this book, we will in general take a profit-maximization view, assuming that the incentives the firm presents to the credit department are appropriate for this view. However, the discussion will also incorporate costs. Credit policy-makers whose managers see them as cost minimizers should concentrate on this aspect of the analysis.

Effects of Credit Policy Decisions

No matter which aspect of credit policy is under consideration (credit investigation, credit-granting, etc.), the policy will affect both the costs and revenues of the selling firm. Revenues come from sales, and credit policy affects both sales volume and the timing of collections on these sales. Less restrictive credit policies increase sales but may stretch the time between sales and collections. More restrictive policies have the opposite effect.

While it is possible for credit decisions to affect almost any of the firm's various costs, the primary effect is likely to be on six different types of costs: costs of sales (the cost of goods or services sold), credit investigation costs, cash discount expense, bad debt expense, accounts receivable carrying costs, and collection and administration costs.[1] We will refer to these types of costs frequently in this book. A brief discussion of each follows.

Costs of Sales—When credit policy affects the firm's sales volume, it also affects its cost of goods or services sold, including direct materials, direct labor, and similar expenses. Credit policies which increase sales also increase these costs, and credit policies which result in lesser sales reduce these costs.

Credit Investigation Costs—These are the out-of-pocket and other costs of assessing the creditworthiness of customers. Credit policies which result in more

---

[1] For a more extensive discussion of the potential effects of credit policy on other aspects of the firm's cost structure, see Frederick C. Scherr, *Modern Working Capital Management: Text and Cases*, Prentice Hall, 1989, pp. 159-162.

credit investigation will increase these costs but (we will see later) may reduce other costs.

Cash Discount Expense—This is the dollar amount of receipts that the firm does not collect because buyers pay within the discount period when the seller offers a cash discount. Higher cash discounts will increase this expense, but may decrease other costs.

Bad Debt Expense—Some buyers will default, and some receivables will therefore go uncollected. While the credit analyst does not know exactly which customers will default (or credit management would be an easy task), the point of credit analysis of customers is to give the analyst some feeling for the default risk class of each customer (how likely the customer is to default). Credit policies which involve granting credit to customers of higher risk classes, all else equal, will result in higher bad debt expenses.

Accounts Receivable Carrying Costs—All assets of the firm must be financed, including accounts receivable, and financing is costly. Therefore, the firm bears a financing cost between the time a receivable is generated and the time it is collected. Credit polices which result in greater sales or longer time between sales and collections will result in higher receivables balances and greater accounts receivable carrying costs.

Collection and Administration Costs—Outstanding accounts receivable must be administered and collected. Included in the costs of these functions are the out-of-pocket costs of collection such as mail costs, telephone charges, and expenses of travel to customers for collection calls. However, these sorts of expenses are generally less than a hidden cost: *the opportunity cost of the credit analyst's time*. Many credit policies result in the granting of credit to buyers who are burdensome to administer: these buyers require extensive amounts of the analyst's time for collection, follow-up, hand-holding, etc. Though the credit analyst's salary will be paid even if these buyers are not granted credit, the analyst's time is diverted from other activities. *In short, the credit analyst's time is not free because the credit analyst could be using this time to perform other useful and productive functions for the firm.* Credit policies which entail higher out-of-pocket collection costs and administrative opportunity costs must be evaluated relative to the benefits (in terms of other costs and revenues) that such policies produce.

While this list may seem long, it is very important that these cost and revenues effects are kept in mind when the credit manager considers credit policy. Most of the important credit policy decisions entail trade-offs between these costs and revenues. The challenge is to formulate policy so that the trade-offs result in the greatest advantage to the firm.

Principles for Analyzing Credit Policy Decisions

Two principles of modern finance guide the evaluation of all financial decisions, including those of credit policy. The first principle is that the only revenues and costs that are relevant to evaluating a policy are changes in costs and revenues relative to the firm's revenues and cost position if that policy is not instituted. This is called the principle of marginality. The second principle is that the evaluation system for these changes in revenues and costs must reflect the three aspects of these that influence stock value: their amount, timing, and risk. This is called the principle of valuation.

The Principle of Marginality—The best way to understand the principle of marginality is by example. Consider a change in credit policy that would increase sales by $2 million and affect the various credit-related costs discussed previously. A hypothetical example is presented in Table 1-1. Rather than focus on the current cost and revenue structure (the structure without the credit policy change) or the resulting structure after the change, the appropriate costs and revenues to consider are those which result from the change, that is, the differences between the two structures.

These differences are portrayed in the right-hand column of Table 1-1. The proposed change increases sales by $2 million, costs of sales by $1.46 million, and all other costs by a total of $440,000, so the net benefit of this credit policy change in terms of yearly profit is $100,000.[2]

As this book proceeds, the reader will find that presenting all three of the present costs and revenues, the new costs and revenues, and the marginal costs and revenues as the difference between these is an unnecessarily burdensome approach. Once the principle of marginality is grasped, analysis can proceed directly to these marginal effects without the burden of presenting the present and new cost and revenue structures. However, the reader should always keep in mind that the cost and revenue effects are marginal changes in the firm's overall cost and revenue picture.

The Principle of Valuation—There are two good ways to reflect the impact of the timing, amount, and risk of marginal revenue and cost effects on the firm: the income statement approach (also know as "profitability analysis") and the present value approach. The advantages and disadvantages of each will be discussed in following sections.

The Income Statement Approach to Analyzing Credit Policy Effects

In the income statement approach, the manager estimates a marginal income statement which includes changes in each type of cost and revenue associated with the proposed credit policy. Estimation of some of these costs and revenue effects is straightforward while estimating others is more complex. In the following paragraphs, we discuss this estimation procedure for each of the six types of revenues and costs.

---

[2] We will discuss methods of calculating these various costs later in this chapter.

Table 1-1.   An Example of the Marginality Principle

Three Income Statements (in thousands)

Item	Without Credit Policy Change	With Credit Policy Change	Marginal Change
Sales	$ 100,000	$ 102,000	$ 2,000
Costs of Sales	73,000	74,460	1,460
Credit Investigation Costs	500	500	0
Cash Discount Expense	1,400	1,440	40
Bad Debt Expense	500	750	250
Account Receivable Carrying Costs	1,300	1,400	100
Collection and Administration Costs	300	350	50
Other Noncredit Expenses	15,000	15,000	0
Earnings	$ 8,000	$ 8,100	$ 100

Change in Sales—This is simply the expected change in sales volume that is expected to result from the proposed credit policy. For sales, the concept of estimating the change is relatively simple, but the estimate that results may be highly uncertain. The precise reaction of customers to a change in credit policy is never completely clear, and competitors may or may not react to the change. Consequently, it is not an easy task to come up with a reliable estimate of the marginal sales revenues that are expected from a credit policy. To deal with this uncertainty in estimation, the credit manager may repeat the analysis of policy for several different levels of sales. This repetition procedure is known as "sensitivity" or "what-if" analysis and will be illustrated at several points in this book.

Change in Cost of Sales—Cost of sales is generally estimated as a percent of sales. In estimating this type of cost, the problem is the extraction of a relevant cost of sales percent for the particular product from the selling firm's product cost accounting system. The problem is reasonably tricky and deserves some examination.[3]

Product cost accounting systems are internal systems set up within firms to produce information for management's use in making decisions. For many marketing decisions (including pricing), full-cost product costing systems are the most useful. Many product costing systems are consequently set up on a full-cost basis. In these systems, all of the firm's costs are allocated to its various products. Included in these product costing statements are costs which are directly associated with producing the products as well as costs which are only indirectly associated with particular products. A simplified example of product costing is presented in Table 1-2.

In this table, the firm has three products: A, B, and C. Total sales for the firm were $100 million and total cost of goods sold was $60 million. The firm's total

---

[3] A more complete discussion of the issues presented here can be found in "What Does it Really Cost?" *Credit Research Digest*, Credit Research Foundation of NACM, February 1994, from which much of the following discussion is taken.

selling expenses were $18 million and general and headquarters expenses were $12 million, so the firm made $10 million before taxes.

However, there are great differences in costs among the products sold, and the credit manager should reflect these differences in analysis of credit policy. A naive way to do this would be to use the total costs/sales ratios for each of the products (see Table 1-2) to estimate the effects of a credit policy on cost of sales. However, this is inappropriate because there are likely to be several expenses on a full-cost product costing statement which are not relevant to most credit policy decisions. They are not relevant because they will not change for the firm as a whole with these decisions (that is, these are costs which are not marginal to the credit decision). Further, the amount of these costs varies among products, so a simple adjustment of total costs/sales is not representative.

These effects can be seen by examining Table 1-2 in detail. There are three types of costs in this statement: (1) direct production costs (cost of goods sold, or CGS), (2) product-related selling expenses, and (3) general and headquarters expenses. For any policy decision (credit or otherwise), which of these is relevant depends on the size of the effect of the policy on sales volume.

If the anticipated change in sales volume is reasonably small (say less than 10 percent of the current figure, which is typical for credit policy decisions), only CGS is likely to change. CGS must change since more or less product or service will have to be produced, resulting in a change in out-of-pocket production costs. For relatively small changes in sale volumes, it is unlikely that more salespeople, product managers, and other personnel will have to be hired, so selling expenses and headquarters expenses generally will not change. A cost ratio based on CGS/sales will generally capture the marginal costs of sales.

One important insight of the marginality principle in determining costs of sales is: Don't be fooled by costs which are allocated based on the sales volume method (as with General and Headquarters Expense in Table 1-2). In allocating costs by the sales volume method, the overall cost for the firm as a whole is apportioned to the products based on each product's percent of the firm's total sales. For example, in Table 1-2, product A has 50 percent of the firm's total sales volume, and is consequently allocated 50 percent of the firm's general and headquarters expense. It is easy to confuse the effects that result from this allocation method with marginal changes in costs. If the credit manager makes a credit policy decision which increases sales for a product, it is true that since its sales have grown relative to the other products, the product will receive a greater allocation of general and headquarters expenses. While this looks like an increase in marginal cost, it really isn't, since the total dollar expense for the firm as a whole is unchanged. The point is that, regardless of the allocation system, unless the increase in sales is sufficiently large to require an actual increase in the overall level of an expense, a shift in allocated burden is irrelevant to credit decisions.

Credit managers will sometimes hear the argument that a full cost basis should be used rather than a marginal cost basis in making credit decisions because fixed

Table 1-2. An Example of Product Costing

(All Entries in Millions of Dollars)

	Entire Firm	*A*	*B*	*C*
		Allocated to Products		
Sales Revenue	$100.0	$50.0	$30.0	$20.0
Costs of Goods Sold (CGS)				
Direct Materials	$48.0	$22.0	$15.0	$11.0
Direct Labor	$5.0	$2.0	$1.5	$1.5
Direct Overhead	7.0	$3.0	$2.0	$2.0
Total CGS	$60.0	$27.0	$18.5	$14.5
Selling Expenses*	$18.0	$11.0	$4.0	$3.0
General and Headquarters Exp.**	$12.0	$6.0	$3.6	$2.4
Total Costs	$90.0	$44.0	$26.1	$19.9
Total Costs/Sales	90.00%	88.00%	87.00%	99.50%
CGS/Sales	60.00%	54.00%	61.67%	72.50%

Notes:
*Actual selling expenses in selling these products.
**General corporate expenses; allocated using percent of sales method.

costs must be absorbed. Unfortunately, while it is true that fixed costs must be paid, making decisions based on full costing does not help pay them. Making credit policy decisions on a full-cost basis can result in rejecting credit policies which would, in fact, contribute to the bottom line if these policies produce revenues which are greater than marginal costs.

Change in Credit Investigation Costs—Two types of credit policy changes will affect credit investigation costs: policies which change the number of customers to which the firm sells, and policies which change the amount of investigation of each customer. In either case, the out-of-pocket costs of credit reports, trade clearances, etc., and the opportunity costs of the credit managers' time to analyze these reports will be affected and are relevant marginal costs in evaluating the new policy relative to the old. For example, suppose that the firm institutes a change in credit policy that will add another 300 customers to the firm's customer base and that, on average, it is expected to cost $75 to assess the credit risk of each customer. In this case, the marginal increase in credit investigation cost would be $22,500 (equal to 300 customers times $75 per customer).

Change in Cash Discount Expense—Many credit policy decisions, particularly those which have to do with terms of sale, result in a change in the firm's expected cash discount expense. For any credit policy, the amount of the cash discount expense is equal to the fraction of the firm's customers that are expected to take the cash discount times the cash discount percent times sales. For example, suppose that under the current credit policy, the firm's expected sales for next year are $50 million. Sixty percent of the firm's customers are expected to take the cash discount, and the cash discount is 2 percent. The expected cash discount expense is then $600,000 (= ($50,000,000)(.60)(.02)).

In evaluating changes in policy, the change in cash discount expense is equal to the difference in the expected cash discount expense under the current policy and the expected cash discount expense after the policy change. Relative to the prior numerical example, suppose that the firm is considering a change in credit policy that would result in the firm's sales increasing to $53 million, and that under this new policy 80 percent of the firm's customers are expected to take the cash discount, which is to remain at 2 percent. The new expected cash discount expense would be $848,000 (= ($53,000,000)(.80)(.02)), so the change in cash discount expense from instituting this policy is an increase in cost of $848,000 – $600,000 = $248,000. This figure would, of course, be weighed against other cost and revenue effects in determining whether the policy change should be implemented.

Change in Bad Debt Expense—Like the change in discount expense, the change in bad debt expense associated with a new credit policy is the difference between the expected bad debt expense under the current policy and the expected bad debt expense under the proposed policy. Most firms will have good historical data on their dollar losses based on their current credit policies. When executing the income statement approach to evaluating credit policy, it is convenient to convert the dollar amount into percents of receivables balance.[4] For example, if a firm's bad debt loss for the last year was $250,000, and receivables averaged $40 million, then bad debt loss as a fraction of receivables balance was $250,000/$40,000,000 = 0.625 percent.

Let's do a numerical example of a change in bad debt expense as a result of a credit policy change. Suppose that, if the current credit policies are continued, the firm's expected sales are $60 million, its receivables turnover is expected to be eight times per year, and bad debts are expected to be 0.50 percent of receivables. Expected bad debt under the current credit policy is then $37,500 (= ($60,000,000)(1/8)(.005)). A change in credit policy is under consideration which would result in expected sales of $62 million, receivables turnover of six times per year, and bad debt expense of 0.75 percent of receivables. The expected bad debt under the proposed policy is $77,500 (= ($62,000,000)(1/6)(.0075)), so the increase in expected bad debt cost for this policy change is $77,500 – $37,500 = $40,000.

Change in Accounts Receivable Carrying Cost—Accounts receivable carrying cost measures the cost that occurs to the firm because collections from sales occur when the receivable is paid rather than at the time of sale. This timing difference results in a receivables asset which the firm must finance. This cost

---

[4] While bad debt expense is frequently expressed as a percent of sales, it is often more useful to express it as a percent of receivables balance because the dollar amount of the firm's bad debt losses depends not only on the sales volume and credit risk of the firm's customers, but also on the turnover of receivables. The slower the receivables turn, the higher will be exposures and the larger will be the loss on each individual customer which defaults. Bad debt as a percent of receivables is equal to bad debt as a percent of sales divided by receivables turnover.

represents the time value of money in the income statement approach to analysis of credit policy. The cost of carrying the receivable is calculated as the receivables balance times a required rate of return. The change in accounts receivable carrying cost attributable to the proposed credit policy is the difference between the expected carrying cost under the current policy and that under the proposed policy.

There has been great debate in the financial research literature as to the appropriate way to cost the firm's investment in accounts receivable and what appropriate required rate of return to use. For purposes of this book, we will express the investment in receivables in terms of the book value of the receivables and use the selling firm's per-year cost of capital as the required return.[5]

Let us do another numerical example. The firm's current credit policies are expected to result in sales of $32 million and an average collection period of 90 days (a turnover of four times per year using a 360-day year). A change in credit policy is contemplated which will result in sales of $30 million and an average collection period of 30 days (12 times per year). The firm's cost of capital is 11 percent per year. The expected accounts receivable balance under the current policy is $32,000,000/4, or $8.0 million, and the expected carrying cost under the current policy is then $880,000 (=($8,000,000).11). The yearly expected receivables balance under the proposed policy is $30,000,000/12, or $2.5 million, and the expected carrying cost under the proposed policy is $275,000 (=($2,500,000).11). The expected reduction in accounts receivable carrying cost from this policy change is $880,000 – $275,000 = $605,000.

Change in Collection and Administration Costs—This cost has two parts: (1) the change on the out-of-pocket costs for telephone, postage, credit reports, and so forth that is associated with managing customer accounts and (2) the change in the opportunity cost that comes with the diversion of credit employees' time from other profitable pursuits.

The firm's past results provide important data on these costs, and a common-sense application of these figures to the credit policy being considered will generally lead to a reasonably reliable cost estimate. Let us assume that a change in credit policy is contemplated which will result in credit being granted to an additional 200 customers. Examining last year's pay and expense records, we find (based on the number of such accounts assigned to current employees) that each account of this sort takes 10 hours per year to analyze, monitor, and collect, and results in $50 in out-of-pocket collection costs. If compensation for the credit personnel who must administer and collect these accounts totals $35 per hour, then the total administration and collection cost of the 200 new accounts will be $80,000 (=200(10)($35) + 200($50)) per year.[6]

---

[5] Alternatives include expressing the investment in receivables on a cost basis using either full cost or production cost. We use receivables balance instead because this is the amount of the cash flow that is delayed because the receivable is uncollected.

[6] In this illustration, the opportunity cost per hour of the time spent by credit personnel in administration and collection is based on their total compensation, that is, their total yearly cost including pay and benefits divided by the number of hours they work. We do this in the interests of simplicity. However, in practice a somewhat higher figure should be used, as the firm receives benefit from these people in excess of their costs, and it is this benefit we are trying to measure.

Arriving at a Decision—In the income statement (profitability) approach to analyzing credit policy, once all the expected changes in costs and revenues from a proposed credit policy have been estimated, it is simply a matter of adding up their effects to get the expected change in yearly profits. Credit policy changes which make positive contributions to expected profits are advantageous and should be seriously considered for implementation.

Advantages and Disadvantages of the Income Statement Approach—The major virtue of the income statement approach to the analysis of credit policy decisions is its simplicity. It is based on the well-known and understood income statement, a format familiar to every sophisticated credit manager. The only important modification to the familiar income statement is the addition of an accounts receivable carrying cost term to represent the time value of money. Because of this major advantage, in this text we will use the income statement approach to analyzing credit policy whenever it is feasible. However, the income statement approach also has disadvantages. Its method for addressing accounts receivable carrying costs contains the inherent assumption that all the revenues and costs from the credit policy decision continue perpetually at their initial values. While this is a reasonable approximation in many circumstances, it is inappropriate in others, particularly when the decision is one where there are future costs and benefits that are contingent on certain events or when the pattern of costs and revenue changes over time.[7] Also, addressing situations where the different components of revenues and costs happen at different times (which occurs in some credit policy decisions) is very burdensome in the income statement approach. Finally, it is very difficult to reflect differences in some aspects of risk among policies when using the income statement approach. While less familiar and more computationally complex, the net present value approach can address all these difficulties. It is discussed in the next section.

The Present Value Approach to Analyzing Credit Policy Effects

Present value analysis is a technique which has come into common use in the analysis of most financial decisions. The major difference between the present value approach and the income statement approach is how the present value approach addresses the time value of money and risk. Rather than having one carrying cost item to account for the time value of money (as in the income statement approach), in present value analysis the amount of each cost and revenue is adjusted to account for both the time value of money and the riskiness of the particular cost or revenue. (In this context, riskiness can be viewed as the amount of uncertainty that the policy maker has about the estimate of the item.) This adjustment is performed by multiplying the dollar amount of the expected cost and revenue by a discount factor. The equation for this process is:

[7] For a more in-depth discussion of this problem with the income statement approach to the analysis of credit policy, see Frederick C. Scherr, *Modern Working Capital: Text and Cases*, Prentice Hall, 1989, pp. 162-165.

$$\textbf{Present value} = E(NCF)(1/(1+k)^t)$$

In this equation, $E(NCF)$ is the expected cash flow from the cost or revenue, with a negative sign for costs and a positive sign for revenues. The $(1/(1+k)^t)$ term is the discount factor. In this term, k is the appropriate discount rate on a yearly basis (which is the firm's cost of capital if the cash flow is of the same riskiness as the average of the firm's other cash flows) and t is the fraction of a year or the number of years until the expected cash flow occurs. For example, suppose that a particular credit policy is expected to require that a cost be $100,000, that this cost will occur in 90 days, and that the firm's cost of capital is 12% per year. The present value calculation is:

$$\begin{aligned}
\textbf{Present value} &= -\$100,000(1/1.12^{90/360}) \\
&= -\$100,000(1/1.02874) \\
&= -\$100,000(.97206) \\
&= -\$97,206
\end{aligned}$$

To make a decision, the credit policy analyst totals up the present values of the various marginal costs and revenues. The sum of the present values of the costs and revenues associated with a decision is called the decision's net present value. Decisions which have positive net present values are advantageous to the firm and should be considered for adoption while decisions which have negative net present values are not advantageous (all else constant). For example, suppose that a cost with a present value of –$97,206 was associated with a policy which would produce a future revenue with a present value of $115,000. The net present value of these two is $17,794 (equal to $115,000 – $97,206), so the policy is advantageous.

Advantages and Disadvantages of the Present Value Approach—The present value approach to the evaluation of credit policy is particularly useful when any of the following occur:

1. The revenues and costs associated with the policy decision cannot be modeled as a perpetuity.

2. The timing of costs and revenues has important effects on the value of the decision.

3. The expected revenues or costs differ greatly in risk.

The disadvantages of present value analysis relative to the income statement approach are its increased mathematical complexity and the fact that most credit managers are less familiar with it than with income statements. There are several situations where the advantages of present value analysis in evaluating credit policy outweigh these disadvantages, and we will employ this technique when such is the case.

Summary of Policy Implications in this Chapter

Credit policy decisions involve trade-offs between the revenues and costs that are affected by credit policy: sales, costs of goods sold, credit investigation expense, accounts receivable carrying costs, discount expense, bad debt costs, and collection and administrative costs. Analysis of credit policy requires that the policy maker consider the revenue and cost effects of credit policy decisions in deciding which policies are advantageous to the firm.

One important insight from this chapter is that the costs and revenues which should be considered in credit policy analysis are those which change, from the standpoint of the firm as a whole, with a change in credit policy: the *marginal* costs and revenues. Costs which do not change with credit policy are irrelevant to the analysis of that policy, even if the policy changes the allocation of these costs changes among the firm's products.

A second important implication concerns the relationship between the organization's structure and those marginal costs and revenues that are appropriately considered in decision-making. In some organizations, credit managers are seen primarily as cost-minimizers. They are evaluated based on cost-based targets and are not given recognition for the revenues that the expenditure of these costs produce. In such organizations, the ability of the credit manager to minimize costs is constrained only by the political consequences of these actions: If actions in pursuit of cost minimization become too severe, they risk conflict with other units of the firm.

When analyzing credit policy in firms with such organizational characteristics, it is inappropriate to consider the effects of credit policy on revenue. In such organizations, the credit manager should evaluate policy in the way the organizational structure conveys: minimize costs subject to the political constraints of the organization and live with the resulting goal conflict between units of the firm. Analysis in such organizations should center around the relative costs of various credit policies, with the policy maker seeking cost minimization.

In other firms, more emphasis is placed on profitability, and credit departments are evaluated and credit managers paid based on this goal (despite the problems in personnel evaluation and organizational structure that this view entails). In such a firm, the analyst of credit policy must consider not only all marginal costs but any marginal revenues that are associated with policy choice. Costs and revenues must be weighed based on their valuation consequences, reflecting the amount, timing, and risk of the marginal costs and revenues associated with the decision. Either the income statement approach or the present value approach can perform this weighing, but both methods have advantages as well as disadvantages. Both will be used at various times in the remainder of this text.

Case for Discussion and Analysis

The Case of the Confused Credit Manager

Tom Easton was a new employee of the Jones Chemical Company, a medium-sized firm located in the eastern United States. Mr. Easton had previously been employed as a middle-ranked credit manager with a much larger firm and had taken the position of General Credit Manager with Jones Chemical a month before.

The credit department at Jones Chemical consisted of Mr. Easton and two credit analysts. The department reported to one of the firm's Assistant Treasurers, who in turn reported to the Treasurer. Mr. Easton had responsibility for collection and administration of the firm's overseas sales (a responsibility entailing mostly paperwork but little credit analysis or credit risk, given the way that Jones Chemical did business), for formulating credit policy, and for the personnel evaluation of the two credit analysts. The prior general credit manager had left for a better-paying job in another city, and it was not felt that either of the analysts had sufficient experience to take over the job at that time.

The Assistant Treasurer to whom the General Credit Manager reported was a gentleman with little expertise in credit management; his training was in accounting. On joining the firm, Mr. Easton asked him what criteria he should use in formulating credit policy, and he received a blank stare in reply. The best the Assistant Treasurer could do was say, "Well, Tom, when we were between people in your position and the analysts came to me with a question, I just gave them the old maxim, 'when in doubt, ship it out.'"

Seeking further direction but unwilling to go over the head of his supervisor, Tom started looking around the organization to assess the state of credit policy. The firm had no credit policy manual or other materials to give direction (the feeling being that the credit department was "too small" for such things). Little policy analysis had been performed by the prior credit manager.

He found several other useful pieces of information. First, the responsibility for sales of individual products rested with the firm's Product Managers, who with a few exceptions were reasonable and understood the trade-offs in policy formulation. When some friction occurred between field sales personnel and the credit analysts regarding credit department decisions, the Product Managers generally saw that these were resolved amicably. Second, the Assistant Treasurer had recently begun to measure its receivables turnover and had begun to set goals based on this turnover. For the upcoming year, this goal was to speed collections from an average of 43 days (not including receivables from overseas sales) to 41 days.

Third, he found that the firm has just completed a sales incentive program in which the firm's Product Managers, salespeople, marketing staff, customer service representatives, and technical sales representatives had participated but credit personnel had not. Finally, he noted that the firm offered no bonuses based on the firm's profitability or stock options to credit people: all compensation was straight salary with raises based on performance reviews.

Suggestions for Analysis

1. Summarize Jones Chemicals' current goal structure for its Credit Department. Which aspects of what Mr. Easton has heard and seen lead you to believe that the role of the Credit Department in this organization is cost minimization? Which aspects lead you to believe it is profit maximization?

2. If you were Mr. Easton, how would you proceed? How should credit policy be made?

2 Credit Investigation Policy

Almost every credit analyst performs credit investigation as part of the credit evaluation process. Credit investigation requires gathering various types of information which enable the credit analyst to assess the credit worthiness of the customer. Gathering information entails costs to the firm, costs which can total a major portion of the firm's credit-related costs. Therefore, policy with respect to credit investigation should be carefully developed.

Unfortunately, policy with respect to credit investigation is not easily formulated because of the subtle trade-offs it involves. In this chapter, these trade-offs are outlined and a conceptual model of the credit investigation process is presented. This model is used to investigate an important policy question: the effects of order size and product profitability on credit investigation policy. A practical approach to actual credit investigation decisions—next-decision analysis—is then introduced. The chapter concludes with a summary of policy implications and a case for analysis and discussion.

Introduction to the Trade-offs in Credit Investigation Policy[8]

Types of Credit Investigation Costs—Let us first review the discussion of credit investigation costs presented in the prior chapter. The firm bears two types of costs as a result of credit investigation: out-of-pocket costs and opportunity costs of the credit analyst's time. Out-of-pocket costs are cash costs which the firm pays to obtain information. Examples include charges for trade clearances obtained from commercial sources and telephone costs of credit inquiries. The opportunity cost of the analyst's time represents the cost of the time spent in obtaining and analyzing credit information.

---

[8] This section of the chapter draws from "Credit Investigation: Can There be Too Much of a Good Thing?," CRF Staff Report, December 1993.

In formulating policy with respect to credit investigation, some credit executives ignore the opportunity cost of the credit analyst's time, arguing that this is a sunk cost, since the firm pays the credit analyst regardless of what the credit analyst is doing. This is correct only when the alternative use of the credit analyst's time (for example, in making collections) has no value to the firm. When the credit analyst's time could be profitably used in performing some other function, there is an opportunity cost in using this time for credit investigation. The amount of this opportunity cost is the profit lost because the other function is not performed or is delayed.

The level of each of these costs will vary with the particular source of credit information that is used. Obtaining and analyzing a commercial trade clearance entails only a small out-of-pocket cost and time cost, whereas a customer visit may be expensive in both respects.

It is important to note the relatively fixed nature of both the out-of-pocket and opportunity costs of any particular source of credit information. The out-of-pocket and opportunity costs of obtaining and analyzing information from any particular source may vary greatly from one source to another but are approximately the same any time a particular source is used. We will see later that this fixed nature has important implications for policy formulation.

Trade-offs in Credit Investigation Policy—The most important tradeoff in credit investigation policy is between the costs of credit investigation and the expected level of bad debt and accounts receivable carrying costs that result from credit-granting decisions. Consider the circumstance in which a credit analyst receives an order from a customer about which he or she knows nothing. One alternative is to approve this order without any credit investigation. In this case, the expected costs to the seller are represented by the expected bad debt expense and payment time of an average customer, since the seller has no information to distinguish the customer under consideration from the average customer. That is, if on average 1 percent of customers default and on average customers who do not default pay in 60 days, and credit is granted to a customer without investigation, the seller can expect to bear bad debt and carrying costs in keeping with these average figures.

Seen in this light, the function of credit investigation is to enable the seller to make more accurate credit decisions by refining estimates of bad debt loss and carrying cost and thus better identify advantageous and disadvantageous customers. For example, the purchase of a trade clearance on a customer may show a series of defaults and extreme slowness in payments. The credit analyst may conclude, based on a high expected level of bad debt expense and carrying costs, that it is not advantageous to grant credit. But it required costly credit investigation to reach this conclusion. The credit analyst traded off the cost of obtaining and analyzing the trade clearance against the reduction in other expenses that resulted from a more informed credit-granting decision.

There is an important policy tradeoff among credit investigation costs, bad debt expense, and carrying costs. Bad debt and carrying costs can be reduced by credit investigation. Two important policy implications flow from this insight.

First, optimum credit policy will always entail some level of bad debt. The firm's credit analysts can always reduce bad debt by performing more credit investigation. However, at some point the costs of additional credit investigation outweigh the benefits in terms of reduced bad debt and carrying costs. Investigation beyond this point will increase rather than decrease total costs.

Second, a policy of full credit investigation for every possible customer is not generally of advantage to the firm. (This policy is sometimes voiced by credit executives as "I want my credit analysts to know everything about their customers!") This is not advantageous because it entails too much credit investigation. Credit investigation expense is not weighed against its benefits in reducing bad debt and carrying expenses.

Controls for Credit Investigation Costs—One beneficial approach to matching credit investigation costs and benefits is the Sequential Method of Credit Investigation. Variations of this method are used by many firms. In this system, the firm makes a list of the sources of credit information available to it with the approximate costs of utilizing each source of information. The list is ordered from the lowest to the highest cost. While these lists vary greatly from firm to firm and industry to industry, a typical list might look like the one presented in Table 2-1.

Using the sequential method, credit investigation policy is formulated to balance the benefits that each level of investigation confers in terms of reductions in bad debt and carrying cost against the costs of that level of investigation. At any point in his or her credit investigation, the credit analyst will make trade-offs of the form: I already know this much; the next level of investigation will cost me this much; this additional investigation is/is not worth the cost for this customer. We will see that this decision is greatly influenced by the size of the order under consideration and the profitability (profit margin before credit costs) of the product or service being sold.

Table 2-1.   A Hypothetical Sequential List of Credit Information Sources and Costs

Source of Information	Investigation Cost of this Source
Ship Order without Credit Investigation	$0
Obtain and Analyze Commercial Credit Report	$10
Obtain and Analyze Trade Clearance	$20
Obtain and Analyze Bank Report	$35
Call Other Trade Supplies to Discuss Account	$75
Obtain, Spread, and Analyze Financial Statements	$150
Visit Customer and Analyze Resulting Information	$500

A Conceptual Model of the Credit Investigation Process

To illustrate the effects of order size and product profitability on credit investigation, we need a conceptual model of the process of credit investigation. Such a model is not simple because it must incorporate both credit investigation and credit-granting decisions; the level of credit investigation undertaken specifies the amount and type of information that will be available to make the credit-granting decision.

The simplest way to visualize the credit investigation process is as a decision tree.[9] In management science, decision-tree analysis is a standard approach to problems where future decisions are contingent on the outcomes of events which, when the initial decision must be made, are not known. In credit investigation, these events are the various sorts of credit investigation that the firm can perform and the outcomes are the information regarding the customer that this investigation provides. This information enables the credit analyst to revise estimates of how long the receivable is expected to be outstanding (and thus the receivable's carrying costs) and of the default risk class of the customer (and thus of the customer's expected bad debt cost).[10]

An Example Problem. By far the best way to understand the decision-tree approach to credit investigation is by example. Consider the following vastly oversimplified but illustrative problem:[11]

A seller is considering credit investigation policy for orders of $500. Two stages of credit investigation are available:

Stage	Cost
1. Check prior payment history	$5
2. Evaluate applicant's financial strength	$25

When an order is received, the firm can accept the order, reject the order, or investigate further. If the order is accepted without further investigation, estimates of default rate and time to pay based on industry averages are appropriate. For the industry to which the firm sells, the chance of default is 5 percent (on average one customer in 20 who is granted credit fails to pay) and the average payment time is 45 days.

If the firm elects to check its payment history for the applicant, the costs of this investigation are $5, and three results are possible: the applicant has paid promptly in the past, the applicant has defaulted in the past, or the firm has no experience with the applicant. Given the firm's customer base, the probabilities of these outcomes are 0.75, 0.05, and 0.20.

---

[9] This approach to the credit investigation problem is generally credited to D. Mehta. See D. Mehta, "The Formulation of Credit Policy Models," *Management Science*, October 1968, pp. B-30 to B-50.

[10] While useful as a conceptual model, the decision tree technique presented here is far too burdensome to use to address real-world credit investigation situations because using the decision-tree technique requires an impractical amount of data collection and estimation (we will discuss this point in detail later in the chapter). This model is presented here only to illustrate the credit investigation process and the tradeoffs involved in this process.

[11] This problem is taken from Frederick C. Scherr, *Modern Working Capital Management: Text and Cases*, Prentice-Hall, 1989, pp. 241-242.

If the seller has experience with the applicant, it is assumed that future credit granting will have the same result as past credit granting. After checking the history of payments, the seller may grant credit to the applicant without further investigation, reject the applicant, or investigate further. (Note that if the seller investigates and finds that it has no experience with the applicant, and credit is granted without further investigation, the seller has learned nothing from the investigation. In this case, the probability of default is 5 percent and the expected time to pay is 45 days.)

If additional credit investigation is undertaken, the next stage is to order a credit report which will give a rough evaluation of the applicant's financial position. This stage of investigation will cost $25 and two outcomes are possible: the applicant may have a relatively strong or weak financial position. Based on analysis of current customers, the seller has found that financially strong customers pay in 30 days and do not default; given the characteristics of the applicant's industry, there is a 70 percent chance the applicant will be financially strong. If the applicant is found to be financially weak (a 30 percent chance), the probability of its default on the order is 15 percent. If the financially weak customer does not default, it is expected that payments will be received in 80 days. If a customer defaults, recoveries are trivial. The seller's cost of capital is 10 percent per year and costs of goods sold are 85 percent of sales.

The decision tree for this problem is presented in Figure 2-1.[12] In this decision tree, a "P" indicates that the customer Paid for an order, a "D" that the customer Defaulted on an order, an "R" that the credit analyst decided to Reject credit, an "I" that the credit analyst decided to Investigate further, an "A" that the credit analyst Accepted the order (granted credit), an "S" that the second-stage credit investigation found the customer to be relatively Strong, and a "W" that this investigation found the customer to be relatively Weak. Circles indicate nodes at which probabilistic chance events occur. Squares indicate nodes at which the credit analyst makes a choice among alternative courses of action.

It pays to study this Figure closely, as much future discussion will be based on it. There are 12 possible outcomes of the credit investigation and payment/default processes.[13] These outcomes are labeled based on the last node from which they originate. (For example, outcome 2D is the default outcome from chance node 2; to get to chance node 2, the credit analyst granted credit without any investigation at decision node 1.) The decision tree contains two chance nodes that represent the results of credit investigations. Node 3 represents the results of a check of the firm's records of customer payments to determine whether the customer has purchased from the firm before and the result of that purchase. Node 6 represents the results of an evaluation of the customer's financial strength (weak or strong).

---

[12] In this problem we assume a simple model of the credit-granting process in which the customer either pays or defaults. Taxes are also ignored. More complex models of credit-granting will be presented in future chapters.

[13] In the interest of simplicity, in this decision tree it is assumed that: (1) the order is rejected if it is found that the applicant has defaulted in the past (outcome 3R); and (2) the order is accepted if it is found that the applicant will pay promptly (outcomes 3PPT and 6S).

The decision tree contains three nodes that represent payment or default: nodes 2, 5, and 8. Node 2 represents the payment or default events that result when credit is granted without any credit investigation, and node 5 represents these events when a check of past experience finds that the customer has not purchased from the firm previously. Node 8 represents the payment or default events when the customer has not purchased previously and an investigation has found that the customer is financially weak.

The decision tree also contains three nodes that represent credit-granting decisions: nodes 1, 4, and 7. Each is different in the sense that the credit analyst has different information when making them. At node 1 the credit analyst knows nothing about the customer; at node 4, the credit analyst knows that the customer has not purchased from the firm previously; and at node 7 the credit analyst knows that the firm has no experience with the customer and that the customer is financially weak.

How much investigation should be performed depends, in this or any other credit investigation situation, on the tradeoff among credit investigation costs, accounts receivable carrying costs, bad debt expense, and also on product profitability. To evaluate this tradeoff, we first need to know the profits from each of the potential outcomes of the credit investigation process should that outcome occur. These calculations appear in Table 2-2.[14]

A review of one of the calculations of these profit numbers is in order. As an example, we will use outcome 8P.[15] If this outcome occurs, both stages of credit investigation will have been utilized, and the customer will have paid in 80 days. Collections from sales will be $500 and the cost of sales will have been .85($500) = $425. Accounts receivable carrying costs of the receivable for 80 days will have been .10(80/360)$500 = $11.11 and credit investigation costs will have been $5 for the first stage and $25 for the second stage. The net profit before tax for this outcome is then $33.89 (= $500–$425–$11.11–$5–$25). The profit figures for each outcome of the decision tree are posted to the tree in Figure 2-2.

To establish the optimal policy for orders of this size, we "roll back" the decision tree, proceeding right to left and using inductive reasoning to decide on the best policies, given that prior decisions led to a particular node. At chance-event nodes, the expected profits of events from that node are computed, and at decision nodes it is assumed that the analyst selects the alternative with the greatest expected profits.

Starting at node 8 (the right most node), if credit is granted, there is an 85 percent chance that the applicant will pay, resulting in a profit of $33.89 on the $500

[14] The profit calculations in this table are for a single order and the level of exposure that results from this order, rather than for yearly sales. Note that repeat orders of the same amount (or less) do not affect credit investigation policy because bad debt and accounts receivable carrying costs are proportional to exposure, not to yearly sales. However, if there is a reasonable expectation that order amounts from a particular credit applicant will rise in the future, and that delays in the credit investigation might affect the approval of such orders (with the potential result of lost sales), then the likely size of the larger future order amount should be used to determine credit investigation strategy.
[15] To get to this outcome, at node 1 the credit analyst decided to perform stage-one credit investigation, leading to node 3; at node 3 there was no past experience with the applicant, leading to node 4; at node 4, the credit manager chose to investigate further, leading to node 6; at node 6, the investigation disclosed a relatively weak financial position, leading to node 7; at node 7, the credit manager granted credit, leading to node 8; and at node 8, the applicant paid in 80 days.

Figure 2-1. Decision Tree for Example Problem

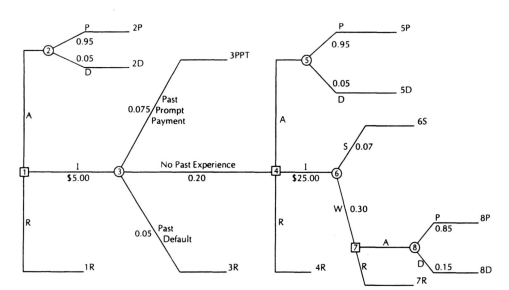

order, and a 15 percent chance that the applicant will default, resulting in a $455.00 loss. The expected profit at this node is then –$39.44 (equal to .85($33.89) plus .15(–$455.00)). At decision node 7, the best alternative is to reject the relatively weak applicants, with a profitability of –$30.00 (from outcome 7R), since this is less costly than to grant credit, which has an expected profit of –$39.44 (the ex-

Figure 2-2. Example Decision Tree with Profit Figures

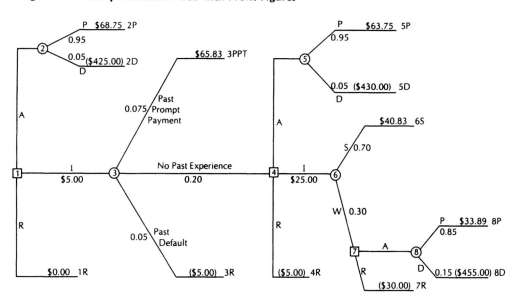

pected profit at node 8). At node 6, since there is a 70 percent chance that the customer will have a strong financial position (with a profit of $40.83) and a 30 percent chance that this position is weak (in which case the best the analyst can do is –$30.00), the expected profit is then $19.58 (= .7($40.83) + .3(–$30.00)). Therefore, at node 4, if the analyst chooses to investigate, the best strategy after this investigation results in expected profits of $19.58.

However, at node 4 the analyst has two other choices: the analyst can reject all applicants (with an expected profit of –$5.00) or the analyst can grant credit without further investigation, with an expected profit of $39.06 (= .95($63.75) + .05(–$430.00)) at node 5. Given these profit figures, the best alternative is not to perform the additional investigation and grant credit to all applicants. Note that this will result in granting credit to some applicants (those with a relatively weak financial position) that, if further investigation were performed, would be rejected. However, for the investigation cost, default probabilities, and the other figures in this problem, *the reduction in other costs is not worth the additional credit investigation cost.*

The remaining calculations of expected profitability are presented in Table 2-3. A completely rolled-back decision tree is presented in Figure 2-3. At node 3, the profitability of rejecting past defaults, accepting past prompts, and accepting past no-experiences is $56.93, which is greater than the expected profitability of $44.06 from granting credit without a first-stage investigation (node 2). Therefore, the optimal strategy for an order size of $500 in this problem is to perform initial investigation to check the applicant's past history of payments to the firm, and to grant credit to all applicants who have not defaulted in the past. It is not advantageous to perform additional credit investigation beyond this point for this order size. This strategy has an expected profitability of $56.93 for orders of $500.

This problem illustrates the tradeoff between credit investigation expense versus bad debt expense and accounts receivable carrying cost that is the essence of credit investigation policy: by spending more on credit investigation, other credit-related costs can be reduced. The challenge is balancing this investigation cost against the reduction in other costs that results. Because this tradeoff is between the fixed cost of a particular stage of credit investigation versus bad debt and receivables carrying costs which increase with the amount of credit granted, the size of the exposure (the order size) plays an important role in credit investigation policy, as will be illustrated in the next section.

The Effects of Exposure on Credit Investigation Policy

Consider again the circumstances faced by the analyst if the analysis reaches node 4 in the prior problem. Our prior numerical analysis found that, for exposures of $500, it was not worth an additional credit investigation expense of $25 in order to be able to distinguish between financially strong customers (who in our ex-

Table 2-2. Profit Calcualtions for Example Problems

Outcome:	1R	2P	2D	3PPT.	3R	4R	5P	5D	6S	8P	8D	7R
Collection on Sales	$0.00	$500.00	$0.00	$500.00	$0.00	$0.00	$500.00	$0.00	$500.00	$500.00	$0.00	$0.00
Cost of Goods Sold	$0.00	$425.00	$425.00	$425.00	$0.00	$0.00	$425.00	$425.00	$425.00	$425.00	$425.00	$0.00
Gross Margin	$0.00	$75.00	($425.00)	$75.00	$0.00	$0.00	$75.00	($425.00)	$75.00	$75.00	($425.00)	$0.00
Credit Costs:												
Accounts rec. carrying cost	$0.00	$6.25	$0.00	$4.17	$0.00	$0.00	$6.25	$0.00	$4.17	$11.11	$0.00	$0.00
First-stage investigation cost	$0.00	$0.00	$0.00	$5.00	$5.00	$5.00	$5.00	$5.00	$5.00	$5.00	$5.00	$5.00
Second-stage investigation cost	$0.00	$0.00	$0.00	$0.00	$0.00	$0.00	$0.00	$0.00	$25.00	$25.00	$25.00	$25.00
Profit after credit-related costs	$0.00	$68.75	($425.00)	$65.83	($5.00)	($5.00)	$63.75	($430.00)	$40.83	$33.89	($455.00)	($30.00)
Other Data:												
Days to Pay		45	45	30			45		30	80		

Table 2-3. Calculation of Expected Profits at Chance Event Nodes for Example Problem

Node	Probability, First Outcome	Profit, First Outcome	Probability, Second Outcome	Profit, Second Outcome	Probability, Third Outcome	Profit, Third Outcome	Expected Profit
8	0.85	$33.89	0.15	($455.00)			($39.44)
6	0.30	($30.00)	0.70	$40.83			$19.58
5	0.05	($430.00)	0.95	$63.75			$39.06
3	0.05	($5.00)	0.20	$39.06	0.75	$65.83	$56.93
2	0.05	($425.00)	0.95	$68.75			$44.06

Figure 2-3. Example Decision Tree With Roll-Back

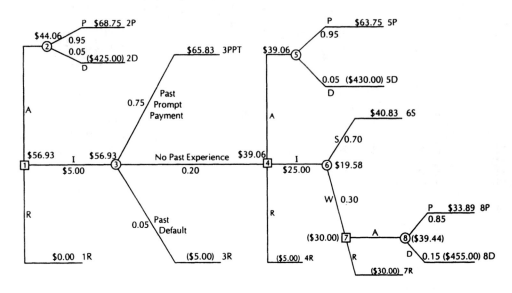

ample are profitable sales) and financially weak customers (who are not profitable because their expected bad debt and carrying costs are too high). But while
the $25 cost of additional investigation is fixed, bad debt costs and accounts re-
ceivable carrying costs depend on exposure. It is logical that for some *higher* levels

Figure 2-4. Portion of Example Decision Tree for Order Size of $10,000

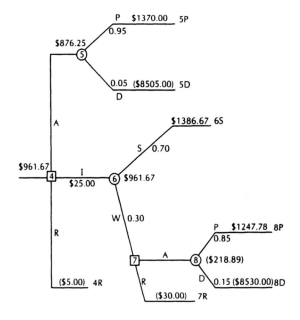

of exposure, distinguishing among customers with strong from weak financial positions *will be warranted.*[16]

To illustrate, let us repeat the appropriate portions of the analysis at nodes 4 through 8 for our example problem, changing the order size to $10,000.[17] The necessary calculations are presented in Table 2-4 and the rolled-back decision tree in Figure 2-4.

The important thing to note in Figure 2-4 is that at node 4 it is now advantageous to investigate further, since the expected profitability at node 6 exceeds that at node 5 (node 5 representing the choice of no further investigation). In fact, in this problem it is advantageous to spend $25 to perform the second-stage investigation as long as the order amount exceeds $2,264, which is the break-even volume for the choice between investigating further and not investigating further at node 4.[18] This break-even situation is illustrated in Table 2-5. Note that the expected profitabilities at nodes 5 and 6 in panel B of this table are essentially equal, the difference being due to rounding.

Further, while sufficiently high volumes trigger stage two investigation, for sufficiently low volumes even stage one investigation (checking prior payment experience in this problem) is not profitable. The important point is that *advantageous credit investigation policy must be tailored to order volume.* Higher exposures increase expected bad debt expense and accounts receivable carrying costs, justifying additional credit investigation expenses aimed at assessing and controlling these costs.

Therefore, a large part of the science of making credit investigation policy concerns the coordination of credit investigation with order volume, frequently by linking levels of exposure to the firm's sequential list of sources of credit information. In this approach, the credit policy maker specifies the level of exposure that is appropriate for each level of credit investigation. If that level of exposure is passed, the next level of credit investigation is performed. In such a system, orders resulting in exposures of less than a certain dollar amount are shipped without credit investigation unless the customer is past due; once the exposure reaches a particular cutoff, the first stage of credit investigation is triggered; and so forth down the sequential list.

The prior analysis shows how optimal credit investigation policy relates to order size. However, product profitability also affects the relationship between the level of exposure and the optimal amount of credit investigation. This relationship is illustrated in the next section.

---

[16] Note the implication in this numerical example that applicants with weak financial positions (who have a relatively high probability of default) will be granted credit for small exposures. However, if their order volumes are sufficiently large to trigger second-stage credit investigation, they will be sorted from stronger applicants and denied credit. Therefore, some applicants will be granted credit for lesser amounts but not for larger amounts, where further investigation reveals their higher credit costs. This subtle point is a perfectly logical consequence of the tradeoff between credit investigation costs, expected bad debt costs, and accounts receivable carrying costs.

[17] It is not necessary to repeat the analysis at nodes 1, 2, and 3, which concern whether the analyst should check prior payment experience (which is the first and cheapest of the credit investigation techniques in this firm's sequential list). This is not necessary because we found previously that this type of investigation was advantageous for a smaller order size ($500), so it will certainly be advantageous for a larger order size.

[18] This break-even point is computed algebraically by setting the expected profits at nodes 5 and 6 equal to each other and solving for order size.

Table 2-4. Calculation of Profits for a $10,000 Order Size

Panel A: Calculation of Profits for Example Problem, Exposure = $10,000

Outcome:	4R	5P	5D	6S	8P	8D	7R
Collections on Sales	$0.00	$10,000.00	$0.00	$10,000.00	$10,000.00	$0.00	$0.00
Cost of Goods Sold	$0.00	$8,500.00	$8,500.00	$8,500.00	$8,500.00	$8,500.00	$0.00
Gross Margin	$0.00	$1,500.00	($8,500.00)	$1,500.00	$1,500.00	($8,500.00)	$0.00
Credit Costs:							
Accounts rec. carrying cost	$0.00	$125.00	$0.00	$83.33	$222.22	$0.00	$0.00
First-stage investigation cost	$5.00	$5.00	$5.00	$5.00	$5.00	$5.00	$5.00
Second-stage investigation cost	$0.00	$0.00	$0.00	$25.00	$25.00	$25.00	$25.00
Profit after credit-related costs	($5.00)	$1,370.00	($8,505.00)	$1,386.67	$1,247.78	($8,530.00)	($30.00)
Other Data:							
Days to pay		45		30	80		

Panel B: Calculation of Expected Profits at Chance Event Nodes, Exposure = $10,000

Node	Probability, First Outcome	Profit, First Outcome	Probability, Second Outcome	Profit, Second Outcome	Expected Profit
8	0.85	$1,247.78	0.15	($8,530.00)	($218.89)
6	0.30	($30.00)	0.70	$1,386.67	$961.67
5	0.05	($8,505.00)	0.95	$1,370.00	$876.25

Table 2-5. Calculation of Profits for a $2,264 Order Size

Panel A: Calculation of Profits for Example Problem, Exposure = $2,264

Outcome:	4R	5P	5D	6S	8P	8D	7R
Collections on Sales	$0.00	$2,264.00	$0.00	$2,264.00	$2,264.00	$0.00	$0.00
Cost of Goods Sold	$0.00	$1,924.40	$1,924.40	$1,924.40	$1,924.40	$1,924.40	$0.00
Gross Margin	$0.00	$339.60	($1,924.40)	$339.60	$339.60	($1,924.40)	$0.00
Credit Costs:							
Accounts rec. carrying cost	$0.00	$28.30	$0.00	$18.87	$50.31	$0.00	$0.00
First-stage investigation cost	$5.00	$5.00	$5.00	$5.00	$5.00	$5.00	$5.00
Second-stage investigation cost	$0.00	$0.00	$0.00	$25.00	$25.00	$25.00	$25.00
Profit after credit-related costs	($5.00)	$306.30	($1,929.40)	$290.73	$259.29	($1,954.40)	($30.00)
Other Data:							
Days to pay		45		30	80		

Panel B: Calculation of Expected Profits at Chance Event Nodes, Exposure = $2,264

Node	Probability, First Outcome	Profit, First Outcome	Probability, Second Outcome	Profit, Second Outcome	Expected Profit
8	0.85	$259.29	0.15	($1,954.40)	($72.76)
6	0.30	($30.00)	0.70	$290.73	$194.51
5	0.05	($1,929.40)	0.95	$306.30	$194.52

The Effects of Profitability on Credit Investigation Policy

As discussed in the prior chapter, the credit policy-maker must formulate policy in line with the system by which the firm evaluates its credit personnel. If the firm is structured such that profitability (as opposed to cost-minimization) is a credit department goal, then the effects of differences in profitability among the firm's products or services (that is, differences in profit margin before credit-related expenses) on credit investigation policy need to be examined. While we will illustrate the relationship mathematically, the intuition is:

1. The greater the profitability of the product or service, the more customers for whom the granting of credit will be advantageous.

2. The more customers for whom credit-granting will be advantageous, the less credit investigation will be needed to distinguish advantageous from disadvantageous customers.

3. Therefore, the higher the product profitability, the less credit investigation should be performed.

That is, *if product profitability is greater, it will require higher exposure levels to trigger additional credit investigation* than when product profitability is lower.

To illustrate this principle, let us turn again to our numerical example. In it, cost of goods sold were 85 percent of sales, and we found that exposures of greater than $2,264 were needed to make second-stage investigation necessary. However, differences in product profitability affect this trigger point. Table 2-6 illustrates how this break point changes with CGS/sales.

In this table, note that when CGS/sales is higher (that is, when product profitability before credit-related costs is lower), the exposure necessary to trigger the investigation is lower, reflecting the greater investigation required when product profit margins are narrower.

One interesting side note from this example problem is that, if CGS/sales falls below some particular level, second-stage credit investigation will never be needed. This is true because, for CGS/sales ratios lower that this level, profits before credit costs are sufficiently large that granting credit even to customers whose financial position would be found to be relatively weak (in credit investigation at node 6) is advantageous. In that case, a second-stage credit investigation is never necessary to distinguish weak from strong applicants. Both are advantageous and thus are granted credit.[19]

Next-Decision Analysis[20]

The decision-tree model of credit investigation previously presented is useful in two respects. First, it shows the trade-offs that are necessary in the formulation of

---

[19] In this problem, this CGS/sales level is 83.1 percent. For example, if CGS/sales is .80 and order size is $500, profitability of outcome 8P is $500-.80($500)-(80/360).1($500)-30 = $58.89 and the loss for outcome 8D is -.80(500)-30 = -$430, so the expected profitability at node 8 is .85($58.89)+.15(-430) = -$14.44, which is greater than the profitability of -$30 from rejecting these customers (outcome 7R), so the best choice is to grant credit.

[20] This section draws from Frederick C. Scherr, "A New Technique for Weighing Credit Benefit Decisions," *Credit and Financial Management Review*, 1995, pp. 32-35.

Table 2-6.   Sensitivity Analysis of Exposure Necessary to Trigger Second-Stage Investigation for Various CGS/Sales in Numerical Example

CGS/Sales	Necessary Exposure	
83.5%	$3,822	
84.0%	$3,109	
84.5%	$2,620	
85.0%	$2,264	Base Case
85.5%	$1,993	
86.0%	$1,780	
86.5%	$1,609	
87.0%	$1,467	
87.5%	$1,348	

credit policy, and second, it allows the illustration of the effects of order size and product profitability on credit investigation strategy via simple numerical examples. This allows the credit policy-maker to understand the principles by which the cutoffs (in terms of exposure) necessary to trigger various stages of credit investigation should be set. These cutoffs are useful guidelines for credit analysts, particularly if the analysts are not very experienced.

Unfortunately, the direct application of this model to the calculation of actual numerical values for these cutoffs, while possible mathematically, is impractical in real situations because of the required expense of data collection and parameter estimation. To use this model in practice, the firm must make an estimate of the time to pay and of the probability of default for *every possible outcome of the credit investigation process*, many of which may never occur. In real credit investigations, there are many thousands of possible combinations of the various informational outcomes of the credit investigation procedure: past payment experiences, credit ratings, assessments of financial strength, and so on. While the procedure could be simplified (for example, by the grouping of outcomes of the assessment of financial strength into "weak" and "strong" in the prior numerical example), each simplification decreases the ability of the model to represent the real world.

A better credit policy, particularly if the firm's credit analysts are relatively experienced, is to train analysts to consider the costs and benefits of additional credit investigation "on the fly" as the analyst investigates a particular account. In this process, the analyst looks at the potential results of the next stage of credit analysis to see whether the benefits, in terms of increased accuracy in making the credit-granting decision, are worth the investigation cost, given the size of the order. We use the term "next-decision analysis" to describe the quantitative analysis of this cost/benefit tradeoff.

An Example Analysis—Next-decision analysis is best illustrated by example. Consider the analyst who has performed sufficient credit investigation so that the next stage requires an expenditure of $150 for the analysis of the customer's financial statements. (This $150 is the sum of opportunity and out-of-pocket in-

Table 2-7.   **Possible Results of Credit Investigation for Example**

Investigation Result	Probability of This Result	Estimate of Chance of Default	Estimate of Time to Pay
Worst Case	0.2	15%	100 days
Current Estimates	0.6	10%	75 days
Best Case	0.2	5%	50 days

vestigation costs.) Based on information generated from credit investigation up to this point, the credit analyst expects that the chance of default for this account is 10 percent, and that payment is expected in 75 days if the account does not default. The order in hand is for $10,000, the cost of this order is 85 percent of sales, and the selling firm's cost of capital is 10 percent per year.

The benefits of additional investigation involve the ability to better estimate the parameters of the credit applicant that determine credit-related costs, in this case the chance of default (which is used to estimate expected bad debt expense) and the time to pay (which is used to estimate accounts receivable carrying costs). One approach to the problem is "best case-worst case" analysis in which the credit analyst analyzes the best and worst-case outcomes relative to what the analyst currently knows.[21] The potential results of further credit investigation are characterized as three cases: (1) the investigation will show that the account is in worse shape than expected, (2) the credit investigation will confirm the analyst's prior estimates, and (3) the investigation will show that the account is in better shape than expected. In this procedure, the analyst estimates values for the chance of default and the time to pay for each of the three outcomes and assigns probabilities to each of these outcomes of investigation. The potential result of such an estimation is presented in Table 2-7.

The spread of probabilities captures the amount of uncertainty that the credit analyst has about the true financial condition of the applicant. The numerical analysis necessary to decide on additional investigation is presented in Table 2-8, with all cost figures calculated as previously discussed.

If the analyst spends the $150 necessary to assess which of the possible outcomes fits the customer, the customer would not be granted credit if it fits the "worst-case" result (since the profit from granting credit is negative), while the customer would be granted credit for the "expected" and "best-case" outcomes. The expected profitability from investigation and these resulting decisions is then $.2(\$0) + .6(\$292) + .2(\$861) = \$347$. Without this credit investigation, credit would be granted even if the customer were in fact "worst case," and the expected profitability of granting credit would be $292 $(= .2(-\$278) + .6(\$292) + .2(\$861))$. Therefore, the gain from investigation allowing for the cost of investigation is –$94 $(= \$347 - \$292 - \$150$, difference due to rounding), and the investigation *should not*

---

[21] This type of analysis is also known as "optimistic-realistic-pessimistic" analysis. We will use it several times in later chapters.

Table 2-8. Next-Decision Analysis of Example Credit Investigation Decision

Situation	Worst Case	Expected Result	Best Case
Sales	$10,000	$10,000	$10,000
Cost of Goods Sold	$8,500	$8,500	$8,500
Margin before Credit Costs	$1,500	$1,500	$1,500
Expected Time to Pay (days)	100	75	50
Carrying Cost	$278	$208	$139
Chance of Default	0.15	0.10	0.05
Expected Bad Debt Expense	$1,500	$1,000	$500
Profit from Granting Credit	($278)	$292	$861
Best Decision	reject	grant	grant
Profit from Best Decision	$0	$292	$861
Probability of this Investigation Outcome	0.2	0.6	0.2
Expected Profitability with Investigation			$347
Expected Profitability without Investigation			$292
Difference			$56
Cost of Next-Stage Investigation			$150
Net Gain from Investigation			($94)

be performed. In this example, the gain in more accurate decision-making is not worth the investigation cost.

Advantages and Disadvantages of Next-Decision Analysis—The traditional method of deciding whether additional credit investigation is warranted is to use pure judgment without the aid of quantitative analysis. In practice, when should credit analysts be instructed to use next-decision analysis rather than this traditional method? This clearly depends on the advantages of next-decision analysis versus the traditional approach.

The advantage of the traditional approach is that it does not require any of the analyst's time to make parameter estimates and perform quantitative analysis, since decisions are made solely on a "feel" for the situation.[22] A primary disadvantage of that technique stems from the natural tendency of credit analysts to over investigate when using this approach. Since the credit analyst has no means to quantitatively assess when enough investigation has been performed, the analyst will tend to hedge by performing the next stage of investigation even when it is not really needed. This raises credit investigation costs beyond required levels. The advantage of next-decision analysis is that it produces an explicit cost-benefit analysis of the credit investigation decision, and is likely to result in investigation decisions that are advantageous to the firm.

---

[22] While this savings in analysis time is not trivial, note that the analysis costs of the next-decision procedure can be reduced considerably if the credit analyst is provided with a series of spreadsheet templates for analyzing various types of investigation decisions. These templates would specify the possible outcomes of the next stage of credit investigation. The analyst would enter estimates of times to pay and default probabilities for each outcome of this next stage, and the template would tell the analyst whether that stage of investigation was worthwhile.

It is clear from the economics of the matter that credit analysts should actually perform the numerical analysis only when the analysis itself is beneficial, as when the next stage of credit investigation is reasonably expensive. Setting aside the hedging problem discussed above, when the cost of the next stage of credit investigation is reasonably small, a quick and dirty judgmental decision aided by the policy-makers' guidelines linking exposure to the level of credit investigation is likely to be sufficient. However, analysts should be instructed to weigh the costs of investigation as well as the other relevant costs in making such judgmental decisions.

Summary of the Policy Implications in this Chapter

The trade-offs between credit investigation cost and the expected costs of bad debt and accounts receivable carrying make the formulation of credit investigation policy a subtle and interesting aspect of credit management. Because credit investigation functions to provide the credit analyst with the information necessary to assess bad debt and accounts receivable carrying costs, increasing credit investigation expenditures serves to reduce the other two. It is up to the credit policy-maker to formulate policy to produce the lowest *total* cost.

It is rare that a solution to any problem that requires the minimization of total cost should resolve to the minimization of one part of this cost, and credit investigation is no exception. Specifically, one way that the oft-heard goal of minimizing bad debt expense can be achieved is by unnecessary expenditures on credit investigation. Advantageous credit policy instead considers the tradeoff between credit expenditures and other expenses, and recognizes that as long as credit investigation is costly, there will be some level of bad debt (representing credit-granting to defaulted customers when a more complete credit investigation was not economical) that is actually of advantage to the firm.

A second insight concerns the effect of exposure on credit policy. Since the cost of utilizing any particular source of credit information is relatively fixed while the expenses that are controlled by credit investigation (expected bad debt and accounts receivable carrying costs) increase with exposure, advantageous credit policy calls for the amount of credit investigation to increase with exposure. This creates the counterintuitive result that some customers will be considered credit worthy if their exposures are low, but will not be granted credit if their exposures are higher, and their costliness is assessed more accurately.

A last major policy implication concerns the effect of product profitability before credit-related costs (that is, of price/cost margin) on credit investigation. The two are inversely related: the higher the product profitability, the lower should be the amount of credit investigation undertaken (and vice versa: lower margins should entail higher levels of credit investigation). This is so because, the higher the margin, the more customers represent profitable sales, and the lower the amount of credit expenditures required to distinguish advantageous from disadvantageous customers. While these insights are useful, it should be kept in mind that credit investigation costs play a major role in credit policy only when the costs of investigation are on the same order of magnitude as other credit-related costs. Since these other credit-related costs increase with exposure, for larger sales volumes expected bad debt and accounts receivable carrying costs are big enough to dwarf credit investigation costs and the firm will be driven to a relatively full investigation of the customer. Analyses of customers who are sufficiently large that the amount of credit investigation is no longer a policy consideration are the subject of the next chapter.

Case for Discussion and Analysis

The Case of the Innovative Investigator

Jane Lopez was one of four credit analysts of Smythe Distribution, a wholesaler of various novelties. One night, while working late, Ms. Lopez paused a moment to muse over the structure of her job. The credit procedures for Smythe Distribution were detailed in the firm's *Credit Handbook*, a voluminous document whose axiom was "Be prepared for any eventuality!" (In fact, the phrase "be prepared" appeared so frequently in the *Handbook* that the credit analysts were given to calling it the *Boy Scout Manual*.)

One aspect of the "be prepared" philosophy was reflected in the firm's policy toward credit investigation. When any new customer placed its first order with Smythe Distribution, the customer filled out the firm's credit application and was required to provide a copy of its latest financial statement. (Copies of prior financial statements were not required but were frequently provided by customers.) The application and financial statements were then faxed to Smythe's credit department. Once received, a credit analyst would order a credit agency report and a trade clearance and would enter the financial figures for all financial statements provided by the customer into the firm's financial statement analysis package, which computed numerous ratios and compared these to median ratios for the customer's industry. (This process was repeated yearly for ongoing customers.) Once the credit agency report and the trade clearance were received and the financial data analyzed, the credit analyst inspected the results and made a decision on the customer's creditworthiness.

While this procedure allowed the credit analysts to make highly informed decisions on each customer, Ms. Lopez was concerned about certain aspects of it. First, the detailed consideration of every new customer diverted the analysts' efforts from other useful duties. Second, while the sales volume to some customers was very large, some customers purchased only a few thousand dollars in goods over an entire year. Others never purchased again after their first purchase. Third, she knew that some customers had been turned away because they would not provide financial statements. Some of these declined customers would have purchased small volumes from the firm while others would have purchased larger volumes. Fourth, she knew that many of the firm's customers were relatively high-risk, and thought that visiting such customers might provide insights into their creditworthiness that the current system did not provide. Finally, she wondered about the effect of differences among the firm's product lines on credit investigation policy. (A statement of profits by product line for Smythe Distribution, as prepared by the firm's cost accounting department, is presented as Table 2-1C.)

Ms. Lopez contemplated whether it might be advisable to suggest some changes in the *Credit Handbook* to her boss, the General Credit Manager, who was in charge

Table 2-1C. Profitability by Product Line for Smythe Distribution

(All Entries in Millions of Dollars)

	Whoopie Cushions	Hand Buzzers	Trickle Glasses	Magic Cards	Total
Sales Revenue	$10.0	$15.0	$12.0	$20.0	$57.00
Costs of Purchase from Manufacturers:					
Cost of Goods	$4.0	$9.0	$3.6	$10.0	$26.60
Cost of Shipping	$0.4	$0.9	$0.4	$1.0	$2.70
Costs of Distribution	$0.6	$1.4	$0.5	$1.5	$4.00
Total CGS	$5.0	$11.3	$4.5	$12.5	$33.30
Other Expenses:*					
Catalog Expense	$0.2	$0.3	$0.2	$0.4	$1.00
Selling Expenses	$1.8	$2.6	$2.1	$3.5	$10.00
General and Headquarters Expense	$1.4	$2.1	$1.7	$2.8	$8.00
Earnings Before Taxes (EBT)	$1.8	($1.0)	$3.7	$1.2	$5.70

Notes: *Allocated by the percent of sales method.

of credit policy. (Smythe's *Credit Handbook* encouraged such suggestions as signs of leadership potential and stated unequivocally, "What any company is looking for in an employee is leadership!")

Suggestions for Analysis

1. Discuss the virtues of Smythe Distribution's current credit investigation policy.

2. Discuss each of Ms. Lopez's concerns regarding the current policy. Give advantageous modifications of this policy, and discuss the trade-offs inherent in implementing these modifications.

3 Credit Granting Decisions

Undoubtedly the most difficult decisions faced by credit analysts in the course of their work are those regarding credit granting to "marginal accounts." Marginal accounts are those where exposures are large but where the account entails substantial credit risk. A major credit policy question concerns the means that analysts should use in the evaluation of these accounts. The credit policy-maker must specify the methodology that analysts are to use in making credit-granting decisions about them. This methodology should list the important aspects of these accounts that should be considered in credit-granting and how the credit-granting decision process should integrate these aspects to produce a decision. Further, the methodology should indicate what factors are generally unimportant to this decision, and the special circumstances under which these generally unimportant factors must be considered.

In this chapter, the traditional methodology for making credit-granting decisions (the "Five Cs of Credit") is first reviewed. The cost and profit tradeoffs inherent in credit-granting policy are then discussed. A model for making credit decisions on individual customers based on the tradeoff between profit on sales and credit costs is presented, and estimation procedures for each of the parameters in this model are given. The chapter's summary of policy implications is followed by a case in which the use of the model is illustrated.

The Traditional Approach to Credit-Granting Decisions

Any decision methodology must tell the decision-maker two things: (1) what factors are important in making the decision and (2) how these factors are to be combined to make the decision. In the traditional approach to the credit-granting decision, five aspects of the customer are important in making the decision: capital, character, collateral, capacity, and conditions. The credit analyst uses the data collected from various sources of credit information (banks, commercial reporting agencies, and so forth) to assess the customer along each of these dimensions. The credit analyst then judges these factors to determine whether the customer is "creditworthy." If the customer passes the test of creditworthiness, credit (in some amount) is granted.

Let us critically evaluate this technique from a policy standpoint based on the cost and benefit concepts presented in prior chapters. At their heart the Five Cs are proxies for some of the credit-related costs which were discussed in Chapter 1. Specifically, they are proxies for expected bad debt expense, accounts receivable carrying costs, and credit and administration costs from granting credit to an account.

For example, consider the analysis of "capital" that is performed under a Five Cs approach. When assessing capital, the analyst looks at liquidity, debt position, and similar aspects of the customer's financial structure. The customer's position on these dimensions is compared to industry norms and is charted over time to detect trends. The analyst reaches some conclusion on the financial strength of the customer relative to other firms in the industry and whether that strength is likely to change in the future.

But what is really being done is an indirect assessment of the costs of granting credit. Liquidity and debt position are guides of the customer's likelihood of default (and thus of expected bad debt expense) and of the time that the customer is likely to take to pay if the customer does not default (and thus of accounts receivable carrying costs). Customers with better liquidity and debt positions are less likely to default (and therefore they have lower expected bad debt expenses) and are more likely to pay quickly (thus they have lower accounts receivable carrying costs). The same logic extends to the other four Cs. The Five Cs methodology is simply a secondhand way of looking at surrogates for some of the costs which the firm bears when credit is granted.

Problems With the Traditional Approach—There are at least two major problems with the Five Cs approach. The first problem has to do with the nature of capital, capacity, and so forth as proxies for the actual costs of granting credit. Since no actual estimates of these costs are made, it is difficult for the credit analyst to: (1) assess tradeoffs among aspects of the customer, and (2) to determine what level of these aspects is sufficient for creditworthiness. How much "capital" is worth how much "character?" How much of both is needed for the customer to be granted credit? These are not easy questions to answer, but they occur frequently and make the Five Cs methodology difficult to apply, particularly for the inexperienced analyst.

The second problem with this analysis system is that within the Five Cs the difference between the selling price of the product or service and the cost of producing that product or service (the product's profitability on sales) is not reflected. This factor must either be included as an additional consideration in the analysis or ignored altogether. Ignoring product profitability considerations is entirely appropriate if the selling firm's organizational structure is such that credit managers are evaluated only on cost-based targets. However, if the firm's credit managers are evaluated based on profitability considerations, this major difficulty further complicates the use of the Five Cs as a decision methodology.

Overall Tradeoffs in Credit-Granting from a Profitability Standpoint: Credit Standards

Problems with the traditional approach to credit-granting decisions can be addressed by using the credit information on the customer in a different way. Instead of using this information to evaluate aspects of the firm which proxy for credit-related costs, a more straightforward approach is to use the information directly to make estimates of these costs, then compare them to the product profitability that results from granting credit. In such a system, there is no question of how to trade off one aspect of the customer against another, since these aspects are expressed in a common denominator: dollars of cost or revenue. There is also no question about what constitutes creditworthiness if credit managers are evaluated on a profitability basis: customers who are expected to add to the firm's profits are creditworthy.[23]

Before discussing the application of the profitability approach to credit-granting strategy at the level of the individual customer (which is the level at which such decisions are generally made), it is useful to consider the conceptual implications of credit-granting strategy for the firm's entire customer base of both existing and potential customers. In the finance literature, this overall view of credit-granting policy is called "credit standards."

In the analysis of credit standards, the selling firm groups customers according to credit costs based on expected days to pay, default probability, and credit and administration costs. These groups are then ordered from highest to lowest profits. The credit standards decision is where to draw the line between groups that get credit and those that do not. This procedure is illustrated in Table 3-1. The firm's customers have been divided into seven groups. Each group has the same potential sales volume ($1,000,000 per year; analysis is for the upcoming year).[24] Cost of goods sold is the same for each group, at 88 percent of sales. Group A has the lowest default probability, expected days to pay, and credit and administration costs, while Group G is the highest in all of these. The "Total Profits" line tracks the cumulative profitability of granting credit and selling to groups of that set of characteristics or lower. (That is, the $181,250 figure for total profits in the column representing Group B is the total of the profits from Group A and Group B. This represents the total profits if the credit standards are such that Groups A and B are granted credit while the other groups are not.)

---

[23] If credit managers are evaluated on the basis of credit costs alone, the question of credit granting is more difficult, as it is far from clear what level of expected costs is "too high" for the customer to be creditworthy.

[24] Equal potential sales volume among groups is not necessary for the procedure; this pattern of potential sales volume is used for simplicity.

Table 3-1. Analysis of Credit Standards

Customer Group	A	B	C	D	E	F	G
Sales to Group if Credit is Granted	$1,000,000	$1,000,000	$1,000,000	$1,000,000	$1,000,000	$1,000,000	$1,000,000
CGS (88% of Sales)	$880,000	$880,000	$880,000	$880,000	$880,000	$880,000	$880,000
Expected Days to Pay for This Group	30	45	60	75	90	105	120
Expected Exposure for This Group	$83,333	$125,000	$166,667	$208,333	$250,000	$291,667	$333,333
Default Probability for This Group	0	0.03	0.06	0.09	0.12	0.15	0.18
Expected Bad Debt Costs for This Group	0	$3,750	$10,000	$18,750	$30,000	$43,750	$60,000
Expected A/R Carrying Costs for This Group (MCC=12%)	$10,000	$15,000	$20,000	$25,000	$30,000	$35,000	$40,000
Expected Collection and Administration Costs for This Group	10,000	$20,000	$30,000	$40,000	$50,000	$60,000	$70,000
Total Costs for This Group	$900,000	$918,750	$940,000	$963,750	$990,000	$1,018,750	$1,050,000
Profits for this Group	$100,000	$81,250	$60,000	$36,250	$10,000	($18,750)	($50,000)
Total Sales	$1,000,000	$2,000,000	$3,000,000	$4,000,000	$5,000,000	$6,000,000	$7,000,000
Total Costs	$900,000	$1,818,750	$2,758,750	$3,722,500	$4,712,500	$5,731,250	$6,781,250
Total Profits	$100,000	$181,250	$241,250	$277,500	$287,500	$268,750	$218,750

The important insight that comes from this analysis flows from a graph of total profits versus credit standards. At some point, profits peak and granting further credit is disadvantageous. Figure 3-1 presents this graph for the product cost structure in Table 3-1. The optimal credit standards policy is to grant credit and sell to customers in Groups A through E but to deny credit to customers in groups F and G, since this cutoff results in maximum total profits of $287,500 for the selling firm (the maximum height of the graph in Figure 3-1).

A second insight is that this policy, like all policy decisions, depends on the selling firm's product cost structure. Lower product costs (due to lower costs of production and/or costs of materials) require looser credit standards, while higher costs require tighter credit standards.[25]

Figure 3-2 illustrates this principle. In addition to the analysis for the cost figures in Table 3-1, this figure presents profits versus credit standards graphs based on two alterations of this analysis: (1) the selling firm's cost of goods sold is 85 percent of sales and (2) the selling firm's cost of goods sold is 91 percent of sales. From this figure, we see that when the firm's cost of goods sold is 85 percent of sales, profits are highest when Groups A-F are granted credit and only group G is rejected. However, when CGS is 91 percent of sales, the optimal credit-granting policy is quite restrictive: only Groups A, B, C, and D are granted credit, while Groups E, F, and G are denied credit. The logic of this example applies regardless of what component of product cost causes this cost difference: optimal credit-granting policy will be looser when product costs are lower and margins are higher.

While this conceptual analysis of overall credit standards provides insights for credit-granting policy in general, it is unrepresentative in that credit-granting decisions are usually made on a case-by-case rather than on a grouped basis. When large amounts of money are involved (as in the case of the classic "marginal account"), it makes sense to include the particularities of each customer in the analysis, so that the conclusion reached is most appropriate for that customer's individual set of circumstances.[26] The next section presents a model for the making of credit-granting decisions on individual customers.

Making Credit Decisions on Individual Accounts: A Present Value Approach

This section provides a quantitative model for making credit-granting decisions on individual customers. The model is an alternative to the traditional Five Cs approach, and balances the benefits of credit-granting in increased sales to its costs. The model reflects the principles of modern finance in that it is based on

---

[25] This point is discussed in more depth in Lynn Tylczak, *Credit and Sales: The Winning Team*, NACM, 1994, pp. 36-38. To facilitate policies which coordinate sales and credit policies, Tylczak suggests that salespeople provide estimates of the profit margins on products to be sold when communicating with the credit department.

[26] Also, commercial law allows credit-granting decisions to be made on a case-by-case basis rather than across the board when it is in the interests of the seller to do so, as for marginal accounts. While case-by-case decisions are allowed in credit-granting, this is not true for other types of credit policy decisions, particularly those regarding terms of sale. More discussion of this issue will be presented in Chapter 7.

Figure 3-1. Analysis of Credit Standards

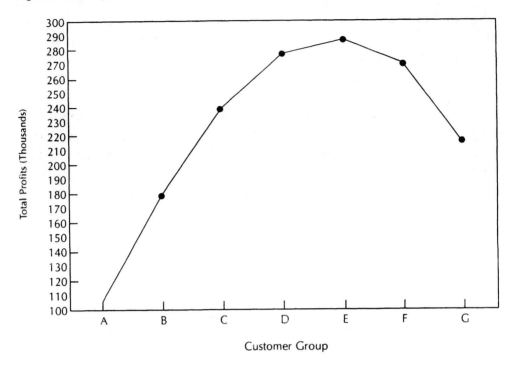

Figure 3-2. Credit Standards for Several CGS/Sales

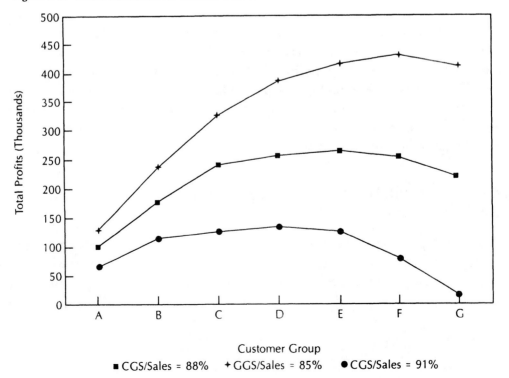

the marginal cash flows that result from the decision and the timing of each marginal cash flow. These principles are used throughout modern financial management, whether the decision concerns the purchase of a piece of equipment, the management of the firm's cash, or the nature and timing of a security issue. Sections following this will deal with the estimation of the parameters necessary to execute the model and analysis of the effects of uncertainty in this parameter estimation on the credit-granting decision.

Some background on the model to be presented is appropriate. In formulating all decision models, there is a tradeoff between simplicity and the ability of the model to represent the real world. Decision models which include more aspects of the real world are more complicated to use because they are more complex and require the estimation of more parameters. Since credit-granting decisions on marginal accounts are so important, this section presents a model which is a reasonably accurate representation of many of the aspects of the credit-granting and payment process (for example, the effects of taxes are included). The cost of this accuracy is some loss of simplicity.

Because the timing of costs and revenues is reasonably important in the credit-granting decision, the model is based on present value. All present value models are based on the marginal cash flows associated with a decision, in this case the decision to grant credit. We will initially limit the cash flows considered to those from the order in hand. Circumstances under which future orders must be considered in making the credit-granting decision will be discussed later in the chapter. Credit investigation costs are ignored since it is assumed that all relevant credit investigation has been performed, and collection and administration expenses are ignored because it is assumed that for marginal accounts these are small relative to the magnitude of the other cash flows from the credit-granting decision. We also assume that only two outcomes occur as the result of granting credit:[27]

1. The customer does not default and pays for the sale. In this case, the seller will receive a cash inflow in the amount of the sale, though the receipt of this cash flow will be delayed by the time it takes the customer to pay. The sale will also generate a tax bill for the seller if the sale is profitable and the seller is taxable, and this bill will result in a cash outflow the next time the seller makes a tax payment.

2. The customer defaults and is liquidated. In this case, the seller will receive the recovery in default at the time the seller is liquidated. Under current U.S. tax law, the seller will still have to pay the initial tax bill on the sale (just as when the customer pays for the sale) even if the customer defaults, but the de-

---

[27] For more discussion of models of this sort, see Frederick C. Scherr, "The Industrial Credit-Granting Decision: Two-State Models including Tax Effects," *Akron Business and Economic Review*, Winter 1985, pp. 7-11, and Frederick C. Scherr, *Modern Working Capital Management: Text and Cases*, Prentice Hall, 1989, pp. 218-230. A simpler and less comprehensive present value model of credit granting is presented in Terry S. Maness and John T. Zietlow, *Short-Term Financial Management: Text, Readings, and Cases*, West Publishing, 1991, pp. 80-81.

When the selling firm offers a cash discount, the two-outcome model does not adequately represent the credit-granting situation. When a cash discount is offered, three outcomes of credit-granting typically occur: payment in the discount period, payment beyond the discount period, and default. A credit-granting decision model for this circumstance is presented in the appendix for this chapter; the value of a cash discount as part of the firm's terms of sale is discussed in Chapter 7.

fault will generate a tax shield in the amount of the loss when the liquidation is adjudicated and the loss is recognized for tax purposes.

In either case the seller will have to pay to replace the inventory sold and for other costs necessary to make the sale. There may be a delay in paying for these expenses. In summary, there are five cash flows in this model:

1. The cash outflow to replenish inventory and pay the other costs of servicing the order. This cash flow occurs whether or not the customer defaults.

2. The initial tax bill on the profit from the sale, which also occurs whether or not the customer defaults.

3. The cash inflow from paying for the sale if the customer makes this payment.

4. The cash inflow from the recovery in the liquidation of the customer if and when the customer is liquidated.

5. The tax reduction due to the writeoff of the bad debt loss if and when the customer is liquidated.

It is useful at this point to use some elementary algebra.

Let: S = The amount of the sale in dollars.
         V = The out-of-pocket cash costs of servicing the order.
         a = The time delay until V is paid.
         T = The firm's income tax rate.
         b = The time delay until the initial tax bill is paid.
         c = The time delay until the customer pays for the sale if the customer does not default.
         k = The selling firm's cost of capital.
         R = The recovery rate in liquidation should the customer liquidate.
         d = The time delay until the customer is liquidated should the customer liquidate.
         X = The probability that the customer defaults and is liquidated.

Using this notation and assuming that the sale will not be made unless credit is granted, we can visualize the credit-granting decision as a simple, one-stage decision tree in which the single uncertain future event is whether the customer pays or defaults. This tree is presented in Figure 3-3, with A, R, P, and D, indicating Accept (grant) credit, Reject credit, Payment, and Default as in Chapter 1. Since X is the probability that the customer will default on the sale and be liquidated, the probability of payment is $(1-X)$, and the expected present value from granting credit is:

$$E(PV) = -V/(1+k)^a - (S-V)T/(1+k)^b + (1-X)S/(1+k)^c + XRS/(1+k)^d + XT(1-R)S/(1+k)^d$$

While this formula looks quite complicated, it is really quite simple when examined one term at a time. There are five terms. Each term represents the contribution to the expected present value of one of the five cash flows. The first term, $-V/(1+k)^a$, is simply the present value of the costs of servicing the order. The second term, $-(S-V)T/(1+k)^b$, is the present value of the tax bill associated from

Figure 3-3. Decision Tree of the Credit-Granting Model

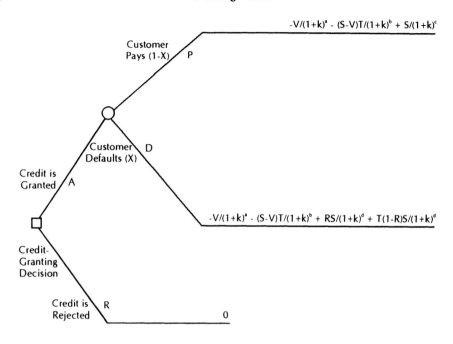

making the sale, since S–V is the profit and T is the income tax rate. In the third term, $S/(1+k)^c$ is the present value of the cash flow if the firm pays and (1–X) is the probability of payment, so the present value of the expected cash flow is $(1–X)S/(1+k)^c$.

In the fourth term, RS is the cash recovery from liquidation if the firm defaults. This occurs with probability X and at time d, so its contribution to the expected present value is $XRS/(1+k)^d$. The fifth term is the present value of the tax savings from the writeoff of the uncollected portion of the receivable. Since RS is collected, (1–R)S is written off at a tax rate of T. Since the writeoff occurs with probability X, its contribution to the expected present value is $XT(1–R)S/(1+k)^d$.

A Numerical Example—Let us illustrate this model by a numerical example in which the parameters of the model have already been estimated. Later in the chapter, methods for estimating each parameter will be discussed. Assume that a credit analyst has an order in hand for $50,000 (=S) and knows that it will cost his firm $40,000 (=V) to service this order, and that payments for the goods and labor necessary to service the order will be made, on average, 30 days (=a) after the order is shipped. The firm pays taxes at a 35 percent rate (=T), and it is 45 days (=b) until the next tax payment is due. The selling firm's cost of capital is 12 percent per year.

The customer under consideration is quite risky, and the credit analyst estimates that it will be 90 days (=c) until the customer pays if the customer pays at all, and that there is a 5 percent chance (=X) that a customer with this customer's risk characteristics will fail before payment is received.[28] If the customer defaults, the analyst expects that only 10 percent (=R) of the receivable will be recovered, and that the liquidation will take one year (=d).

The formula is executed in Table 3-2. Going through this calculation term by term, the outflow for the order is -$40,000 (the negative sign indicates a cost) and payment for it occurs in 30 days, so its present value is $-\$40,000/(1.12^{30/360}) = -\$39,624$. The profit from the sale will be $10,000 (=$50,000-$40,000), resulting in a $3,500 tax bill (=.35($10,000)). Given that this tax bill is payable in 45 days, its present value is $-\$3,451(=-\$3,500/(1.12^{45/360})$. There is a 95 percent probability that payment will be made, so the firm expects to receive .95($50,000) = $47,500 in 90 days, with a present value of $46,173 (=$47,500/1.12^{90/360})$.

If the customer defaults, the seller expects to recover $5,000 (=.10($50,000). There is a 5 percent probability of default, so the expected cash flow from recovery is $250 (=.05($5,000)), occurring one year in the future and with a present value of $223 (=$250/1.12^{1.0})$. If default occurs, the remaining balance of $45,000 will be written off, resulting in a tax savings of $15,750 (=.35($45,000)). Since the probability of nonpayment has been estimated at 5 percent, the expected cash flow associated with this tax savings is $788 (=.05($15,750)), and its present value is $703 (=$788/1.12^{1.0})$.

The sum of these five components is the expected present value of granting credit and making the sale, and is $4,025, so the sale should be made. Another way of looking at this is that, since a zero value for collection and administration costs was assumed, as long as these costs are not in fact greater than $4,025, then granting credit to this customer is advantageous.

Advantages of the Present Value Approach—Given the venerable history of the traditional approach to credit-granting decisions, some credit managers are likely to be skeptical of basing credit-granting policy on the present value approach. It is important to note that the two analysis systems use the same sorts of credit information, but that they use it in different ways. In the Five Cs, this information forms the basis for assessments of capital, character, etc. A credit analyst then judges whether the levels of the five are sufficient for "creditworthiness." By contrast, in the present value decision model this same information is used to estimate parameters of the customer which represent costs and time delays (the b, X, etc., in the model). The financial principles represented in the model weigh their effects on the benefits of granting credit. The credit analyst's expertise is used to translate credit information into figures that actually represent costs, rather than in trying to interpret this information in terms of five reasonably imprecise concepts.

There are several advantages of the present value approach as a policy alternative to the traditional approach in making credit-granting decisions. First, as pre-

[28] That is to say, the credit analyst estimates that one in 20 customers with these risk characteristics will fail before payment is made and that the remaining 19 will make payment.

Table 3-2. A Present Value Model for Credit-Granting Model Decisions

Parameters:

Symbol	Meaning	Estimate
S	Sale in dollars	$50,000
V	Cost of sale in dollars	$40,000
a	Time until V is paid (days)	30
T	Tax rate	35%
b	Time until tax is paid (days)	45
c	Customer's time to pay (days)	90
k	Seller's yearly cost of capital	12%
R	Recovery rate	10%
d	Time until recovery (years)	1
X	Probability of nonpayment	5%

Value of Term 1: $-V/(1+k)^a$	($39,624)
Value of Term 2: $-(S-V)T/(1+k)^b$	($3,451)
Value of Term 3: $(1-X)S/(1+k)^c$	$46,173
Value of Term 4: $XRS/(1+k)^d$	$223
Value of Term 5: $XT(1-R)S/(1+k)^d$	$703
Present Value of Granting Credit	$4,025

viously discussed, the model allows tradeoffs among the various types of costs and revenues that are associated with the credit-granting decision because all are expressed in dollars, and the model clearly indicates whether granting credit is of advantage to the firm. Second, we will see later in the chapter that the effects of the analyst's uncertainty about these cost estimates on the credit-granting decision can be easily evaluated. This is a difficult procedure if the Five Cs is in use.

Third, the model is in keeping with the financial technology which is generally used to make other types of financial decisions by most large firms. The use of such a common set of principles enables better communication and mobility between the credit department and other finance functions within the firm. Finally, the model aligns the decisions that are made by the credit analyst with those that shareholders would prefer. That is, it results in decisions which maximize the value of the firm, a result to which the Five Cs is not specifically oriented.

Set against these advantages are two major drawbacks. First, models of this sort are not in common use by credit analysts, so some retraining is required. Second, any model which counts benefits from sales is inappropriate when the credit department is evaluated solely on the minimization of credit costs.

A Side Note on Taxes—While this model is in many ways an advantageous alternative to traditional decision methods in analyzing credit-granting decisions, it also provides interesting insights regarding the effect of taxes on credit-granting. One of these effects is relatively obvious: margins (against which credit costs must be compared) are never as large as they seem because a sale will always trigger a tax bill. Taxes are a cost like any other cost.

However, there is a counteracting effect: when the selling firm is taxable, tax savings engendered by the writeoff of the uncollected receivable limits the minimum cash inflow that can occur after credit is granted. For a taxable firm's receivable of $10,000, at a 35 percent tax rate the minimum cash inflow that can occur, even if nothing is recovered in liquidation, is $3,500.

In practice, whenever the corporate policy-maker chooses to include the effect of taxes in the analysis of credit-granting policy, both the effects of taxes in terms of reduced margin and the effects of the tax writeoff in limiting downside risk must be considered. It is easy to incorporate the first of these in analysis but to forget the second. However, the two tend to balance out (though not on a one-for-one basis) since they act in opposite directions on the expected present value of the sale (the initial tax bill reduces the present value while the eventual tax writeoff increases it).

Parameter Estimation for the Present Value Approach

The present value model for making credit-granting decisions involves 10 parameters: S, V, a, T, b, c, k, R, d, and X. Of these, five (V, a, T, b, and k) are parameters related to the selling firm and its products. The other five (S, c, R, d, and X) are related to the particular customer under consideration. Quite different techniques are required to estimate these two types of parameters.

Estimating Seller-Related Parameters—Seller-related parameters do not vary from one customer to another as long as the customers purchase the same product or service. While values for these parameters must be updated periodically, their estimation represents only a modest challenge. The V parameter is the cost of sales for the good or service being provided to the customer. This includes the out-of-pocket costs of any services that are required for the order and the cost of replacing any inventory that has been sold. Data of these sorts is available from the selling firm's product costing statements, the only complication being that the analyst must be careful to center on marginal rather than full costs (see the extensive discussion of this issue in Chapter 2). Once these product-cost records are examined, V is frequently estimated as a percent of S, the amount of the sale.

In the model, a is the average delay until these product or service costs are paid. This will vary from one source of product cost to another. For example, payment for products purchased for resale will typically be made in keeping with the vendor's terms of sale (often 30 days). However, payments for labor services will be delayed until the next pay cycle, which may be as short as a week or as long as a month. For example, consider a product one-half of whose costs consist of goods purchased for resale on terms of 30 days and one-half of labor expense, and that the firm pays labor every two weeks. Since paychecks are issued every two weeks, on average it is 7 days between the time when a labor expense is incurred and when it is paid and the average time between when V is incurred and it is paid is $(.5)30 + .5(7) = 18.5$ days. This is the firm's estimate of a.

The T parameter is the firm's tax rate. This rate depends on two factors: (1) the statutory income tax rate schedule in effect at the time of the sale; and (2) the firm's taxability. Income tax schedules are, of course, set legislatively. Rates and cutoffs for these rates are changed periodically based on political considerations. In the United States, there is some graduation of these rates such that corporations with very low incomes (typically a few tens of thousands of dollars) pay at lower marginal rates, while firms with higher incomes pay at the maximum rate.

Whatever rate applies to additions to the seller's income should be used to estimate T, subject to the seller's taxability. Taxability includes not only whether the firm is tax-exempt (in which case T is zero), but also whether the firm has any losses in the current year or in prior years that are to be used to reduce taxable income. For example, an otherwise taxable firm may have tax loss carry forwards which reduce its tax rate to zero in some years. Of course, taxes are not paid immediately at the time that the tax bill is incurred. Most firms make income tax payments on a periodic basis, frequently making quarterly payments as the tax year proceeds and making final payment when the tax year is complete. The b parameter captures the average delay between the time when a tax liability is incurred and when it is paid. If the firm makes quarterly tax payments on income from that quarter (that is, it makes payments every 90 days), then on average there will be 45 days from the time a sale is made and a tax liability is incurred and the time that the tax payment for that liability is made.

In present value models, when a cash flow is of the same risk as the average cash flow that occurs to a firm, the required rate of return on that cash flow is the firm's cost of capital, which is k in the credit-granting decision model. The cost of capital is a weighted average of the costs of the various stock, debt, and other funds that investors provide to the selling firm, and will vary from firm to firm based on the mix of sources of funding used. In practice, k typically ranges between 10 and 20 percent per year. Since this parameter is so widely used, the finance department of most firms will have it readily available, and the credit manager should seek information from that source.[29]

Estimating Buyer-Related Parameters—Two of the five buyer-related parameters are relatively simple to assess. These are S and d. In the present value model, S is the amount in dollars of the current order being considered for credit. Only this current order should be considered in S.[30] The d parameter is the time delay until the customer is liquidated if the customer defaults. This will largely be a function of efficiency of the particular courts where the liquidation would be performed, and will be at least a year. Legal researchers keep of statistics of these sorts, and the credit analyst needs to keep tabs on the current levels and trends.

While estimations of the seven previously-discussed parameters are important, the majority of the credit analyst's effort and expertise must go into the estimation of the remaining three parameters. They greatly determine whether the customer will be an advantageous credit risk, and depend on the customer's "credit position" as the term is usually used. These parameters are R, the recovery rate in liquidation, c, the time to pay should the customer pay, and X, the probability of default.[31]

Estimating the Recovery Rate in Default—The fraction of the receivable the seller recovers if the customer is liquidated (R) depends on the quality and type of the customer's assets, the structure of the customer's liabilities, and the extent to which these liabilities are collateralized by security interests in assets.[32] Customers whose assets have a relatively high market value when liquidated, who have fewer debts, and whose debts are not secured against assets will have higher recoveries than other firms.

There are at least two good ways to estimate recoveries in default. One is to compare the customer's circumstances to those of other firms that have been liquidated. To do this, first the credit manager develops a sample of firms that have been liquidated. This can be done from the seller's own credit files, if these contain records for a sufficient number of firms (at least 10) that have been liquidated in the past several years, or the information can be obtained from credit reporting agencies or trade reporting groups. Then the credit analyst compiles data on the financial positions of these liquidated firms and the recoveries after liquidation. Relevant aspects of these data are then averaged to obtain a profile of the typical liquidated firm and the recoveries in default from that firm. Included in this profile are all the aspects of the firm that could affect recoveries in liquidation: measures of asset quality (such as the fixed asset turnover ratio, accounts receivable turnover ratio, and the inventory turnover ratio), debt as a percentage of assets, percent of assets pledged as security, and so forth.[33]

This profile is useful as a benchmark against which other customers can be compared. For example, suppose the profile of liquidations finds that the average accounts receivable turnover for liquidated firms when credit was granted was 4.50 times per year, the average inventory turnover was 5.00, and that the average recovery in default is 20 percent. Credit applicants with turnover ratios lower than this are likely to also have lower recoveries than the benchmark. Firms with higher turnover ratios are likely to have higher recoveries.

While it might seem that the gathering of these data on liquidated firms is burdensome, a few comments are in order. First, the well-managed firm will as a matter of course examine the result of all of its decisions (including credit-granting) to determine how its policy-making procedures can be improved. The compilation of these data involve little effort beyond this examination. Second, these

---

[31] Other discussion of the estimation of these parameters can be found in Frederick C. Scherr, *Modern Working Capital: Text and Cases*, Prentice Hall, 1989, pp. 231-235.

[32] Much of the Five Cs analysis under "collateral" and the portion of the analysis of "capital" that deals with asset quality is in fact an assessment of these factors.

[33] Note also that this examination of prior liquidations also provides insight into the time from credit-granting to liquidation recovery (the d parameter).

benchmarks are developed for broad use in estimating the recovery rates from many customers, so the cost of developing them is spread over many decisions.

Another approach to the estimation of recovery rate is the "simulated liquidation" approach. The credit analyst starts with the most recent balance sheet of the customer. Based on past experience and the analyst's knowledge of the customer's business, the analyst makes an estimate of the percent of book value that would be recovered from the sale of each of the customer's assets and applies this to the book value of the asset to get the dollar estimated recovery. (For example, the analyst might estimate that in liquidation 70 percent of the value of the customer's accounts receivable would be obtained once the liquidation was complete. If the book value of accounts receivable were $200,000, the estimated recovery is then $140,000.). These recoveries on the customer's various assets are totaled and payments to secured and priority claims deducted to get the estimated recovery, in dollars, to general creditors. Dividing this estimated recovery by the current amount owed to general creditors gives expected recovery in liquidation.[34]

Because it centers on the particular asset structure and values for the individual customer, the simulated liquidation method is likely to be more accurate in estimating the recovery rate than a simple comparison of the customer with benchmarks derived from past defaults. However, the simulated asset liquidation method is also more burdensome computationally. In either case, the effects of an analyst's uncertainty about his or her estimate of this parameter on the credit-granting decision can be assessed via sensitivity analysis, a technique we will discuss later in the chapter.

Estimating the Time to Pay—The time that the customer will take to pay for the order, if the customer pays rather than defaults (the c parameter), depends on both the customer's ability to pay and the customer's policy in paying trade creditors. One way to assess ability to pay is to inspect the customer's financial ratios which measure the customer's liquidity, such as the current ratio and quick ratios and to some extent the accounts receivable turnover and inventory turnover ratios. The current and quick ratios measure the relationship between those assets which are short-term sources of funds and those liabilities which are short-term uses of funds. The two turnover ratios measure the quality (liquidity) of the two assets from which much of the firm's short-term funds flow comes.

Comparing these four ratios with those of other firms in the industry or with those of the seller's other customers tells the credit analyst much about the time it will take for the customer to make payment. Customers who are lower in liquidity than the average firm in the industry are less able to make payments to the trade as fast as do other firms.

A second method of assessing likely payment time, and one which takes into account both the customer's ability to make trade payments and its payment

---

[34]Of course, this procedure must be adjusted for any particular legal circumstances that would be involved in the individual customer's liquidation: cash offset, subordinated claims, and so forth.

policies, is to examine the customer's accounts payable turnover ratio. This ratio measures the average time that the customer makes payments to the trade. To compute this ratio, the analyst divides the total purchases from suppliers during a period (data obtained from the customer's income statement) by the customer's period-ending accounts payable. Like any turnover ratio, this one can be converted into a time period by dividing it into the number of days in a year. For example, suppose that the customer purchased $4 million in materials and services during the last fiscal year, and that $500,000 was owed to suppliers at the end of that year. Ignoring seasonality in purchases, the turnover ratio is $4,000,000/$500,000 = 8 times per year, which corresponds to an average of 360/8 = 45 days to pay suppliers.

A third method of assessing time to pay is simply to review the customer's payments to the trade as reflected in trade clearances. In addition to revealing how the customer pays the trade as a whole, this can reveal patterns in trade payments which the analyst may reflect in estimates of time to pay. For example, it is not unknown for customers to: (1) pay all suppliers who offer discount terms during the cash discount period while stretching other suppliers for extended periods; (2) pay suppliers of one type of good or service faster than others; or (3) pay all suppliers in the same time (for example, in 60 days) regardless of their terms of sale. Inspection of the trade clearance can reveal policies of these sorts.

A reliable estimate of c will utilize as many of these three methods as the analyst has data to execute. Contrasting these methods can reveal as much about the customer as does examining them individually. For example, consider a customer with high liquidity ratios but slow payments to the trade. This divergence may indicate either that: (1) the customer has a policy of taking as long to pay as possible (which leads to a larger estimate of c than the liquidity ratios might indicate) or (2) the customer's financial statements are not representative of its true financial condition. If the customer's financial statements are not representative, any estimates made using them are suspect, not only estimates of c but also estimates of default probability (X).

Estimating the Probability of Default—Represented by X in the present value model, the probability of default is often the most critical parameter in determining whether the customer represents an advantageous sale and is frequently the most difficult parameter to estimate. Much of the analysis of "capital," "capacity," and "conditions" in the traditional Five Cs approach is relevant to the estimation of this parameter, which is the essence of "credit risk" as the term is usually defined. In this section, we discuss the estimation of X for a customer based on benchmarks for this statistic and on factors which predict X.

Let us turn first to examination of the probability itself and some benchmarks that the analyst can develop regarding this probability. Since the present value model deals with only a single order (the order currently in hand), keep in mind that the default probability is for this single order only; it is the probability that the customer will fail before payment on that order is made. One benchmark regarding this probability is the past fraction of orders for which the seller has not received payment. The seller can determine this from examining its bad debt and sales records. For example, suppose that examination reveals that the seller has experienced default on 1 percent of its past orders.[35] This means that, on average, a customer who passes the firm's credit standards and is granted credit has a 1 percent chance of default. New customers who meet these credit standards but are riskier than average have a higher default probability than one percent, while less risky customers have a lower probability.

Benchmark default probabilities can also be obtained from those commercial sources of credit information which publish default rates by industry. However, it is important to inspect carefully the way in which these default rates are expressed. Commercial sources often express these default rates in terms of the fraction of firms in a particular industry that fail during a year. The present value model looks at default rate only between the time the sale is made and when the payment is expected to be received (time c). If the customer defaults after the sale has been collected, there is no effect on value of the sale to the seller.

When the benchmark default rate is expressed on a yearly basis, an adjustment is necessary to obtain a per-order benchmark figure for X. To make the necessary adjustment from a yearly default rate, the yearly rate must be divided by 360/c. For example, suppose that the analyst finds that the yearly default rate in an industry is 9 percent, and that the analyst expects to be paid in 60 days if payment is made. The 360/c calculation is the 360/60 = 6, and the per-order default rate is 0.09/6 = 0.015, which would be the benchmark estimate of X. After this benchmark is established, the analyst compares measures which are predictive of default for the customer (financial ratios, etc.) to average figures for the industry and makes the necessary adjustments in order to obtain an estimate of X for the customer.

Left unsaid in the above discussion is what measures are predictive of default and consequently what the analyst should examine in adjusting X relative to benchmarks. Traditional financial ratios which measure the customer's risks and returns, such as profitability, liquidity, and debt are very important indicators of a customer's default probability, and are among the more important measures to inspect. Not only is the relationship between these ratios and default or nondefault intuitively strong, but it has been shown to hold empirically in many studies contrasting defaulted and nondefaulted firms. Firms with greater liquidity, greater profitability, and lower debt relative to equity are less likely to default.

In addition to these ratios, which are computed based on accrual accounting conventions, the analysis of cash flows (FASB 95 analysis) which is presented in many modern finance texts is also of use in assessing default probability. Cash flow analysis of this sort tracks the pattern of cash flow through the customer's

---

[35] Note that the language refers specifically to number of orders rather than sales volume. A default rate of one percent of the number of orders is a bad debt loss of 1 percent of sales only if the orders which defaulted were of average size.

business as cash is generated and used.[36] Cash flow analysis is particularly relevant to the estimation of default probability because, for survival purposes, cash is king. A firm with large cash flows and a strong cash position is unlikely to default, regardless of its other aspects, whereas a firm poorer in these respects may have a substantial default risk.

While financial measures can tell a good part of the story on default risk, other aspects of the firm are also important, though their predictive value in forecasting default has not received much attention in the default research literature. It is well known that the default rate for newer firms and for smaller firms is higher than average, and these factors must be reflected in making an estimate of default probability for any particular customer.

On Statistical Default Forecasting—Starting with benchmarks of default risk, the analyst must take the information that has been gathered on a particular customer and use this to make an estimate of X relative to the benchmark. This is primarily a judgmental process involving weighing various aspects. However, attempts have been made to weigh these aspects on a statistical rather than judgmental basis to increase accuracy in forecasting. These statistical procedures will be discussed in Chapter 6.

Sensitivity Analysis of Parameter Estimates

Because the process of estimating the critical R, c, and X variables in the present value model involves judgment, the analyst should be concerned with the effects of this estimation procedure on the credit decision, asking: "If my estimate is wrong, will a poor decision be made?" The way to test the effects of these parameter estimates on the credit decision is to use the "what-if" procedures of "sensitivity analysis." In sensitivity analysis, the analyst tests the criticality of estimates by changing these estimates to see if the decision involved (the credit-granting decision in this case) is affected.

Optimistic-Realistic-Pessimistic Analysis—The most basic of sensitivity analysis is "optimistic-realistic-pessimistic" analysis. A version of this was presented as part of the "next decision analysis" of credit investigation in Chapter 2. In optimistic-realistic-pessimistic analysis, the analyst says, "I have made my best estimates of these parameters [the realistic estimate]. What is the best [optimistic] and worst [pessimistic] estimate of these values that I think could possibly occur?" The analysis is done using each of these three estimates (if all are needed) to assess whether the decision is affected.

To see how this works, let us revisit the numerical analysis presented in Table 3-2 and test it on R, c, and X. Recall that in the original analysis, the estimates were R = 10 percent, c = 90 days, and X = 5 percent. The present value of the sale for these parameters was $4,025. Let us assume that the analyst's rock-bottom

---

[36] A review of cash flow analysis can be found in Charles L. Gahala, *Credit Management: Principles and Practices*, NACM, 1996, pp. 158-167.

Table 3-3.   Execution of the Present Value Model for "Pessimistic" Estimates of R, c, and X

Parameters:

Symbol	Meaning	Estimate
S	Sale in dollars	$50,000
V	Cost of Sale in dollars	$40,000
a	Time until V is paid (days)	30
T	Tax rate	35%
b	Time until tax is paid (days)	45
c	Customer's time to pay (days)	150
k	Seller's yearly cost of capital	12%
R	Recovery rate	0%
d	Time until recovery (years)	1
X	Probability of Nonpayment	10%

Value of Term 1: $-V/(1+k)^a$	($39,624)
Value of Term 2: $-(S-V)T/(1+k)^b$	($3,451)
Value of Term 3: $(1-X)S/(1+k)^c$	$42,924
Value of Term 4: $XRS/(1+k)^d$	$0
Value of Term 5: $XT(1-R)S/(1+k)^d$	$1,563
Present Value of Granting Credit	$1,412

pessimistic estimates of these parameters were $R=0$ percent, $c=150$ days, and $X=10$ percent.[37]

The resulting analysis is presented in Table 3-3. The net expected present value is $1,412, so it is still advantageous to grant credit to the customer. If these estimates of R, c, and X represent the most disadvantageous estimates that the credit analyst believes are reasonable, then the credit analyst can be reasonably certain that the decision to grant credit is a good one.

Single-Parameter Sensitivity Analysis—Optimistic-realistic-pessimistic analysis looks at the worst- and best-case values of each of the uncertain parameters taken together. Another way to test the sensitivity of the decision to changes in estimates is to look at the uncertain parameters one at a time and see what values of each of these parameters are necessary to alter the decision, given the "realistic" values of the other parameters.[38] What we are looking for here are the break-even points: those points which tip the decision from granting credit to refusing credit. The values for these break-even points are then examined to see whether there is a reasonable chance they might occur.

Table 3-4 portrays this analysis for our example where R is varied from 0 to 50 percent, c is varied from 30 days to 360 days, and X is varied from 0 to 50 percent. Results are graphed in Figures 3-4 (for R), 3-5 (for c) and 3-6 (for X).

---

[37] In interpreting this estimate of X, remember that the estimated default rate is for the period of c. A 10 percent estimate for X, given a c of 150 days, means the analyst is estimating a default probability of (360/150)10% = 24% for the upcoming year.

In this case it is unnecessary to perform the "optimistic" analysis since it will not change the decision; the customer is creditworthy for the "realistic" estimates of R, c, and X; lower estimates of c and X and higher estimates of R simply result in higher expected present values.

[38] The analysis that follows is easily performed with modern spreadsheet software, but it would be extremely burdensome if done other ways.

Table 3-4. Sensitivity Analysis of Present Value of Numerical Example for Various Estimates of R, c, and X

R	E(PV)	c	E(PV)	X	E(PV)
0%	$3,880	30	$4,905	0%	$5,528
5%	$3,952	60	$4,463	5%	$4,025*
10%	$4,025*	90	$4,025*	10%	$2,521
15%	$4,097	120	$3,591	15%	$1,017
20%	$4,170	150	$3,161	20%	($487)
25%	$4,242	180	$2,735	25%	($1,991)
30%	$4,315	210	$2,313	30%	($3,494)
35%	$4,387	240	$1,895	35%	($4,998)
40%	$4,460	270	$1,481	40%	($6,502)
45%	$4,532	300	$1,071	45%	($8,006)
50%	$4,605	330	$665	50%	($9,510)
		360	$262		

Note: an * next to a figure indicates that this estimate of the parameter represents the "realistic" case.

Estimates of R between 0 and 50 percent do not affect the decision, as the expected present values of granting credit for all these values of R are positive. Similarly, the expected values of granting credit are also positive for all values of c between 30 and 360 days, though payment in times longer than this would

Figure 3-4. Sensitivity Analysis of R

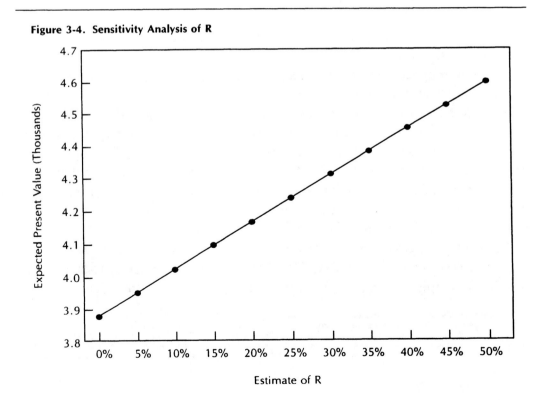

Figure 3-5. Sensitivity Analysis of c

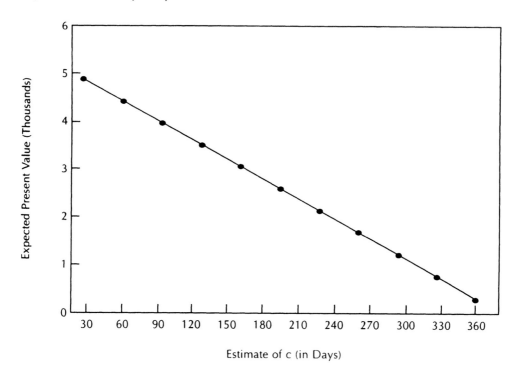

Figure 3-6. Sensitivity Analysis of X

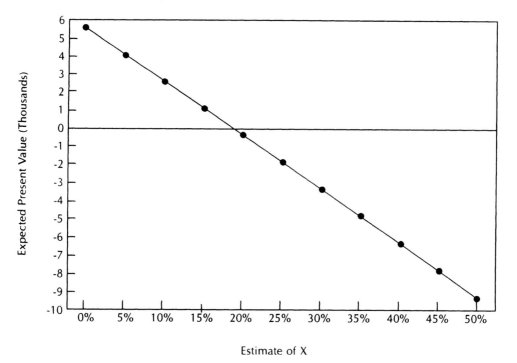

probably result in negative expected present values, since the present value of granting credit if the customer pays in 360 days is only $262.

For this numerical example, only the sensitivity analysis of X presents circumstances where the decision would be changed if the estimate were in error. Specifically, if the default probability on the order in hand is above 15 percent, credit should not be granted. However, this is a very high (and likely improbable) level of default risk, as it is equivalent to a probability estimate that the firm will default during the upcoming year of 60 percent (360/90 times 15 percent).

Based on this sensitivity analysis of individual parameters, we therefore conclude that the customer represents an advantageous credit risk, given the margin on the product and other considerations. Credit would be granted. However, if this decision had been shown to be sensitive to the analyst's estimates of R, c, or X, then the seller might consider refusing credit or negotiating for credit enhancements which would raise the present value of the sale. These enhancements will be discussed in Chapter 4.

Issues in Credit-Granting Decisions

The present value model previously presented evaluates customers based on the narrowest of considerations: the value of a single order. Building a model on such narrow considerations simplifies the modeling and parameter estimation process. If the credit analyst finds the customer to be creditworthy on this basis, then credit should be granted; consideration of any future orders can be deferred until these orders occur, if and when they do. However, suppose the customer is not creditworthy based on this single-order approach, and further that the negotiation and credit-enhancement strategies presented in Chapter 4 fail to produce a positive present value. What other circumstances still make the customer acceptable? This section analyzes several such circumstances and illustrates the contexts under which they require consideration.

Lost Future Orders—When a customer is denied credit for the current order, the issue of the impact of this decision on future orders is frequently raised, with the argument being that denying credit now forecloses advantageous future sales.[39] This argument has a good deal of face validity, and many a credit analyst has been swayed by it. But as a credit policy matter, when does it make sense? The key to understanding the circumstances under which this argument is relevant is in the words "advantageous" and "forecloses." For this argument to be valid, future orders must be both advantageous and foreclosed by the negative credit-granting decision on the current order.

Let us first consider the advantageousness of future orders. This aspect of the argument focuses on the premise that the seller should grant credit now, when the customer *is not* creditworthy, in order to gain future orders later when the

---

[39] For additional discussion of the relevance of future orders to the credit-granting decision, see "Who Cares About Future Orders?" *CRF Staff Report*, December 1992.

customer *is* creditworthy. For this to be true, the customer's creditworthiness must be expected to change over time, from less creditworthy to more creditworthy. If the creditworthiness of the customer is not expected to change over time, there is no sense in considering future orders in the analysis. Just as are current orders, these orders are not good credit risks, and the fact that they are precluded by denying the customer credit for the current order is irrelevant.

There are two ways such a change in creditworthiness over time can occur. The first is when the *actual parameters* of the customer that determine creditworthiness (chiefly R, c, and X) are expected to change such that future orders will have positive expected present values though the current order does not. The second is when the *analyst's estimate* of creditworthiness improves if the customer pays in response to the granting of credit. This occurs when, despite performing as complete a credit investigation as is feasible, the credit manager is still quite uncertain about the customer's creditworthiness. In that case, the receipt of a payment in response to an initial granting of credit sends a signal to the credit manager that the customer's creditworthiness is greater than initially estimated.

The second assumption of the "lost future orders" argument is that refusing credit for the current order *actually forecloses* later sales when the customer's creditworthiness improves. That is, it is an assumption that the customer is brand loyal. If the customer is not brand loyal, there is no reason for the credit manager to grant credit now, when the risk is high, in order to gain access to lower-risk orders later. Instead, the credit manager can simply wait out the high-risk period, thereby avoiding the risk, and sell later when risk is lower (as when the customer's financial position has improved or when the customer has proved itself creditworthy by payments to the trade).

Any time that *either* of these two conditions are invalid, a current-order framework is adequate for credit-granting decisions. Whether they are valid or not is an issue that varies from customer to customer. For example, for very new firms there is good reason to believe their default probabilities will fall over time as they overcome the "liability of newness." In other cases, there is little or no expectation of improvement in creditworthiness. The best example is the well-known established customer with a history of low liquidity and slow payments to the trade. In this case, credit risk is high and payments slow, with no anticipation of improvement. Finally, some industries are characterized by great brand loyalty while in others customers switch from one supplier to another, searching for the best current deal.

Therefore, if analysis of the current order is negative, to assess whether a multi-order view is necessary for the customer the analyst should be instructed to ask two questions:

1. Is either of the following true?
   a. There is a reasonable expectation that the customer will become more creditworthy over time.

  b. A payment in response to my granting of credit would cause me to change my estimates of R, c, or X.

2. Is the customer brand loyal, or will the customer be likely to go to another supplier after my firm has borne the initial credit risk?

If the answer to *either* of these two questions is no, then there is no need to go beyond a single order framework and the customer should not be granted credit. If, however, the answer to *both* is yes, then the customer must be evaluated based not only on revenues and costs from the current order but on the revenues and costs from future orders. Unfortunately, while it is reasonable to employ a cost-benefit model of credit-granting in a single-order framework, multi-order models of this sort involve the estimation of an impracticably large number of parameters and/or questionable assumptions about how the customer's creditworthiness evolves over time. Consequently, when a multi-order framework is required, it is probably best as a policy matter to use the traditional Five Cs approach, allowing product profitability to be considered as the "sixth C." It should be stressed, however, that this procedure is best regarded as a last rather than a first resort.

  Market Penetration Considerations—Related to the "lost future orders" argument is the "market penetration argument." In this argument, it is maintained that the customer should be granted credit, not on the basis of that customer's future sales potential, but based on the effect of granting credit to the customer on sales to other firms in the customer's geographic area or business line. The contention is that credit should be granted based on strategic marketing considerations in addition to considerations of creditworthiness.[40]

  This argument makes perfect sense when the customer is, in fact, necessary for some strategic marketing purpose. Perhaps the customer intends to demonstrate the use of the seller's products in a new application, or perhaps the customer is located in a geographic area where the seller is not well represented. In the later case, competitors may have locked up customers who are better credit risks, and only a customer who is a marginal credit risk may be willing to purchase from a new seller.

  However, there is no reason that the evaluation of a customer who presents market penetration advantages need be on any basis other than the single-order framework previously described, since the sales that are contingent on granting credit to the customer depend only on the fact of the current sale. Instead, the negative present value of granting credit should be weighed against the strategic marketing advantages of selling the current order. If it is felt that these advantages more than compensate for the expected loss from the sale, credit should be granted, but *the comparison should be made explicitly based on this expected loss.*

---

[40] More discussion of the types of strategic marketing considerations that are relevant to the credit decision is provided in Lynn Tylczak's, *Credit and Sales: The Winning Team*, NACM, 1994, pp. 5-6.

Summary of the Policy Implications in this Chapter

This chapter deals with credit-granting decisions on "marginal accounts," which are customers to whom potential sales volume is large but where there is significant credit risk. The traditional method of making credit-granting decisions regarding these customers is to apply the Five Cs of Credit as a system of organizing and evaluating credit information. In the Five Cs method, the costs of granting credit to a customer are not estimated directly. Instead, each of the Five Cs are indirect indicators of one or more of the costs the firms bears as a result of credit-granting.

While certainly tried and true (the method has been used by credit managers in essentially its present form for about a century), the Five Cs methodology presents difficulties for the analyst in making tradeoffs among the factors that affect creditworthiness and in deciding how creditworthy a customer must be in order for credit to be granted. As a policy alternative to the use of the Five Cs, this chapter introduces a model for making credit-granting decisions based on expected present value, a widely-used technique in making other financial decisions. In this technique, the analyst uses the same credit information as in the Five Cs, but uses it in a different way: to make estimates of factors which affect credit costs. The model compares the revenues from credit-granting with these costs, adjusted for their timing, to make a credit decision.

Of the estimates necessary to execute the model, the most difficult to make are three related to the particular customer under consideration: the recovery in default (should the customer not pay for the order), the time for the customer to pay (if payment is made), and the probability of default. The recovery in default determines the amount of the loss should the customer default and along with the probability of default determines the expected bad debt loss from granting credit. The time to pay determines accounts receivable carrying costs. Methods for estimating each of these three parameters were discussed, and methods for assessing the impact of uncertainty in their estimation on the credit-granting decision were presented. One policy implication, whether this approach is used in aggregate to determine credit standards or to assess customers individually, is that higher product profitability (greater price-cost margins) leads to looser credit-granting, while lower margins lead to tighter credit-granting.

Another policy implication concerns the time horizon that is appropriate to consider in making credit-granting decisions. Making such decisions based only on considerations relevant to the order in hand is simplest for the credit analyst, and the present value credit-granting decision model presented in this chapter is based on this view. However, when the credit-granting decision on the current order is negative and this decision affects the ability of the firm to get future orders from the customer, there are some conditions under which a longer view of the credit relationship must be taken, though these conditions are reasonably restrictive. First, the analyst must expect the customer's creditworthiness to improve over time, either because of an expected improvement in the customer's financial condition or because the customer's continued existence evidences better creditworthiness than the analyst originally estimated. Second, the customer must be brand loyal and expected to commit to the use of the seller's products.

If either of these conditions are absent, the single-order approach will produce the same decisions as longer-term analysis. The logical policy implication is for the credit analyst to perform initial analysis using the single-order view. If the customer is creditworthy under this view, the order is approved and no additional analysis is necessary. If the customer is not creditworthy on this basis, the analyst asks whether both of the prior conditions hold. If either condition does not hold, credit should not be granted. If they both hold, a longer-term analysis is required to make the decision properly. Because the present value approach (and the related profitability approach) are not practical beyond consideration of a single order, this longer-term analysis should be conducted under the fallback Five Cs approach, though product profitability should also play an important role in the decision.

As an introduction to the topic, this chapter models the credit-granting decision as a take-it-or-leave-it proposition in which the seller's only option is to grant or refuse credit on an open-credit basis. In the real world, if open-credit conditions are not acceptable to the seller, the customer and the credit manager can bargain, using various mechanisms to change the characteristics of credit-granting. We consider this negotiation process in the next chapter.

Case for Discussion and Analysis

The Case of the Meritorious Molder (Part 1)

Chad Martin was a credit analyst in the employ of Monumental Chemical Company. Among other products, Monumental produced plastic resins. Plastic resins of various types (polyethylene, polypropylene, and others) are manufactured by large chemical companies in the United States and worldwide, and are sold by weight in the form of small pellets. The business was quite competitive, as there were many sellers of each product and the properties of each type of plastic were largely the same among suppliers. These plastics were essentially commodity items.

Plastic resins are formed into plastic products by several processes, including injection molding, extruding, and vacuum forming. In these processes, the pellets of resin are first melted, then formed into the desired shape. Few of the forming processes are technologically sophisticated, and the equipment necessary to perform them is available from many manufacturers.

There were two major types of customers for plastic resins. Much of the volume was sold directly to large firms who molded their own plastic products, usually for use as part of consumer goods. However, plastics were also sold to smaller firms who did plastic molding under contract for larger firms, frequently receiving orders at peak times when the larger firms had run out of molding capacity. Many of the smaller firms were fringe producers, poorly capitalized and only occasionally profitable.

One such firm was Meritorious Plastic Products. Located just outside Detroit, Meritorious Plastics picked up sales volume from the auto manufacturers. Many other firms were in the same business, and margins were thin. Meritorious, like its competitors, bought resin from many suppliers, always searching for the best available deal. Meritorious had placed an order for $30,000 from Monumental. This was the first order that had been received from Meritorious in several years (Meritorious was about 10 years old, but had not been purchasing from Monumental recently).

The order was to be sold with stated terms of sale of 30 days, if Mr. Martin elected to grant credit. Otherwise, the order would go to the competition. Monumental sold to many other firms that molded plastic for the auto industry. No market penetration considerations were involved.

Mr. Martin's review of the available credit information indicated that recent years had not been kind to Meritorious Plastics. Losses had eroded the firm's financial position relative to other firms in the industry. (See Table 3-1C for the financial ratios that Mr. Martin calculated based on Meritorious' recent financial statement, as well as median, upper quartile, and lower quartile ratios for the industry.) Trade clearances indicated that Meritorious was paying the trade in 120 days, a payment cycle Mr. Martin confirmed by comparing it to the firm's accounts payable turnover ratio. Further, Mr. Martin knew that times were tough for plastic molders. Based on his experience with the industry and past data, he

Table 3-1C. Ratio Analysis for Meritorious Plastics

Ratio	:	Industry Ratios			:	Ratios for Meritorious
	:	Upper Quartile	Median Ratio	Lower Quartile	:	
Current Ratio	:	2.2	1.5	1.2	:	0.7
Quick Ratio	:	1.2	0.8	0.7	:	0.4
Sale/Receivables	:	9.4	7.5	6.2	:	4.5
Cost of Sales/Inventory	:	9.7	6.4	4.8	:	3.5
Debt/Equity	:	0.8	1.5	2.8	:	4.5

estimated that 10 percent of the plastic molding companies would not survive the year.

Because plastic molders usually owned plastic molding machines which had a ready resale market, banks frequently provided term loan and credit line facilities for them, with these borrowings secured by liens on the machines and other assets. While advantageous for the molders, these secured claims reduced recoveries to trade creditors in the event the molder failed. Mr. Martin's experience was that substantial recoveries were rare. His records indicated that recoveries averaged five cents on the dollar and that these recoveries were typically delayed for 18 months (from the time of the sale) while the bankruptcy court supervised the liquidation or reorganization of the debtor. He did not see any reason to believe the situation for Meritorious would be atypical should the firm default.

Mr. Martin knew his own firm paid taxes at a 35 percent income tax rate. Margins were not high on the type of plastic that Meritorious intended to purchase. Mr. Martin expected the out-of-pocket costs of producing and shipping this material would total 85 percent of sales. On average, there would be a 20-day delay from the time these costs were incurred until they were paid. The cost of capital for Monumental was 15 percent per year.

Suggestions for Analysis

1. Based on the facts of this case, utilize the present value model presented in the chapter to make a credit-granting decision on the $30,000 order for Meritorious. Justify all parameter estimates.

2. Test the sensitivity of your decision to uncertainty in your estimate of the probability of default by performing a single-parameter sensitivity analysis of the X parameter, varying the default probability between zero and 25 percent.

3. Is this a situation where a multi-order view of the credit granting decision is appropriate? Discuss why it is or is not based on the facts of the case.

Appendix to Chapter 3

An Expected Present Value Model of Credit-Granting With a Cash Discount

When the selling firm offers a cash discount for payment within a given time, this cash discount is usually of sufficient size and timing so as to make taking this discount economically attractive for most customers. For example, the effective cost of not taking the discount and paying at the net date under terms of 2 percent 10 net 30 is over 40 percent per year (we will discuss the cost of these discounts in greater detail in Chapter 7). When the discount is this large, even firms that are illiquid and of marginal creditworthiness will sometimes pay within the discount period. In such a situation, the credit-granting model presented in the chapter must be modified to include a third outcome from credit-granting, in addition to payment of the face amount of the invoice and default. The third outcome is payment of the invoice less the cash discount.

To model this we need to change the notation somewhat from the present value model presented in the body of this chapter. Let X_1 (rather than X) be the probability of default and X_2 be the probability of payment during the discount period. The probability of payment beyond the discount period is then $(1-X_1-X_2)$. If C is the cash discount fraction, then the amount received if the customer pays in the cash discount period will be $(1-C)S$. Let e be the time we expect the customer to pay if payment is made during the cash discount period.

Under this notation, the decision tree facing the credit manager will be the one illustrated in Figure 3-1B, and the expected present value of granting credit will be:

$$E(PV) = -V/(1+k)^a - (S(1-CX_2)-V)T/(1+k)^b + (1-X_1-X_2)S/(1+k)^c + X_2S(1-C)/(1+k)^e$$
$$+ X_1RS/(1+k)^d + X_1T(1-R)S/(1+k)^d$$

Note the differences between this equation and the present value model presented in the body of this chapter. First, the initial tax bill has been reduced by $(1-CX_2)$, where CX_2 is the expected cash discount as a fraction of the sale amount. Second, the cash inflow from payment outside the discount period now has a probability of $(1-X_1-X_2)$ instead of $(1-X)$, reflecting the additional chance (X_2) that payment will be made in the discount period. Third, there is a new term, $X_2S(1-C)/(1+k)^e$, which reflects the contribution to expected present value of payment during the cash discount period.

A Numerical Example—Let us modify the numerical example presented in the chapter to reflect cash discount terms. Recall that the parameters of this example were:

S	= $50,000	k	= 12 percent per year
V	= $40,000	c	= 90 days
a	= 30 days	R	= 10 percent
T	= 35 percent	d	= 1 year
b	= 45 days		

Figure 3-1A.   Decision Tree of the Credit-Granting Model with Cash Discount

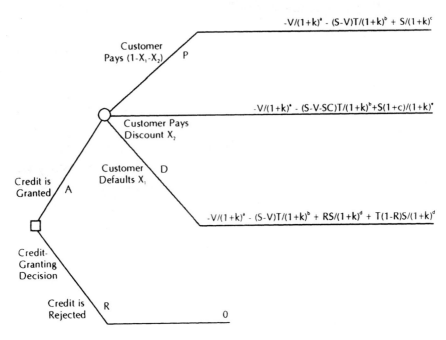

In the original example, the probability of default was 5 percent and the probability of payment was 95 percent. Let us assume that, if the firm offers discount terms of sale of 1.5 percent 10 days, net 30 days, the customer will have a 50 percent chance of paying in 10 days and taking the discount, a 47 percent chance of paying in 90 days, and a 3 percent chance of defaulting.[41] Then:

$$X_1 = 3 \text{ percent}$$
$$X_2 = 50 \text{ percent}$$
$$C = 1.5 \text{ percent}$$
$$e = 10 \text{ days}$$

The formula is executed in Table 3-1A. In this table, the terms representing the contribution to expected present value of the customer paying beyond discount (the $(1-X_1-X_2)S/(1+k)^e$ term) and at discount (the $X_2S(1-C)/(1+k)^e$ term) are labeled as terms 3A and 3B so that the other terms will have the same term numbers as in Table 3-2. Term 1, representing the contribution to expected present value from the outflow for materials, etc., is unchanged in value at –$39,624. Terms 4 and 5 (the contributions from the recoveries in default and from the tax savings due to the writeoff of the uncollected receivable in default) are reduced in value because the probability of default (X_1 in this model) is lower than is X in Table 3-2 (see footnote 41).

---

[41] Because the customer is encouraged by the discount to pay (on average) more quickly, there is less chance of default than in the model presented in the chapter, and the estimated probability of default must reflect this. In the numerical example in the text, the expected time to pay, if the customer pays, was 90 days and the probability of default was 5 percent. In this cash discount example, the expected time to pay is the probability-weighted average of paying in 10 and 90 days, which is (0.50/(0.47+0.50))(10 days) + (0.47/(0.47+0.50))(90 days) or about 48.8 days, so the appropriate probability of default is (48.8/90)0.05 or about 3 percent.

Table 3-1A.   A Present Value Model for Credit-Granting Decisions with Cash Discounts

Parameters:

Symbol	Meaning	Estimate
S	Sale in dollars	$50,000
V	Cost of Sale in dollars	$40,000
a	Time until V is paid (days)	30
T	Tax rate	35%
b	Time until tax is paid (days)	45
c	Customer's time to pay (days)	90
k	Seller's yearly cost of capital	12%
R	Recovery rate	10%
d	Time until recovery (years)	1
X_1	Probability of Nonpayment	3%
X_2	Probability of Paying at Discount	50%
C	Cash Discount Percent	1.5%
e	Time to Pay if Paid in Discount (days)	10

Value of Term 1: $-V/(1+k)^a$	($39,624)
Value of Term 2: $-(S(1-CX2)-V)T/(1+k)^b$	($3,321)
Value of Term 3A: $(1-X1-X2)S/(1+k)^c$	$22,844
Value of Term 3B: $X2S(1-C)/(1+k)^e$	$24,548
Value of Term 4: $X1RS/(1+k)^d$	$134
Value of Term 5: $X1T(1-R)S/(1+k)^d$	$422
Present Value of Granting Credit	$5,002

In term 2, the expected cash discount, is $50,000 times 0.50 times 0.015, since we estimate a 50 percent probability that the customer will take the discount and since the discount is 1.5 percent. The amount of this expected discount is $375, which reduces taxable income to $50,000–$40,000–$375 = $9,625, producing a $9,625(.35) = $3,389 tax bill, which has a present value of –$3,321 at a 12 percent discount rate for 45 days.

Terms 3A and 3B model the contribution to present value from payments beyond the discount time (term 3) and within the discount time (term 3A). Since in this example the probability of paying beyond discount is 47 percent, the expected cash flow is 0.47($50,000) = $23,500, and the present value of this cash flow over 90 days is $22,844. If the firm pays at discount, the cash flow is (1–.015)$50,000 = $49,250; since the probability of this event is 50 percent, the expected cash flow is $24,625. The present value of this over 10 days is $24,548, and the expected present value of the sale is $5,002.

While the present value of tax bill and the cash flows after default are affected by the cash discount, the major increase in the present value between this example and that presented in Table 3-2 comes from the difference in the contribution to present value of the cash inflows if the customer does not default. In Table 3-2, this value is that of term 3, which is $46,173. In the cash discount model, the value of these is the sum of terms 3A and 3B, which is

$22,844 + $24,548 = $47,392, a $1,219 increase. There are two reasons for this increase. First, in the cash discount model while the firm has to bear the cost of a 1.5 percent cash discount if the customer pays in discount, the probability of default is reduced by a larger amount: from 5 percent to 3 percent (which increases the expected cash flows). Second, in the cash discount model a great part of the expected cash flow from granting credit (the expected cash flow if the customer pays at discount) occurs at 10 days (where it has a higher time value) rather than at 90 days.

4 Negotiating the Conditions of Credit-Granting

In Chapter 3, a model was presented for determining the value of a sale. The model was applied to determine the value of a sale made on open-account terms. However, when a customer represents a large enough sales volume to warrant the additional effort, the seller may attempt to raise the sale's value by bargaining with the customer to enhance the conditions of sale.

Enhancement strategies can either increase the value of a sale which is already advantageous when made on open-account terms, or they can turn a sale which is not advantageous into one that is. This chapter discusses the effects of enhancements on credit-granting. In addition, it discusses the negotiation process by which credit analysts obtain these enhancements.

What Credit Enhancements Do

Enhancements act to increase the value of the sale by reducing credit-related costs. Though the types of credit-related costs that are reduced depend on the nature of the particular enhancement, the usual effect is to reduce expected bad debt expense and account receivable carrying cost. However, many types of enhancements require the expenditure of administrative and other costs, and the effects of these costs must also be considered in evaluating enhancement strategies.

Credit analysts face two types of decisions in evaluating enhancement strategies for a particular customer. First, several different enhancements may be proposed by the credit analyst or the customer. The credit analyst must evaluate these various enhancement strategies to determine which of these offers the most advantage. Which strategy offers the most advantage will depend on the characteristics of the customer and of the enhancement, and through these the size of the reductions in various credit-related costs that are produced by the enhancement. Second, for customers who would not be creditworthy without the enhancement, the credit analyst must decide whether a particular enhancement or set of enhancements provides sufficient reduction in credit costs to make the customer creditworthy.

Both of these decisions revolve around the value of the enhancements to the selling firm. For the first, the credit analyst should choose the alternative that adds the most value. For the second, the customer is creditworthy if, with enhancements, the sale has a positive value. The important policy question, then, is how the value of enhancements should be evaluated.

The credit analyst's unaided judgment can, of course, be used to assess value. However, whether the credit department is evaluated on a cost-minimization or a profit-maximization basis, the expected present value model presented in Chapter 3 can be used to assess the effects of enhancements on the value of granting credit. The great advantage of the present value approach is that it gives an explicit basis for evaluation: the effect of the enhancement on the expected dollar value of the sale.

Valuing Credit Enhancements

The formula for the expected present value of granting credit that was developed in Chapter 3 is:

$$E(PV) = -V/(1+k)^a - (S-V)T/(1+k)^b + (1-X)S/(1+k)^c + XRS/(1+k)^d + XT(1-R)S/(1+k)^d$$

Within this formula, enhancements generally act to increase expected present value by one or more of the following mechanisms:

1. Reducing c (the time before payment is expected to be received; this feature captures accounts receivable carrying cost).
2. Reducing X (the probability of nonpayment).
3. Increasing R (the recovery rate in default; along with X, this feature captures bad debt expense).

In this present value framework, the value of the enhancement is the increase in the expected present value over making the sale on open-account terms less any costs of administering the enhancement. To see how this works, let us examine the effects on net present value of four common types of enhancements: (1) security interests in assets; (2) personal guarantees of account; (3) ability to debit; and (4) downpayments.

We center on these four enhancements in the interest of brevity. There are many types of enhancements, but a substantial portion of them are particular to individual industries. For example, firms supplying the construction industry can use the mechanic's lien to increase recoveries in default, and in some industries trade acceptances are an accepted enhancement. The principles illustrated in examining these four types of enhancements can be applied in evaluating any other type of enhancement.[42]

---

[42] For more discussion of the effect of credit enhancements on the present value of credit-granting, and on credit negotiations between the buyer and the seller in general, see Frederick C. Scherr, "Bargaining in Trade Credit-Granting: A Preliminary Analysis," *Journal of the Midwest Finance Association*, Volume 18, 1989.

Table 4-1.   Numerical Example of the Effect of a Security Interest on the Present Value of Credit-Granting

Parameters:

Symbol	Meaning	Estimate (No Security)	Estimate (With Security)
S	Sale in dollars	$50,000	$50,000
V	Cost of sale in dollars	$40,000	$40,000
a	Time until V is paid (days)	30	30
T	Tax rate	35%	35%
b	Time until tax is paid (days)	45	45
c	Customer's time to pay (days)	90	90
k	Seller's yearly cost of capital	12%	12%
R	Recovery rate	10%	50%
d	Time until recovery (years)	1	1
X	Probability of nonpayment	5%	5%
Value of Term 1: $-V/(1+k)^a$		($39,624)	($39,624)
Value of Term 2: $-(S-V)T/(1+k)^b$		($3,451)	($3,451)
Value of Term 3: $(1-X)S/(1+k)^c$		$46,173	$46,173
Value of Term 4: $XRS/(1+k)^d$		$223	$1,116
Value of Term 5: $XT(1-R)S/(1+k)^d$		$703	$391
Present Value of Granting Credit		$4,025	$4,605

Security Interests—If the creditor perfects a security interest in one or more assets of the debtor, the creditor will have a claim on the proceeds of that asset in liquidation that precedes the claims of general creditors. The intent of having this claim is to increase the creditor's recovery if the debtor fails. The amount of the increase in recoveries will depend on the value of the asset which has been pledged, the size of the creditor's claim, and the position of the creditor's security interest relative to other security interests in the same asset.

To estimate the value of a security interest, the credit analyst needs to evaluate the effects of the latter three factors. To illustrate how this is done, let us return to our original numerical example from Chapter 3. The sale was for $50,000 and the expected recovery rate was 10 percent if the sale was unsecured. Assume the seller is able to negotiate with the customer and obtain a lien on the customer's accounts receivable, inventory, and fixed assets, with this position subordinate to the lending bank's lien on the same assets. Based on knowledge of the industry and inspection of the collateral, the analyst estimates that these assets will fetch $125,000 if the customer is liquidated. If the bank's claim is $100,000, there will be $25,000 left for the seller, and the expected recovery rate is therefore 50 percent (= $25,000/$50,000) ignoring for simplicity any additional recoveries on the remaining balance.

The effects of the enhancement on the expected present value of the sale are portrayed in Table 4-1. The value of the sale is increased from $4,025 (the value of the sale on open account) to $4,605, an increase of $580, ignoring for the moment any costs of administering the security interest. This occurs because the contribution of the expected recovery in default to the expected present value (term 4 in the expected present value equation) increases, though this increase is somewhat offset by the reduction in the contribution to expected present value of the tax savings from the writeoffs of the uncollected portion of the receivable (term 5).

The gain in value must be weighed against any cost of instituting and administering the security arrangement. It is important to note that, since the security arrangement will likely be in place for several orders (since filing a floating lien confers security for an extended period of time), its cost must be compared to the savings on all orders covered, which in this case is $580 per order for an order size of $50,000. Note that firms whose credit departments are evaluated on cost-minimization rather the profit-based goals can also use this $580 figure in decision-making since the gain is entirely due to cost reduction.

Note also how the characteristics of the customer act to affect the value of the security interest (or any other credit enhancement strategy) on the sale. Since the security interest reduces losses in default, the impact of having this collateral is larger, the larger is the customer's probability of default. This is so since, for higher probabilities of default, the reduction in bad debt expense from having the security interest is greater. To see this, let us change the parameters of our original numerical example, increasing the estimated probability of nonpayment from 5 percent to 20 percent. This analysis is presented in Table 4-2.

A much greater gain (of $1,348 in present value terms) is achieved in this example than in the prior one because the probability of default is greater. In this

Table 4-2. Numerical Example of the Effect of a Security Interest on the Present Value of Credit-Granting with X = 20%

Parameters:

Symbol	Meaning	Estimate (No Security)	Estimate (With Security)
S	Sale in dollars	$50,000	$50,000
V	Cost of sale in dollars	$40,000	$40,000
a	Time until V is paid (days)	30	30
T	Tax rate	35%	35%
b	Time until tax is paid (days)	45	45
c	Customer's time to pay (days)	90	90
k	Seller's yearly cost of capital	12%	12%
R	Recovery rate	10%	50%
d	Time until recovery (years)	1	1
X	Probability of nonpayment	20%	20%
Value of Term 1: $-V/(1+k)^a$		($39,624)	($39,624)
Value of Term 2: $-(S-V)T/(1+k)^b$		($3,451)	($3,451)
Value of Term 3: $(1-X)S/(1+k)^c$		$38,883	$38,883
Value of Term 4: $XRS/(1+k)^d$		$893	$4,464
Value of Term 5: $XT(1-R)S/(1+k)^d$		$2,813	$1,563
Present Value of Granting Credit		($487)	$1,835

case, the gain in value from the enhancement swings the customer from an unprofitable sale to a profitable one.

Personal Guarantees—When the debtor is incorporated, creditors may negotiate to obtain the personal backing of debts by one or more of the buyer's principals. Such a guarantee will increase recoveries in default in the same fashion as a security interest. The amount of the increase in recoveries will depend on the assets owned by the principal, the amount of the firm's debts, and the claims of others holding guarantees.

However, the effects of having a personal guarantee go beyond increases in R. When a principal personally guarantees the debts of the firm, that principal will be considerably more reluctant to allow the firm to fail. The principal may put money into the firm to see it through hard times, or may be more careful in monitoring the firm's expenditures of funds, particularly for extraneous expenses. That is, in addition to providing the creditor with increased recoveries when the incorporated customer issues a personal guarantee it is also somewhat less likely that the customer will fail, and this factor should be included in the analyst's estimate of the probability of failure (X).

Returning to our original numerical example, suppose that the credit analyst is considering negotiating with the debtor for a personal guarantee. Given the assets of the principal and the other claims against these assets, the analyst estimates that the expected recovery in default will be increased from 10 percent to 30 percent. Also, due to the effects the debtor's failure would have on the principal who is guaranteeing the debt, the analyst estimates a reduction in the probability of failure from 5 percent to 3 percent.

The value of this guarantee is computed in Table 4-3. Having the guarantee increases the present value of the sale by \$775 (= \$4,800 − \$4,025). This increase comes from the higher expected cash flow from collection of the receivable (term 3) due to the higher probability of this collection, and from the higher expected recovery in default (term 4), mitigated by the lower tax shield from the writeoff in default (term 5).

Ability to Debit—Unlike security interests and guarantees, the intent of the creditor in obtaining the ability to debit the debtor's account to get payment is not primarily to increase the recovery in default. Instead, this and similar enhancement techniques are intended to increase the value of the sale by reducing the time to payment (c). A more subtle but equally important effect is the reduction in X that also results: because the creditor is in and out of the account more quickly, it is less likely that some unfortunate event will occur which causes the debtor to fail while the creditor is exposed. In our original numerical example, the customer was expected to take 90 days to pay and the probability of failure was 5 percent over this time. Suppose that the creditor is able to obtain the ability to debit or some other device which requires the debtor to pay in 30 days. In this case, c would be reduced to 30 days, and X to

Table 4-3. Numerical Example of the Effect of a Personal Guarantee on the Present Value of Credit-Granting

Parameters:

Symbol	Meaning	Estimate (No Guarantee)	Estimate (With Guarantee)
S	Sale in dollars	$50,000	$50,000
V	Cost of Sale in dollars	$40,000	$40,000
a	Time until V is paid (days)	30	30
T	Tax rate	35%	35%
b	Time until tax is paid (days)	45	45
c	Customer's time to pay (days)	90	90
k	Seller's yearly cost of capital	12%	12%
R	Recovery rate	10%	30%
d	Time until recovery (years)	1	1
X	Probability of Nonpayment	5%	3%
Value of Term 1: $-V/(1+k)^a$		($39,624)	($39,624)
Value of Term 2: $-(S-V)T/(1+k)^b$		($3,451)	($3,451)
Value of Term 3: $(1-X)S/(1+k)^c$		$46,173	$47,145
Value of Term 4: $XRS/(1+k)^d$		$223	$402
Value of Term 5: $XT(1-R)S/(1+k)^d$		$703	$328
Present Value of Granting Credit		$4,025	$4,800

1.67 percent (= 30/90 x 5 percent). The result is a $1,914 increase in the expected value of the sale (see Table 4-4).

Downpayments—Downpayments, like some other enhancement devices, require modification of the present value model for proper evaluation. When the

Table 4-4. Numerical Example of the Effect of Ability to Debit on the Present Value of Credit-Granting

Parameters:

Symbol	Meaning	Estimate (No Debiting)	Estimate (With Debiting)
S	Sale in dollars	$50,000	$50,000
V	Cost of Sale in dollars	$40,000	$40,000
a	Time until V is paid (days)	30	30
T	Tax rate	35%	35%
b	Time until tax is paid (days)	45	45
c	Customer's time to pay (days)	90	30
k	Seller's yearly cost of capital	12%	12%
R	Recovery rate	10%	10%
d	Time until recovery (years)	1	1
X	Probability of Nonpayment	5%	1.67%
Value of Term 1: $-V/(1+k)^a$		($39,624)	($39,624)
Value of Term 2: $-(S-V)T/(1+k)^b$		($3,451)	($3,451)
Value of Term 3: $(1-X)S/(1+k)^c$		$46,173	$48,705
Value of Term 4: $XRS/(1+k)^d$		$223	$74
Value of Term 5: $XT(1-R)S/(1+k)^d$		$703	$234
Present Value of Granting Credit		$4,025	$5,939

customer makes a downpayment, there are two cash inflows associated with the customer's payment for the sale: the downpayment itself (call the amount of this downpayment D) and the cash inflow should the customer pay, whose amount will now be S–D. An additional term in the equation is needed to represent this downpayment inflow, and the amount of the cash flow in the term representing the customer's future payment must be modified. The last two terms of the present value formula (which represent the present value of recovery in default and of the tax savings from the writeoff) must also be modified, as S–D is now the maximum recovery in default and the maximum tax writeoff. Assuming the downpayment is made at the time of the sale, the resulting formula is:

$$E(PV) = -V/(1+k)^a - (S-V)T/(1+k)^b + D + (1-X)(S-D)/(1+k)^c + XR(S-D)/(1+k)^d + XT(1-R)(S-D)/(1+k)^d$$

Let us contrast the original numerical example with one where the credit analyst is able to successfully negotiate to obtain a downpayment of $15,000 against the $50,000 order. The calculations are presented in Table 4-5. The downpayment reduces the carrying costs of the receivable and the expected bad debt loss since the new receivable amount, S–D, is only $35,000. This increases the value of the sale by $870 (= $4,895 – $4,025) over the sale made on an open-account basis.

These four enhancement strategies are representative of many others in their influence on the value of the sale. By employing expected present value as an evaluation tool, credit analysts can estimate the effects of enhancements such as

---

Table 4-5   The Effect of a $15,000 Down Payment on the Present Value of Credit-Granting

Parameters:

Symbol	Meaning	Estimate
S	Sale in dollars	$50,000
D	Down payment in dollars	$15,000
V	Cost of sale in dollars	$40,000
a	Time until V is paid (days)	30
T	Tax rate	35%
b	Time until tax is paid (days)	45
c	Customer's time to pay (days)	90
k	Seller's yearly cost of capital	12%
R	Recovery rate	10%
d	Time until recovery (years)	1
X	Probability of nonpayment	5%

Present value without down payment:

Value of Term 1: $-V/(1+k)^a$	($39,624)
Value of Term 2: $-(S-V)T/(1+k)^b$	($3,451)
Value of Term 3: $(1-X)S/(1+k)^c$	$46,173
Value of Term 4: $XRS/(1+k)^d$	$223
Value of Term 5: $XT(1-R)S/(1+k)^d$	$703
Present Value of Granting Credit	$4,025

Present value with down payment:

Value of Term 1: $-V/(1+k)^a$	($39,624)
Value of Term 2: $-(S-V)T/(1+k)^b$	($3,451)
Value of Term 3: $+D$	$15,000
Value of Term 4: $(1-X)(S-D)/(1+k)^c$	$32,321
Value of Term 5: $XR(S-D)/(1+k)^d$	$156
Value of Term 6: $XT(1-R)(S-D)/(1+k)^d$	$492
Present Value of Granting Credit	$4,895

these, or combinations of enhancements, on the value of credit-granting. These increases in value must be weighed against any administrative or other costs associated with the enhancements to determine which enhancement has the most value for a particular customer and whether the enhancements are sufficient to make the customer an advantageous sale.

Negotiating Credit Terms

With a technique in hand for judging the value of particular modifications to open-account terms, the credit analyst is equipped to participate in the bargaining process with regard to credit granting. However, most credit analysts have little education in the theory and art of negotiation. This section outlines the basics of negotiation in a credit context.

Basics of Negotiation—All negotiation and bargaining situations involve a series of offers and counteroffers. At any time, either party is free to accept the counterparty's offer, to propose a counteroffer, or to withdraw from the negotiation. A key concept in negotiation is the "reservation price" of the two parties. For the seller, the reservation price is the lowest value that the seller is willing to accept. For the buyer, it is the highest value that the buyer is willing to give up. The overlap between the two is the "bargaining range." Deals advantageous to both parties fall in this range. If there is no overlap between the highest value that the buyer is willing to pay and the lowest value that the seller is willing to accept, there is no bargaining range, and no deal which is advantageous to both parties can be struck.

When there is a bargaining range, the point within this range at which the deal is made determines who gains the most advantage from the deal. Deals near the buyer's reservation price give greatest advantage to the seller. Deals near the seller's reservation price give the greatest advantage to the buyer. Where within the bargaining range the deal is struck depends on the negotiation skills of the two parties. Each can hold out for a deal near what they believe to be the other's reservation price, but in doing so may cause the interaction to deadlock, to the detriment of both parties.

As an illustration of this feature of bargaining, consider a very simple negotiation situation: the purchase of a car. The buyer will have a maximum price that he or she is willing to pay for the car, say $20,000. The seller will have a minimum price that he or she is willing to take for the car, say $17,000. The bargaining range is between $17,000 and $20,000, and each party will accept a deal in this range. However, deals nearer $17,000 are more advantageous to the buyer, while deals nearer $20,000 are more advantageous to the seller. However, if either party bargains too hard, the negotiation may deadlock, to the advantage of neither party.

While the point within the bargaining range where the deal is struck depends to some extent on the personal qualities of the bargainers, one important principal of negotiation is to *hide your reservation price* as much as is reasonable and ethical. In the car bargaining example, the seller who inadvertently suggests that he or she will take $17,000 for the car is much more likely to receive a price near that than near $20,000. Skillful negotiators keep their reservation prices to themselves for as long as possible.

However, one way that reservation price is revealed during negotiation is via the "concession rates" of the parties. The concession rate is the pace at which the party concedes aspects of the deal which are valuable. The "hard bargainer" concedes slowly, implying a reservation price that is close to the current offer (since when a party's reservation price is close to the current offer, the party can concede little).

Negotiation of Credit Terms—For several reasons, negotiating credit terms is a much more complicated situation than negotiating the price of a car. First, unlike negotiations where only one aspect of the sale is being bargained (the price), credit negotiations are multifaceted. There are many possible enhancements from standard open-account terms that can be employed, each with its own characteristics.

Second, even if they wanted to do so, the parties to the credit negotiation process would be hard put to reveal their "reservation prices" to the counterparty in a credible way.[43] The value of the sale to the seller depends on the seller's margin on the sale (the relationship between S and V), its cost of capital, its estimates of the likelihood of the buyer's default, and other factors. To the buyer, the value of the purchase depends on its need for the particular product, its need for the financing that trade credit provides, its true payment policies and default risk, etc. All these aspects of the deal are not easily communicable to the other party, and they are not easily confirmable. There is little way to know whether the counterparty is bluffing.

For example, a buyer might say that he can easily get a product of comparable quality and price from another supplier, and may refuse to grant any credit enhancements. This could be fact or it could be a bluff, and there is no simple way for the credit analyst to assess which.

Third, unlike the car price negotiation, negotiations for credit terms are not necessarily a "zero-sum" situation. In zero-sum negotiations, what one party gains, the other loses. In credit negotiations, however, one party can frequently give up something that has a greater value to the other party, so the net value of the sale for the two parties together increases. For example, suppose that a seller is negotiating with a young incorporated firm which has little operating history. The seller knows that the failure rates for young firms are high, and consequently estimates a relatively high value for X. However, the principals of the buyer know they have a substantial volume of advantageous business already under

---

[43] When negotiation is within the bargaining range, it is of most advantage to keep one's reservation price a secret. However, when one party insists on a deal which violates the other party's reservation price, it is sometimes useful to reveal one's reservation price, and to make a deal of minimal advantage, which is better than no deal at all.

contract which will sustain the firm for years, but cannot credibly communicate this information to the seller (because the seller knows the buyer may be bluffing). In such a case, the buyer may be quite willing to grant a personal guarantee, knowing there is little chance the guarantee will be exercised. The seller, on the other hand, will see this guarantee as very valuable.

Finally, this personal guarantee example illustrates the complex signaling aspects that are inherent in credit terms negotiations. Like simpler negotiations, the concession rate is important, but so are *what aspects* of terms the counterparty proposes to modify and *when* the modification proposal is made. In a multifaceted negotiation, parties will naturally negotiate hard and early over things that are most important to them, and will try not to give up things that are very costly to them. As the negotiation proceeds, observation of this pattern enables the other party to revise its estimates of the value of the sale.

For example, if the buyer is reluctant to grant enhancements that lead to earlier payment (for example, the ability to debit), it may be reasonable to conclude that the buyer is short of cash, or expects substantial cash needs in the near future, regardless of other information the seller may have obtained on the buyer's cash flow position. In the prior example of the young firm, granting a personal guarantee may signal that the probability of the firm's default is lower than what might otherwise be indicated.

There is no magic strategy for the seller to use in obtaining the best bargain in negotiation over credit terms. However, the prepared negotiator: (1) is aware of the various enhancement options and their effects on the value of the particular sale; (2) looks for enhancements which add to the total value of the sale; and (3) is sensitive to the implications of how the buyer makes and responds to offers and what types of offers are made.

Summary of Policy Implications in this Chapter

For large marginal customers, it is frequently worth the selling firm's time and effort to negotiate for sales on credit terms which provide superior value to sales made on an open-account basis. The credit analyst must understand the process of credit terms negotiation and must be able to assess the value of credit enhancements which are proposed during this negotiation.

Negotiation of credit terms is a more complex bargaining situation than most. Numerous types of enhancements are available to the credit analyst, each with their own effects on the time to pay, probability of default, and recovery rate in default. Some enhancements will raise the total value of the deal to the two parties, benefiting one more than the other. In the course of the negotiation, the credit analyst must be ready to modify his or her assessment of credit risk and time to pay based on the credit enhancements proposed as well as those rejected by the buyer.

As a matter of credit policy, the credit manager must choose a framework for the firm to use in assessing the effect of credit enhancements on the value of the sale. While pure judgment can be employed, this chapter uses the expected net present value model presented in Chapter 3 for this purpose. The advantage of this approach is that it allows enhancement alternatives to be compared on a common-denominator basis. This common denominator is the effect on the dollar value of the sale. Using this model, the evaluation of four commonly-used credit enhancements was illustrated: a security interest in the debtor's assets, a personal guarantee of the debtor's principals, the ability to debit the debtor's bank account, and a downpayment. In this model, the difference in present value between making the sale on an open-account basis and the present value when making the sale with the credit enhancement captures the reduction in credit costs from the enhancement. Firms whose credit departments are evaluated on a cost-minimization basis will want to use this cost reduction figure to compare the value of various enhancements and to bargain hard for every dollar of cost reduction. Credit personnel who are evaluated in a more profit-oriented way, while they want to negotiate the best deal possible, will want to make sure the deal is made on *some* terms as long as the expected present value is positive. Credit personnel who are evaluated on this basis will be less willing to risk deadlock in the negotiation process once terms with a positive present value have been accepted by the buyer.

As with any mathematical model, the firm may choose not to utilize the present value model directly as a calculative device, but instead employ only the principles that the model illustrates. In the present value model, these principles are that enhancement strategies are valuable only to the extent that they reduce the expected time to payment, increase the expected recovery in default, and reduce the probability of default. The price that is paid if these principles rather than the model itself are used is the loss of the ability to assess the effects of various credit enhancements on a dollar value basis.

Case for Discussion and Analysis

The Case of the Meritorious Molder (Part 2)

Monumental Chemical Company had received an order for $30,000 worth of plastic products from Meritorious Plastic Products (for more on these firms, see the case in Chapter 3). Monumental had assigned Chad Martin, one of the firm's credit analysts, to determine whether the order represented an advantageous sale. Using the expected present value approach, Mr. Martin had determined that the order had a negative expected value. See Table 4-1C for Mr. Martin's estimates and calculations.

When Mr. Martin advised the managers of Meritorious regarding the situation, they were dismayed, and indicated they were very interested in getting access to Monumental's plastic resins, but would not pay cash for the entire amount of the order. They offered two alternatives to cash terms: a standby letter of credit and a downpayment.

The Standby Letter of Credit Proposal—Because Meritorious' bank's position was protected by its security interest in all the firm's assets, the bank was willing to continue to lend to Meritorious, despite the firm's gruesome financial position. As part of this lending relationship, the bank was willing to issue a standby letter of credit to back up Meritorious' payment to Monumental. In this deal, if Meritorious did not pay the $30,000 promptly, Monumental would present the past-due item to the bank, which would then pay it. However, the bank advised that there would be an up-front cost associated with setting up this letter

---

Table 4-1C.   A Present Value Analysis of Meritorious Plastics

Parameters:

Symbol	Meaning	Estimate
S	Sale in dollars	$30,000
V	Cost of sale in dollars	$25,500
a	Time until V is paid (days)	20
T	Tax rate	35%
b	Time until tax is paid (days)	45
c	Customer's time to pay (days)	120
k	Seller's yearly cost of capital	15%
R	Recovery rate	5%
d	Time until recovery (years)	1.5
X	Probability of nonpayment	13%

Value of Term 1: $-V/(1+k)^a$	($25,303)
Value of Term 2: $-(S-V)T/(1+k)^b$	($1,548)
Value of Term 3: $(1-X)S/(1+k)^c$	$24,912
Value of Term 4: $XRS/(1+k)^d$	$158
Value of Term 5: $XT(1-R)S/(1+k)^d$	$1,052
Present Value of Granting Credit	($729)

of credit: a steep 1 percent of the amount involved.[44] In negotiation, Meritorious took the position that Monumental should pay this cost if the standby letter of credit arrangement was used.

The Downpayment Proposal—With this arrangement, Meritorious would immediately give Monumental a check for $5,000, then be granted credit for the balance of $25,000 on open-account terms.

Suggestions for Analysis

1. Use the present value model to obtain a value for the order under the standby letter of credit proposal, assuming that Monumental will present the invoice for payment to the bank when the invoice is 45 days old and that the invoice will be paid at that time.

2. Use the present value model of sales with downpayments presented in the chapter to evaluate the downpayment proposal.

3. Which proposal is best? Should credit be granted under either proposal? What should Mr. Martin do at this point?

---

[44] Fees for standby letters of credit typically are much lower than this; a more typical fee is one-half of 1 percent of the amount involved.

5 Credit Limits

Probably the most common tool in the management of trade credit is the credit limit. Surveys of large firms indicate that they use credit limits in connection with the vast majority of their sales.[45] Unfortunately, despite the prevalence of this technique, there is little consensus among credit managers about exactly what credit limits are supposed to do or how they are supposed to do it. When asked what their credit limits do, credit managers generally respond that these limits are employed "to control risk," but are unable to say exactly what type of risk is controlled or how it is controlled.

From a policy standpoint, having credit analysts assign and employ credit limits based on such a fuzzy conception is unlikely to lead to advantageous credit management. The challenge is instead to formulate credit limits policy that directly captures the goals of the selling firm with respect to the specific risks associated with credit granting. Addressing this challenge requires that the policy maker think very clearly regarding the link between credit limits and risk.

The purpose of this chapter is to provide a basis for this clear thinking. We discuss specific types of credit risk and show how these can be controlled by credit limits of various sorts. The relevance of each type of credit risk in granting credit to a particular customer will depend on certain characteristics of the customer and of the selling firm. Advantageous credit policy requires that credit analysts be trained to identify situations where these characteristics occur and to properly assign credit limits in those situations.

Distinctions Among Credit Limits

Two distinctions among the various types of credit limits are important in formulating credit policy. First, some credit limits are for *internal use within the selling firm*

---

[45] Recent surveys of credit limits practice are presented in W. Beranek and F.C. Scherr, "On the Significance of Trade Credit Limits," *Financial Practice and Education*, Fall/Winter 1991, pp. 39-44, and S. Besley and J.S. Osteryoung, "Survey of Current Practices in Establishing Trade Credit Limits," *Financial Review*, February 1985, pp. 70-81.

and are intended to be confidential while others are for *external use* and are revealed to the customer. Internal credit limits are intended to trigger action by the seller if and when the customer's exposure exceeds this limit. The action triggered *may or may not involve the customer*, so it would be misleading to advise the customer of the amount of an internal limit. For external limits, the customer is advised of the amount of this limit.

The second distinction is between *binding* and *nonbinding* limits. Binding credit limits give the maximum amount of credit that is to be extended. If the customer places an order that would result in an exposure greater than this amount, payment of some sort is required to reduce exposure before new credit is granted.[46] Violation of a nonbinding credit limit, however, does not necessarily require that a payment be made. Instead, some other action may be triggered, such as a review of the customer's creditworthiness.

It is usually advantageous that binding credit limits also be external and thus revealed to the customer. This is useful because it facilitates understanding between the firm and the customer about how much credit the firm is willing to extend, and therefore how much the customer can purchase before a payment must be made. This avoids untimely delays and confusion when orders are placed. On the other hand, nonbinding credit limits are usually best kept confidential, so that the customer does not misunderstand this limit to be binding when it is not. Then the buyer will not restrict purchases when no restrictions are required. We will see that the decision to assign either an external and binding credit limit or to assign a nonbinding and internal one depends on the type of risk being controlled by the credit limit.

Credit Limits and Credit Investigation

One type of risk that credit limits may be employed to control is the risk that the customer may be less creditworthy than the credit analyst currently believes. This is *information risk*: the firm's current estimates of the creditworthiness of the customer may be incorrect because not enough information has been collected (that is, not enough credit investigation has been performed).[47]

The tradeoffs inherent in credit investigation policy are discussed in Chapter 2. To summarize, credit investigation is a mechanism by which credit analysts can make distinctions between profitable and unprofitable accounts, granting or refusing credit accordingly. However, there is a tradeoff between credit investigation costs versus bad debt expenses and accounts receivable carrying costs. By spending more on credit investigation, bad debt and carrying costs can be reduced. Optimal policy balances reductions in bad debt and carrying cost against credit investigation expenses. Also, the costs of any particular type of credit investigation (purchasing and examining a trade clearance, calling other trade sup-

---

[46] The borrowing limits ("credit lines") on consumer credit cards are examples of binding credit limits.
[47] The following discussion is drawn from "Credit Limits: Two Modern Applications," *CRF Staff Report*, February 1993.

pliers, etc.) are relatively fixed in nature, while bad debt expense and carrying costs increase with exposure. The result is that the firm should follow a sequential procedure for credit investigation. In this procedure, the firm makes a list of potential sources of credit information, starting with the least costly and proceeding to the most costly. Credit investigation strategy involves utilizing more expensive sources of credit information (those further down the list) when investigating accounts where exposure is higher, while limiting such expenses when exposure is lower.

To control information risk, a tool is needed to tell the credit analyst when the information risk of the account is sufficient to warrant additional credit investigation. One way to do this is to assign an *information credit limit* to every account on which a complete credit investigation has not been performed (that is, on every account where there are still sources of credit information on the sequential list which have not yet been utilized). Set as a dollar amount (like any other credit limit), comparing exposure to the information credit limit tells the credit analyst when additional credit investigation is needed.

To set the information credit limit, the credit analyst first uses the sequential credit investigation procedure to make a credit-granting decision. The credit analyst then sets the information credit limit at the exposure which, in the credit analyst's view, warrants undertaking the *next level* of credit investigation. Additional credit investigation on the account is not undertaken until orders are in hand (or are expected to be forthcoming) such that granting credit for these orders results in a level of exposure greater than the information credit limit.[48]

Setting Information Credit Limits—Information credit limits can be set judgmentally or in conjunction with the numerical next-decision analysis technique presented in Chapter 2. Let us discuss the judgmental approach first. Suppose that the credit analyst has received an initial order for $5,000 from a new customer and is faced with the sources of credit information given in Table 2-1, reprinted for reference here as Table 5-1.

Table 5-1.   A Hypothetical Sequential List of Credit Information Sources and Costs (from Table 2-1)

Source of Information	Investigation Cost of this Source
Ship order without credit investigation	$0
Obtain and analyze commercial credit report	$10
Obtain and analyze trade clearance	$20
Obtain and analyze bank report	$35
Call other trade suppliers to discuss account	$75
Obtain, spread, and analyze financial statements	$150
Visit customer and analyze resulting information	$500

---

[48] Note that the use of an information credit limit does not preclude the use of other credit limits or mechanisms to control other aspects of the account, such as past-due balance or other risks.

Table 5-2 (from Table 2-8). Next-Decision Analysis of Example Credit Investigation Decision

Situation	Worst Case	Expected Result	Best Case
Sales	$10,000	$10,000	$10,000
Costs of Goods Sold	$8,500	$8,500	$8,500
Margin Before Credit Costs	$1,500	$1,500	$1,500
Expected Time to Pay (days)	100	75	50
Carrying Cost	$278	$208	$139
Chance of Default	0.15	0.10	0.05
Expected Bad Debt Expense	$1,500	$1,000	$500
Profit from Granting Credit	($278)	$292	$861
Best Decision	reject	grant	grant
Profit from Best Decision	$0	$292	$861
Probability of this Investigation Outcome	0.2	0.6	0.2
Expected Profitability with Investigation	$347		
Expected Profitability without Investigation	$292		
Difference	$56		
Cost of Next-Stage Investigation	$150		
Net Gain from Investigation	($94)		

In the sequential investigation system, the credit analyst will go down the list of sequentially more expensive sources until the credit analyst believes that the advantage of utilizing the next source of credit information is not worth its price. Let us suppose that the last source used is "Obtain and Analyze Bank Report." Given the profit margin for the products to be sold and the credit analyst's uncertainty about the credit risk of the customer, the credit analyst asks what level of exposure would be sufficient for the *next* level of credit investigation to be advantageous. (In Table 5-1, this next level is "Call Other Trade Suppliers to Discuss the Account.") Suppose that the credit analyst decides, given the cost of this next procedure, that it would not be warranted until exposures reach $10,000. This $10,000 figure is the customer's information credit limit.

While this judgmental approach will produce a credit limit, this limit can also be computed numerically if the firm is using next-decision analysis to make credit investigation decisions.[49] The computation is done by repeating the analysis to find the sales volume at which the next stage of analysis becomes advantageous. To see how this works, consider the example next-decision analysis from Chapter 2, reprinted here as Table 5-2.

For an exposure of $10,000 (the "Sales" amount in this table), in this example it is not advantageous to perform the next stage of credit investigation since the net gain from investigation is negative. However, for some larger sales volume, the gains in reduction of accounts receivable carrying costs and expected bad

---

[49] This procedure for setting information credit limits is illustrated in Frederick C. Scherr, "A New Technique for Weighing Credit Benefit Decisions," *Credit and Financial Management Review*, 1995 (annual), pp. 32-35.

debt expense from being able to identify the customer who is a "Worst Case" are sufficiently large that it is better to investigate. To find this sales volume, the analyst increases the sales figure in the next-decision analysis until the gain from investigation becomes positive. Table 5-3 illustrates the relationship between the gain from investigation and sales volume for this example for increments to sales of $2,500. Since the lowest dollar value where the gain from credit investigation is positive occurs for sales of $27,500, the information credit limit should be set at this level, and no further investigation should be performed until this exposure is reached.

Implementing Information Credit Limits Policy—It is very important to understand how information credit limits differ from other types of credit limits. Information credit limits are internal control mechanisms and, unlike some other types of credit limits, are *not generally binding on the customer*. They are *not intended to limit exposure*, but instead to provide easily-used mechanisms to control credit investigation costs. The only circumstance under which the information credit limit is binding on the customer is when the next step in the credit investigation process requires that the customer provide information (for example, when the next level in the sequential investigation process requires the credit analyst to obtain financial statements from the customer and to analyze them).

However, instances where the customer's participation in the credit investigation process is required are much less common than instances where credit information is gathered from other sources. Most of the time, the violation of an information credit limit triggers an action which is internal to the selling firm. The major danger in the use of information credit limits or any other nonbinding internal credit limit is misinterpretation by the sales force, the customer, or a novice credit analyst. If the dollar amount of a customer's information credit limit is revealed to the customer or to the sales force, it may be misinterpreted as

---

Table 5-3.   Sensitivity Analysis of Net Gain from Investigation for Example Next-Decision Analysis Problem

Sales	Gain
$10,000	($94)
$12,500	($81)
$15,000	($67)
$17,500	($53)
$20,000	($39)
$22,500	($25)
$25,000	($11)
$27,500	$3
$30,000	$17
$32,500	$31
$35,000	$44
$37,500	$58
$40,000	$72

a binding limit on exposure and thus on sales. This is not what such a limit is intended to convey. If a salesperson incorrectly believes that a potentially advantageous customer is limited in purchases, the salesperson may de-emphasize his or her selling effort with respect to that customer, resulting in lost profitable sales. Similarly, if a customer believes his or her credit to be limited, he or she may not place orders which would, on investigation, be advantageous to the seller. Since internal credit limits are so easily misinterpreted, except in the case where the customer's participation is required in the next level of credit investigation, it is *very important* that information credit limits be *kept confidential* within the credit department.

Credit Limits and Other Risks

Unlike information credit limits, the limits discussed in this section *are intended to be binding* on the customer; they set as maximum exposures. These limits are used to control other types of risk to the seller besides information risk. The type of risk involved and the relevance of risk of this type to the selling firm will determine whether such a binding credit limit should be assigned and the basis on which this assignment should be made. We call these types of binding credit limits *risk credit limits* to distinguish them from nonbinding information credit limits.

Unfortunately, there are few practical models for setting risk credit limits, regardless of the type of risk involved. The following discussion is limited to outlining the concepts and principles underlying each type of risk and their implications for credit policy. Risk credit limits must be set judgmentally based on these considerations.

Risk of Loss—This risk concept argues that, as the exposure on an account grows, so does expected bad debt expense and accounts receivable carrying cost. Consequently, credit limits should be set to limit these potential costs.

Whether it is advantageous to set credit limits based on this risk concept depends on how the credit department is evaluated: based on profitability or based on credit costs. This risk concept ignores the increases in profits before credit costs that the firm receives from increasing sales. Consider the profitability analysis in Table 5-4. In this numerical example, the credit costs and net profit from granting credit to a customer are examined for order sizes from $10,000 to $80,000, given that production costs are 85 percent of sales, the firm's cost of capital is 10 percent, the expected time to pay is 75 days, and the probability of default on the order is 10 percent. As order sizes increase, so do total credit costs, and a credit limit could be placed on this customer to control these costs. To control credit costs, the credit limit should be set at the lowest level that the other parts of the selling firm will accept.

Note that this logic does not hold if the credit department is judged on a profitability basis. If the parameters of the customer (the probability of default, the

Table 5-4.   Profit and Credit Costs Versus Order Size

(Expected Time to Pay and Probability of Default Constant)

Sale Size	$10,000	$20,000	$30,000	$40,000	$50,000	$60,000	$70,000	$80,000
Costs of Production	$8,500	$17,000	$25,500	$34,000	$42,500	$51,000	$59,500	$68,000
Margin Before Credit Costs	$1,500	$3,000	$4,500	$6,000	$7,500	$9,000	$10,500	$12,000
Expected Time to Pay (days)	75	75	75	75	75	75	75	75
Carrying Cost	$208	$417	$625	$833	$1,042	$1,250	$1,458	$1,667
Default Probability	0.10	0.10	0.10	0.10	0.10	0.10	0.10	0.10
Expected Bad Debt Expense	$1,000	$2,000	$3,000	$4,000	$5,000	$6,000	$7,000	$8,000
Total Credit Costs	$1,208	$2,417	$3,625	$4,833	$6,042	$7,250	$8,458	$9,667
Profit From Granting Credit	$292	$583	$875	$1,167	$1,458	$1,750	$2,042	$2,333

Table 5-5.   Profit and Credit Costs Versus Order Size

(Probability of Default Increases with Order Size)

Sale Size	$10,000	$20,000	$30,000	$40,000	$50,000	$60,000	$70,000	$80,000
Costs of Production	$8,500	$17,000	$25,500	$34,000	$42,500	$51,000	$59,500	$68,000
Margin Before Credit Costs	$1,500	$3,000	$4,500	$6,000	$7,500	$9,000	$10,500	$12,000
Expected Time to Pay (days)	75	75	75	75	75	75	75	75
Carrying Cost	$208	$417	$625	$833	$1,042	$1,250	$1,458	$1,667
Default Probability	0.100	0.105	0.110	0.115	0.120	0.125	0.130	0.135
Expected Bad Debt Expense	$1,000	$2,100	$3,300	$4,600	$6,000	$7,500	$9,100	$10,800
Total Credit Costs	$1,208	$2,517	$3,925	$5,433	$7,042	$8,750	$10,558	$12,467
Profit From Granting Credit	$292	$483	$575	$567	$458	$250	($58)	($467)

expected time to pay, etc.) do not increase as the amount of the order size grows, then the customer is even more profitable at higher order sizes than at lower ones. In this situation, as long as profitability is the basis of the credit department's performance evaluation, there is generally no reason to limit order size. Therefore a risk credit limit is inappropriate.[50]

The Domino Effect—However, there is one special circumstance where controlling the risk of loss requires a credit limit even if the credit department is evaluated on a profitability basis. This circumstance occurs when the default of the customer triggers other costs besides the usual credit costs for the selling firm, in particular when the default of the customer puts the selling firm's *own* survival in danger. We call this the "domino effect" because the default of the customer has the potential to topple the seller as well.[51]

The domino effect and its relevance for credit policy require some explanation.[52] For most firms, the primary source of cash inflows comes from the collection of accounts receivable. As sales to one customer grow (sales to other customers constant), a larger portion of the seller's cash inflows comes from that particular customer, and a smaller fraction from other customers. If this large customer fails, the seller will be denied a substantial portion of its inflows and will have to find another source of money to pay bills. Finding and borrowing from the additional source of funds imposes costs on the seller, and may cause the seller to default if another source of funds is not found. Therefore, this risk concept argues, credit limits should be imposed on large accounts to limit the portion of the firm's cash inflows that come from that particular customer.

For several reasons, the domino effect and its implications for credit limits are primarily relevant for smaller selling firms. First, smaller firms frequently have one customer who purchases a substantial portion of their total sales. This situation is less common for bigger firms. Second, larger firms are more likely to have alternate sources of cash to tap in emergencies since they are more able to sell debt and equity and to borrow from banks. The domino effect and its implications for credit policy will be discussed in more depth in Chapter 9, which deals in part with the special credit policy problems that face small firms.

Changes in Creditworthiness with Amount of Credit Granted—We previously showed that the "risk of loss" concept does not result in a credit limit for a firm whose credit department is evaluated on a profitability basis, except in the special case where the domino effect applies. As long as the probability of default and the expected time to pay do not increase with the amount of credit granted, increases in profits before credit costs are always sufficient to make the customer a more profitable sale for higher sales volumes.

---

[50] See Frederick C. Scherr, "Improve the Odds of Prompt Payment," *Business Credit*, October 1990, pp. 18-19 for more discussion of this issue.

[51] The domino effect is the reason that banks are limited by statute in the amount of their maximum lending to a particular borrower. Banks are particularly vulnerable to the domino effect because of their relatively thin capitalization.

[52] A mathematical model of the domino effect and its relevance for credit policy is presented in Frederick C. Scherr, "Credit-Granting Decisions Under Risk," *Engineering Economist*, Spring 1992.

Figure 5-1. Profits vs. Order Size, Changing X

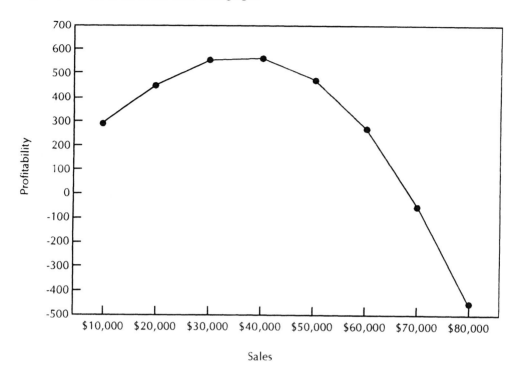

However, assignment of risk credit limits can be advantageous if, for one reason or another, creditworthiness decreases as the amount purchased increases. Starting with the numerical example presented in Table 5-4, assume that the probability of default (X in prior notation) increases as the amount purchased increases from its initial value of 10 percent by 0.5 percent for each additional $10,000 purchased.[53] The profitability analysis of such a situation is presented in Table 5-5. The profits figure from this table is plotted versus order size in Figure 5-1. Because the expected bad debt loss now increases at a faster rate than does the margin before credit costs, there is an optimal amount of credit to be granted (in this case, $30,000) which maximizes the profitability of the sale (the maximum profit is $575). The risk credit limit should be set at this level.

If increases in default probability or time to pay with amount of credit granted are the basis for credit limits, the credit analyst must be trained to detect circumstances in which increases in these parameters are likely to occur, and to separate these from circumstances in which this occurrence is unlikely.[54] In considering whether creditworthiness decreases with purchase volume, it is important to un-

---

[53] Survey evidence indicates that many credit managers believe such increases occur for some of their customers; see W. Beranek and F.C. Scherr, "On the Significance of Trade Credit Limits," *Financial Practice and Education*, Fall/Winter 1991, pp. 39-44. The same logic as that presented in this illustration applies if the time to pay rather than the default probability increases with amount purchased, or if both increase with amount purchased.

[54] See Frederick C. Scherr, "Improve the Odds of Prompt Payment," *Business Credit*, October 1990, pp. 18-19 for additional discussion of the following issues.

derstand the effect of these purchases on the buyer's cash flows. The business buyer makes trade purchases (which require cash outflows) in order to produce salable goods and services (which result in cash inflows). Any change in default risk arising from a trade purchase must result from the *effects of the trade purchase on the buyer's pattern of outflows and inflows.*

Viewed in this context, it is easy to see two circumstances in which increases in trade purchases from a particular supplier will *not* affect the buyer's default risk. First, any increase in purchases which results from a simple replacement of one supplier with another does not affect the amount of required outflows (though the payments are made to different suppliers) or the pattern of inflows (since the buyer's sales are unchanged).

Second, any increase in purchases which results for a simple increase in the buyer's sales volume with its current customers does not increase default risk as long as the buyer finances the required increases in assets with the same mix of financing that was used in the past. When this simple expansion occurs, the amounts of inflows and outflows increase, but the increases in the two are proportional, and default risk is unaffected.

Alternatively, there are three circumstances in which default risk *clearly does* increase with the amount purchased. The first is when the availability of credit causes the customer to purchase more goods and services than are actually needed. In this case, the amount of the customer's outflows increases without a proportional increase in inflows, and default probability increases.[55]

The second occurs when the firm is expanding its sales but has not made the necessary financial arrangements to support the higher sales volume, including appropriate financing of the required purchases of long-term assets. In this case, inflows will rise, but outflows will rise more, and the default probability is consequently increased. A third possibility is that the buyer's increases in sales volume may come from sales to customers who are riskier than the buyer's prior customers. In this case, the buyer's default risk increases because of the increasing default risk of its customer base. All three of these circumstances can be detected by careful observation of the buyer's financial position, including inventory turnover, debt position, and accounts receivable turnover.[56]

From a policy standpoint, the most important implication of this discussion is for the credit manager to make analysts aware of the conditions under *which increases in purchases are associated with increases in default risk and those where they are not.* When the credit department is evaluated on a profitability basis, the imposition of a risk credit limit is required only in conditions where default risk increases. The great danger when credit limits policy is based on increases in default risk

---

[55] This "overbuying" effect is certainly the reason for limitations on consumer borrowing by credit card firms and other consumer lenders. Unlike a business, when a consumer makes a purchase, no inflows are generated, though outflows increase. There is only so much debt that a consumer can repay from his or her inflows. The consumer credit limit acts to limit debt so that repayment can be made.

[56] See Frederick C. Scherr, "Improve the Odds of Prompt Payment," *Business Credit*, October 1990, pp. 18-19 for additional discussion. Note that if the rate of decrease in creditworthiness with increases in sales could be estimated (as in Table 4-5, where default probability increases 0.5 percent for each $10,000 increase in sales volume), it would be a simple matter to calculate optimal credit limits based on increases in default risk. However, making such estimates with any degree of confidence is clearly impractical in practice.

with amount purchased is that credit analysts will impose credit limits when they are not warranted, resulting in lost profitable sales.

Other Rationales for Risk Credit Limits—Risk of loss, the domino effect, and decreases in creditworthiness with increases in purchases are all based on risk concepts which are relevant for some selling firms and some customers. When circumstances arise which make these risk concepts relevant, the imposition of binding risk credit limits is warranted. There are other rationales for the imposition of risk credit limits, and credit managers should have at least a passing familiarity with these rationales. However, the conditions under which these other rationales should be used are much more limited than those previously discussed.

One of these other rationales is funds constraints. This occurs when, for one reason or another, the seller's management chooses to constrain the total dollar amount of investment in its receivables asset. When this constraint is in place, credit limits on individual customers can be used to maximize the value of the receivables asset.[57] However, surveys of credit managers indicate that this constraint simply is not imposed very often.[58]

Another rationale is increases in production costs. This occurs when a buyer purchases so much from the seller that the seller must schedule overtime, utilize less efficient production capacity, etc., to service the buyer's needs, raising the per-unit cost of servicing the customer as more is purchased.[59] While this situation can result in a credit limit, as with funds constraints it is very rare for this circumstance to arise. Unless the seller is very small, buyers whose potential volume of purchases is sufficiently large to change the seller's per-unit production costs are few and far between.

To summarize, funds constraints and increases in production costs are circumstances where it is advantageous to apply binding credit limits. However, these circumstances probably do not occur very frequently for most firms.

Interactions Between Information and Risk Credit Limits

Depending on its circumstances, a firm may choose to employ information credit limits, risk credit limits, or both in its credit policy. When it chooses to employ both types, there will be interactions between the two that policy must address. This section deals with these interactions, with particular emphasis on those aspects which are counterintuitive.

When both information and risk credit limits are assigned to a customer, the lower one of these limits will be encountered first as sales volumes climb, and therefore the lower limit will generally determine the next action to be taken. For

---

[57] A mathematical model is presented in S. Besley and J.S. Osteryoung, "Accounts Receivable Management: The Development of a General Credit-Granting Algorithm for Determining Credit Limits Under Funds Constraints," a paper presented at the Financial Management Association's 1984 meeting.

[58] See S. Besley and J.S. Osteryoung, "Survey of Current Practices in Establishing Trade-Credit Limits," *Financial Review*, February 1985, pp. 70-81.

[59] See Jess Chua, "A Trade Credit Decision Model with Order-Size Dependent Credit Risks," working paper, University of Calgary, for a credit limits model based on this risk concept.

any particular customer, there are two possible circumstances: the information limit is lower than the risk limit, or visa versa.[60]

The Information Credit Limit is Lower than the Risk Credit Limit—In this case, the next action taken by the credit analyst will be additional credit investigation, which enables the credit analyst to make better credit decisions by enhancing the estimate of the customer's creditworthiness. In some cases, the analyst will find that the customer is, in fact, a better credit risk than was previously estimated. For these customers, the risk credit limit will be increased as a consequence of the investigation. In other cases, the analyst will find that the customer is less creditworthy than previously thought. For these customers, the risk credit limit will be reduced.

The idea that increased credit investigation triggered by increased sales volume might result in a *reduced* risk credit limit is not obvious.[61] Examination of a prior numerical example helps understand what is going on.

Consider the credit decision portrayed in Table 5-2, where for customers with these characteristics further credit investigation would reveal that 20 percent of these customers are not creditworthy and 80 percent are creditworthy. If an order for $10,000 is received from a customer with these characteristics, the order will be approved. However, if the order is instead for $30,000, an additional level of credit investigation will be undertaken. After this investigation, there is only an 80 percent chance that the $30,000 order will be approved since only 80 percent of customers with these characteristics are in fact creditworthy. The obvious question is: "How can a customer be approved for $10,000 but not for $30,000?"

The answer is that for an order size of $10,000, there are in fact some customers who are not creditworthy, but for that order size it is not efficient to find out who they are. However, for an order size of $30,000, it is worth the time and expense to separate out the advantageous customers from the disadvantageous ones. Another way of saying this is that for an order size of $30,000, "serious money" is involved (relative to the costs of investigation), and we need to investigate more completely. More complete investigation is of course more likely to detect inappropriate risks.

The Risk Credit Limit is Lower than the Information Credit Limit—When order size is sufficiently small that a complete credit investigation has not been performed, the customer is assigned an information credit limit to trigger the next stage of credit investigation. The risk credit limit assigned to these customers will be based on the average riskiness of all different types of customers that further investigation would reveal and separate. When some of these types of customers are quite risky, the risk credit limit can be less than the information credit limit, and the risk credit limit will govern further action.

---

[60] Numerical illustrations of the following situations can be found in Frederick C. Scherr, "Optimal Trade Credit Limits," *Financial Management*, 1996.
[61] Though it is discussed here in the context of credit limits, careful readers will recognize that this particular effect of the economics of credit investigation also appeared in Chapter 2.

In this situation, exposures will be limited to the risk credit limit until potential sales volumes are large enough to warrant additional credit investigation. Sometimes this investigation will reveal a very risky customer, and require that the risk credit limit be lowered. Sometimes investigation will reveal a less risky customer, and the risk credit limit will be raised. For example, suppose that a customer has been assigned a risk credit limit of $15,000 and an information credit limit of $25,000. An order is received which would result in exposures of $20,000. Because of the current risk credit limit, exposures should be held to $15,000 by requiring payment of past invoices or other methods.

But suppose that an order is received which would instead require exposures of $35,000. In this case, additional credit investigation would be undertaken since the potential exposure is now higher than the information credit limit. As a result of this investigation, for some customer characteristics risk credit limits will be reduced, while for others they will be increased. The natural question is: "How could the customer be creditworthy for $35,000 but not for $20,000?"

The answer again revolves around the cost of information and its role in credit investigation. At exposures of $15,000, the credit analyst knew that some fraction of customers would default, but it was too costly to find out who they were. At this level of exposure, it was more profitable to incur the costs of bad debt and carrying than to sort out various types of customers. Exposures of $25,000, however, constitute "serious money" relative to the costs of credit investigation, and the credit analyst must be more careful about the customers to whom credit is granted. Finding out more about the customer may lead to upward revisions of estimated creditworthiness or may lead to downward ones.

To summarize this section, when the selling firm faces both information risk and other risks, unexpected and counter-intuitive results occur. Customers will be judged creditworthy for small amounts but not for larger amounts, or for larger amounts but not smaller amounts. These results are, however, perfectly rational once the economics of credit investigation and credit granting are understood. In modern corporations, where there is little extra time and money to perform credit investigation beyond what is economical, these unusual results will occur frequently, and the credit manager should be ready to explain them to others in the organization.

Summary of the Policy Implications in this Chapter

Practicing credit analysts need tools which focus their attention to those customers for whom some sort of action is needed. Credit limits serve this "management by exception" principle. Once orders are received such that the customer's exposure will pass the credit limit, the credit limit signals the credit analyst to perform. This useful functioning as a triggering mechanism explains the credit limit's wide adoption among credit departments.

In this chapter, two advantageous uses for credit limits were outlined, both of which serve to control credit risk of one sort or another. Information credit limits address information risk: the risk that the customer may not be as credit-worthy as the credit analyst currently estimates. These types of credit limits are not binding on customer exposures. Instead, they are signals that further credit investigation is required to address the information risk problem. For best results, it is important that information credit limits be kept confidential within the credit department, as they can easily be misinterpreted by those not familiar with their purpose.

The assignment of risk credit limits is another way that credit limits can be employed. These can be used to limit the risk of loss, address the domino effect (in which the default of a customer threatens the selling firm's survival), or account for the decreases in creditworthiness that occur for some customers as purchase volumes increase. Whether a risk credit limit should be imposed depends on the characteristics of both the customer and the selling firm, including the basis on which the performance of the seller's credit department is evaluated. Credit limits which are imposed to limit the risk of loss, for example, are appropriate if the credit department is evaluated based on its effects on credit costs, but not if the credit department is evaluated based on profitability. Risk credit limits are binding on exposures, and the action triggered by the violation of this limit is the credit analyst's request for payment by the customer to reduce this exposure. To avoid misunderstandings between the seller and the customer, it is advantageous that the amount of the risk credit limit be discussed with the customer.

For those credit departments who are evaluated on a profitability basis, a bit should be said about the effects of profit margin before credit costs on credit limits. The greater is the profitability of the product, the greater is the sale's advantage, and the more risk (of whatever type) that the firm can afford to bear. Therefore, customers buying products with higher profit margins should be assigned higher credit limits, and those buying products with lower margins should be assigned lower credit limits.

Credit limits are so useful that most firms adopt them as part of their credit policy as a matter of course. The great danger is that this tool will be used without careful consideration of the needs and circumstances of the seller. What aspects of credit risk are relevant to the particular seller? Which customers manifest these risks? How will credit limits be used to specifically manage these risks? Without clear thinking on these issues, credit limits policy can be ill-founded.

Case for Discussion and Analysis

The Case of the Expanding Electrician

Sparky Switches was a large manufacturer of electrical devices for use in the home. For fiscal 1995, Sparky had annual sales of $50 million. Natalie Anastasia was one of the credit analysts for Sparky Switches, handling a receivables portfolio containing mostly wholesalers. These wholesalers purchased Sparky's products for resale to retailers. The credit department at Sparky was evaluated based on budgets for credit investigation expenses, accounts receivable investment, and bad debt expense, as well as the profitability of sales made to marginal customers.

One of Ms. Anastasia's customers was Smith Electrical Supply, Inc. Smith bought a wide range of products from Sparky on net 30 day terms. Total sales to Smith last year had been about $250,000; $35,0000 was currently owing, of which $20,000 was current and $15,000 was 15 days past due. Sales volume to Smith had been growing rapidly, reflecting Smith's own growth. Smith's sales had grown 18 percent during 1994 and 20 percent during 1995. Ms. Anastasia's credit file on Smith contained a current commercial credit report, a report from Smith's bank (obtained via Sparky's bank), past and current trade clearances, and recent financial statements. The trade clearance showed that Smith was currently paying the trade 15-30 days past terms, as it had over the last several years.

Ms. Anastasia had performed ratio analysis on Smith's statements for the last three years. The results are shown in Table 5-1C. This analysis showed Smith to be a typical wholesale customer. Its latest financial ratios were near the industry means for firms of this type and size. While Ms. Anastasia had examined these financial statements in detail, she had yet to visit Smith to assess the firm's management, examine the premises, and obtain the other information that only a visit to a customer can provide.

Suggestions for Analysis

1. Given the facts in the case, should an information credit limit be assigned to Smith? Justify why it should or should not.

2. Given the facts in the case, should a risk credit limit be assigned to Smith? Justify why it should or should not with reference to the type of risk that this limit is intended to control and how the risk limit would control this risk.

Table 5-1C.   Financial Statements and Ratio Analysis.

Smith Electrical Supply, Inc. (all figures in rounded thousands)

	1993	*1994*	*1995*
Sales	$12,000	$14,160	$16,992
Cost of Sales	$9,528	$11,243	$13,492
Selling and Other Expenses	$1,920	$2,266	$2,719
Profit Before Taxes	$552	$651	$781
Taxes	$193	$228	$273
Earnings After Taxes	$359	$423	$508
Dividends	$40	$45	$50
Additions to Retained Earnings	$319	$378	$458
Cash	$257	$301	$361
Accounts Receivable	$1,613	$1,936	$2,284
Inventory	$2,023	$2,347	$2,863
Other Current Assets	$119	$139	$168
Total Current Assets	$4,012	$4,723	$5,676
Fixed and Other Assets	$747	$892	$1,062
Total Assets	$4,759	$5,615	$6,738
Due to Banks, Short-Term	$400	$476	$566
Trade Payables	$1,133	$1,359	$1,590
Other Current Liabilities	$528	$607	$729
Total Current Liabilities	$2,061	$2,442	$2,885
Long-Term Debt	$556	$653	$875
Equity	$2,142	$2,520	$2,978
Total Liabilities and Equity	$4,759	$5,615	$6,738
Liquidity Ratios			
Current Ratio	1.95	1.93	1.97
Quick Ratio	0.97	0.97	0.98
Turnover Ratios			
Accounts Receivable Turnover	7.44	7.31	7.44
Inv. Turnover (CoS/Inv.)	4.71	4.79	4.71
Total Assets Turnover	2.52	2.52	2.52
CoS/Trade Payables	8.41	8.27	8.49
Debt Ratios			
Total Debt/Total Assets	0.55	0.55	0.56
Total Debt/Net Worth	1.22	1.23	1.26
Profitability Ratios			
Earnings After Taxes/Sales	3.0%	3.0%	3.0%
Earnings After Taxes/Assets	7.5%	7.5%	7.5%
Earnings After Taxes/Equity	16.8%	16.8%	17.1%

6 Expert and Statistical Scoring Systems

Among the most important processes inherent in credit granting is the integration of credit information into an estimate of creditworthiness. This process requires the devotion of considerable effort by credit analysts, whose time is a scarce and valuable commodity.

The firm may elect to shorten the time necessary for the integration process, and obtain other benefits as well, by adopting either "expert system" or "statistical scoring" methodologies as part of its credit policy. Expert and statistical scoring techniques are included within many modern computer packages for credit analysis and management.[62] Both of these techniques use mathematical or other rules to integrate credit information about customers into assessments of creditworthiness.[63] The credit manager must be aware of the advantages and limitations of these systems in deciding whether to adopt them as part of the firm's credit policy.

Advantages of Expert and Statistical Scoring Systems

Regardless of whether an expert or a statistical scoring system is employed, using the system is much the same: the credit analyst gives the system certain information, and the system gives back an integration of this information. The integration given back by the system may be in terms of an accept/reject credit decision, a credit limit, or some sort of score which is indicative of the customer's credit risk.

Though their costs and disadvantages differ widely, the benefits of expert systems and statistical scoring systems are similar. Four such benefits are discussed in the following paragraphs.

Reductions in Analysis Time—Expert and statistical scoring systems may be used in two ways: in place of traditional credit analysis or in addition to this

---

[62] For discussion of several modern credit analysis packages, including the expert and statistical scoring systems they contain, see "Credit Scoring and Analysis: 1995 Software Reviews," *Business Credit*, May 1995, pp. 20-23.
[63] Some expert systems also include rules for credit investigation itself.

analysis. When used in place of this analysis, the analyst does not have to spend the time to consider the credit information that has been accumulated on a customer in order develop an estimate of creditworthiness. Instead, the system tells the analyst to enter specified information, which is integrated by the system, resulting in a time savings for the analyst. The advantage is greatest when the system directly produces an accept/reject decision or a credit limit rather than a risk score which requires further interpretation.

Reduction in the Required Expertise of the Analyst—Veteran credit analysts can use credit information to accurately estimate credit risk. This is partly because, over time, they have learned useful analysis methods and because experience has taught them how to process credit information effectively, picking out the most important information and evaluating its interactions with other types of information. When expert or statistical systems are used, these systems substitute in part for the expertise of the experienced credit analyst. Therefore, credit analysts can function with a lower level of expertise. A greater proportion of novice credit analysts can be employed by the firm, saving salary costs.

Reduced Errors in Decision-Making—Related to the above is the effect of the use of an expert or statistical system on the errors that a credit analyst makes in the credit decisions.

There are two types of these errors: (1) credit can be granted to a customer who is not creditworthy, or (2) credit can be denied to a customer who is creditworthy. Unless the firm hires only very experienced credit analysts, these errors will be made as novice analysts gain experience, and the errors will be costly to the firm. A frequently-cited advantage of expert or statistical systems is that they can improve decision-making by less-experienced analysts and reduce the costs of these errors. Unfortunately, while this error reduction occurs for some credit decisions, in others new errors are introduced which even an inexperienced analysis might not make. (We will discuss this issue at length later in the chapter.)

Increased Consistency Among Analysts—Even among experienced credit analysts, the estimation of creditworthiness is, in part, subjective. Therefore, decisions will vary from analyst to analyst. This makes the firm's credit decision-making process seem arbitrary to others within the firm. Utilizing a single decision-making system leads all analysts to make the same or very similar credit decisions.[64] Further, these systems can be explained and justified to those without credit expertise more easily than can the traditional credit analysis process.

Set against these advantages are several problems, costs, and other difficulties which occur for expert systems and for statistical scoring systems. These problems differ between the two approaches, and understanding them requires a knowledge of how these two approaches work.

---

[64] This consistency also helps the firm in addressing complaints of discrimination in credit-granting based on ethnicity or gender. See Charles L. Gahala, *Credit Management: Principles and Practices*, NACM, 1995, pp. 96-102, for an interesting discussion of these and other issues related to the use of expert and statistical scoring systems.

Principles of Expert Systems for Credit Decisions

Expert systems, in various forms, have been used in credit management since the 1930s. They are called "expert" not because the system itself has any expertise, but because they *attempt to replicate the judgment that an expert would make* if faced with the same decision. This expert provides the knowledge from which the expert system is developed. Expert systems can be simple paper-and-pencil systems or elaborate computer programs.

In any expert system, the goal is to capture the expert's knowledge of credit analysis without having the expert present. To accomplish this, the expert carefully chooses the dimensions of creditworthiness that he or she believes are most relevant and incorporates these into the expert system. However, there is a tradeoff between the costs of developing and using the system and the comprehensiveness of the system. (Comprehensiveness is the ability of the system to deal with unusual circumstances or special cases.) By spending more time in developing the system, the credit expert can produce a more comprehensive decision system which produces fewer errors in credit-granting. However, in addition to the higher costs of their development, more complex and comprehensive systems take more time for the analyst to execute, partly defeating a major advantage of expert systems: reduction in analysis time. Various types of expert systems differ in development time, error rate, and ease of use.

Checklist Expert Systems—Checklists are the simplest, least comprehensive form of expert systems. In checklist expert systems, the initial part of the credit evaluation process consists of answering yes or no to a series of questions. There may be any number of questions. A hypothetical 10-question checklist system is presented in Table 6-1.

In developing a checklist system, the expert must formulate the questions and specify a decision rule for using the tally of yes and no answers to make the credit-granting decision. In the hypothetical checklist in Table 6-1, for example, the expert might require that at least seven questions be answered "yes" in order for credit to be granted.

Table 6-1.   A Hypothetical Checklist Expert System for Credit-Granting

	Yes	No
1. Is the customer's current ratio greater than 2.0?	___	___
2. Is the customer's quick ratio greater than 1.0?	___	___
3. Is the customer's debt/assets ratio less than 0.5?	___	___
4. Is the customer's accounts receivable turnover ratio greater than 8.0?	___	___
5. Is the customer's inventory turnover ratio greater than 6.0?	___	___
6. Did the customer show a profit for the last fiscal year?	___	___
7. Has the customer been in business for more than five years?	___	___
9. Does the customer pay the trade less than 30 days beyond terms?	___	___
9. Are the customer's assets free of security encumbrances?	___	___
10. Is the profit margin on the products to be sold greater than 20 percent?	___	___

Table 6-2.   A Hypothetical Point-Scoring Decision System

			Points:		
Customer Factors	_0_	_1_	_2_	_3_	_4_
Current ratio	below 1.0	1.0 to 1.49	1.50 to 1.99	2.00 to 2.50	above 2.50
Debt/total assets ratio	above .75	0.60 to 0.75	0.45 to 0.59	0.30 to 0.44	below 0.30
Years in business	less than 1	1 to 3	4 to 6	6 to 10	more than 10
Payments to trade	slow over 60	slow 30-60	slow 10-30	slow to 10	ppt. and disc.

Decision rule: Grant credit if customer has over 10 points.

This hypothetical checklist system provides an illustration of the cost/benefit tradeoffs related to the complexity of the expert system. The system is simple and quick to execute, but can make costly errors. For example, there is no question asking whether there are any suits or judgments outstanding against the customer. (If there were, an experienced credit manager would probably be very reluctant to grant credit.) Questions of this sort can be added to the list, but each question added increases the analysis time and reduces the advantage of the expert system.

While checklist systems have the virtue of simplicity, this virtue comes at a cost: checklist systems are not suited to the detection of subtle but important differences among customers. For example, question one in Table 6-1 gives one "yes" credit to the customer if the customer's current ratio is greater than 2.0. This methodology makes no distinction between current ratios of 2.01 and 5.0, yet such a difference clearly has impact on creditworthiness. This problem may be addressed by adopting a point-scoring expert system rather than a checklist system.

Point-Scoring Expert Systems—In these sorts of expert systems, customers score points along various dimensions of creditworthiness rather than receiving a simple yes-no on each of these dimensions. As in checklist systems, the expert decides what dimensions of creditworthiness are to be assessed. In addition, along each dimension the expert also decides the cutoffs in determining the point scores, how many points are to be scored for each response, and the total score that is sufficient for credit to be granted.

A hypothetical point-scoring system is presented in Table 6-2. In this system, four dimensions of the customer's creditworthiness are included: current ratio, debt/assets, years in business, and payments to the trade. Various point values are assigned to levels of each of these.

As with the checklist system, the more aspects of the credit-granting system the expert includes, the more complex and burdensome the system will be to execute, but the fewer costly errors it will produce. Compared to checklist systems, point scoring systems are generally more costly both because they require more effort to develop (to determine cutoffs, scores, etc.) and are more complex to use, but they may produce fewer decision errors.

Computer-Based Expert Systems—The burden of executing checklist and point-scoring expert systems can be eased somewhat by incorporating the system into the firm's credit analysis computer package. However, the main application of computer technology in this area is in the development of the expert system itself. Software for developing expert systems has been available since the early 1980s. Expert systems software has application to any decision requiring expertise, be it credit or otherwise. One early application was in medical diagnosis and treatment. Early systems were mainframe-based, but most modern software runs on a microcomputer. Expert systems software allows for the development of much more complex expert systems, reducing the errors in credit decisions that simpler systems make.

Computer-designed expert systems are developed by the expert, typically with the aid of a "knowledge engineer" who is trained to construct such systems. Computer-designed expert systems are composed of three parts: the "knowledge base," the "inference engine," and the "interface." The knowledge base is all the information needed to execute the system, including the if-then rules by which the system makes decisions. The inference engine selects the applicable rules to be invoked at any particular time. The interface is a set of computer displays that interact with the credit analyst, asking for data and displaying results.

Because of their complexity, illustration of even the most basic of computer-developed expert systems is beyond the scope of this book. (In Srinivasan and Kim's case study of a Fortune 500 firm's computerized expert system for credit granting decisions, the knowledge base for each customer consists in part of measurements of 28 different aspects of the customer's creditworthiness, including many financial ratios and their trends.)[65] In developing such an expert system, in addition to identifying each aspect of creditworthiness and deciding how each aspect is to be measured, decisions must be made on how the aspects are to be combined by the program into a credit-granting decision. It is safe to say that developing a system of this sort entails a substantial commitment of the firm's resources.[66]

Problems in Using Expert Systems—There are two major problems in using any sort of expert system for credit decisions. The first, which was previously discussed, concerns the tradeoff between development costs, ease of use, and errors in decisions.

In any expert system, the number of aspects of the credit decision that are incorporated within the system and the rules based on these aspects will determine how accurate the system is in making credit decisions. This is so since expert systems have no common sense. If some aspect of the credit decision is important in a particular case but is not among those aspects incorporated in the

---

[65] See Venkat Srinivasan and Yong H. Kim, "Designing Expert Financial Systems: A Case Study of Corporate Credit Management," *Financial Management*, Autumn 1988, pp. 32-44.

[66] Gahala estimates that the development and installation of a scoring system could cost from $50,000 to $100,000 (*Credit Management: Principles and Practices*, p. 102). Coats cites a study which claims that moderate sized expert systems typically cost $250,000 to $500,000 just to design (Pamela K. Coats, "Why Expert Systems Fail," *Financial Management*, Autumn 1988, p. 83).

expert system, this aspect is ignored regardless of its value. The more aspects of the credit decision that are incorporated within the expert system, the less likely this is to happen, but the more expensive the expert system is to develop and to use.[67] Checklist and point-scoring systems are cheap to develop and easy to use, but ignore many factors. Decision systems developed using expert system software can take into account many factors and complex interactions of these factors, but are very expensive to develop.

The second problem concerns the basic nature of the expert systems approach itself as a model of the behavior of a designated expert. The problem is that if the expert's judgment is inaccurate, so is the expert system based on this judgment. In the expert systems approach, the system only models the behavior of a particular person. Particularly when the expert system is executed on a computer, there is a tendency for users to believe that the expert system contains an optimization procedure that produces the best possible credit decisions. This belief often occurs if a great deal of time and effort has gone into developing the system, and thus when people have an emotional stake in it.

But *there is no magic in the box*. Any expert system is simply the quantification of someone's opinion. This problem is important because, while an expert will make better decisions than a novice, there are several reasons to believe that even an expert credit manager's opinion may be incorrect in systematic ways. First, even with years of service, the expert's experience with particular events is limited. This is particularly true with defaults. Only a few defaults occur each year; the vast majority of customers survive. Suppose that some aspects of a particular expert credit manager's defaults happen by chance to be atypical of defaults in general. In such a circumstance, that expert would almost certainly include those aspects in his or her expert system, and weight them heavily, even though they were not truly determinants of default in general.

Second, in making decisions there is a natural tendency for people to put too much weight on recent events, under weighting things further in the past. This phenomenon is well documented in the psychological literature. This means that everyone's judgment is systematically biased by recent events, even when a longer-term view is warranted. Because of this, in developing the expert system the credit expert will naturally put too much weight on the causes of his or her last few defaults, and will underweight factors that caused prior defaults.

Finally, while experience tends to bring the expert's judgment in line with the firm's goals, it is quite possible that the expert is too conservative or too liberal in his or her credit decisions relative to what is best for the firm. This problem is particularly important if the firm evaluates credit personnel based on cost targets. When cost targets are used, it is hard for any credit person to know exactly what constitutes creditworthiness. The natural tendency is to be overly cautious to

---

[67] These problems are discussed in Coats, "Why Expert Systems Fail," *Financial Management*, Autumn 1988, pp. 77-86 with reference to expert systems developed using expert systems software.

minimize accounts receivable carrying and bad debt costs. When an expert system is developed based on these judgments, it will contain such a bias.

One way to address any biases that may come from developing an expert system based on a single expert credit manager is to design the system based on the options of several credit managers. However, this geometrically increases the cost of expert system development, as the experts must agree on the aspects of creditworthiness to include, how these are to be used, and so forth.

Should You Use an Expert System in Your Credit Department?—Employing expert systems to make credit-granting decisions is clearly a policy with both advantages and disadvantages. A review of the literature finds four characteristics to be common in successful applications of expert systems.[68] Some of these are apt descriptions of trade credit-granting while others are not:

1. *There are recognized experts who are provably better than amateurs.* This is certainly true for credit decision-making.

2. *The experts routinely teach this skill to novices, so that they are accustomed to putting their procedures into words.* This is true in some selling firms but not in others. Some firms have adequate training programs using veteran credit managers and policy manuals to guide new credit analysts while others do not; novices instead learn by trial and error.

3. *The task is highly specialized, has a very limited domain, rules are static, and no common sense is required.* This is clearly not true for credit decisions. There are many aspects of the credit situation to be considered, including many factors concerning the customer and the selling firm. The domain is not limited, and a great deal of common sense and insight are required to make decisions.

4. *The cost of an incorrect decision is low.* This is true for some credit decisions but not for others. If potential sales volumes to a customer are small, granting or denying credit inappropriately will not entail large costs to the firm. If volumes are higher, much can be lost by either error.

In summary, there is a lot to recommend the use of expert systems of one sort or another as long as the sales volume involved is small. In that case, not much can be lost by an incorrect decision and only a minimal expenditure of analyst's time is warranted. Expert systems save analyst's time and are thus advantageous. When sales volume is larger, and the cost of errors higher, the limitations of this approach become significant and another sort of credit analysis is necessary. Sadly, there is no magic in the box.

Developing a Statistical Scoring System

One of the major problems in using the expert systems approach is that this approach models the credit decisions of a particular expert, and these decisions

---

[68] These four are abstracted from Coats, "Why Expert Systems Fail," *Financial Management*, Autumn 1988, p. 84.

might not be the best ones that can be made. Statistical credit scoring takes a different approach: it allows the data itself to tell the story. Statistical scoring models use statistical comparisons between firms that have defaulted and those that have not defaulted in the past to lend insight into the chance of the future default of a new customer.

Beyond this difference, statistical methodologies and expert systems perform the same task. The task is to take a set of data on a customer's creditworthiness and to provide a mechanism which integrates all or part of these data into a single measure of credit risk. In expert systems, the integration mechanism is developed by an expert. In statistical scoring, it is done by analyzing the data statistically.

If the firm decides to adopt statistical scoring to aid in credit analysis, there is a basic choice to be made: whether to (1) develop the statistical scoring model internally or (2) to utilize a public-domain model or commercial model. (The most popular public-domain model is Altman's Z Score.) Developing the model in-house has several advantages:

1. *The data are likely to be more current.* This is particularly true relative to models which are in the public domain, many of which were developed using data which is decades old. If the firm develops its own model, it can select more recent data, which are likely to be more representative of current conditions.
2. *A single-industry model can be developed that captures the special credit risk factors in each of the industries to which the firm sells.* Public-domain models and commercial models generally utilize data from several industries.
3. *The statistical technology utilized to develop some of the older public-domain models is obsolete.* The firm can use more recent technology to develop its own model.

Set against these advantages are two disadvantages. First, developing a statistical scoring model entails substantial development costs to collect data, perform the statistical analysis, and so forth.[69] Second, public-domain statistical scoring systems (particularly older ones) and commercial systems have a supporting literature detailing their use and limitations. If the firm develops its own statistical scoring system, it has to develop this experience itself.

If the firm chooses to develop its own statistical model, there are three steps in the process: data collection, model development, and model validation. Each of these steps must be done carefully.

Data Collection—To perform the statistical analysis, samples of defaulted and nondefaulted firms must be identified and data collected. There are a number of important considerations in sample development, the first of which is sample size.

To utilize a statistical methodology, the firm will need samples of at least 30 defaulted and 30 nondefaulted firms for each scoring model that it wishes to develop. The larger the number of firms in the samples, the better the model that will result, but the larger the cost of developing the sample. It should be noted that it serves no purpose to increase the sample size of either the defaulted or

---

[69] It should be noted that this procedure will require the time and attention of a statistician and well as the credit manager. While this section provides an introduction, the statistical techniques involved are not simple and require a statistician's expertise to employ properly.

nondefaulted group without increasing the size of the other. The size of the smallest group governs the power of the statistical model. Further, it is very important that the nondefaulted firms should be randomly selected (rather than selecting "best cases" or "best examples") so that the statistical scoring model is applicable to any new credit applicant.

There are two very important and interconnected questions that have to be answered and that affect sample size. The first is whether the firm desires to develop a statistical scoring model for each of the industries to which it sells. The second is whether the firm elects to develop the samples from its own credit records or to buy the samples from a commercial information vendor (such as Dun & Bradstreet). If the firm wants to develop a statistical scoring model for each industry to which it sells, it will need to find data on at least 30 defaulted customers in each of these industries within its credit files and on a corresponding number of nondefaulted customers. Most firms will find this data requirement very difficult to meet. Since default rates are fairly low in most industries, only the very largest firms will find data on enough recently defaulted customers for each industry in which they participate.

Firms that wish to formulate industry-specific statistical models but do not have enough recent data on defaults have three options. First, they can forego industry-specific models and pool data from several industries. The resulting model will not generally detect industry-specific factors which cause default. Second, they can enlarge the time frame over which data are collected, going back more years in each industry to increase sample size. The resulting model will not identify any factors which cause default that have arisen recently. Finally, they can buy the data rather than collecting it themselves. This allows for industry-specific models but may increase collection data costs.

It should be noted that buying the data from a commercial vendor who collects data on all firms has an additional advantage: it mitigates *exclusion bias*. Exclusion bias occurs because the sample of customers that defaulted to the firm are those that met the firm's credit criteria and were therefore granted credit. The credit screening process eliminates the least creditworthy firms from the defaulted sample. The resulting statistical model does not represent them. Instead, it most appropriately applies only to firms that have passed the initial credit screen. This problem is avoided if a broader, more representative sample of defaults is used.[70]

A second important consideration in sample development is the data to collect on each firm in the sample. The measures usually used are financial ratios, but data on any measure which the seller believes is related to default and on which quantitative data or qualitative ratings can be collected can be used in the statistical procedure.

However, there is a pitfall in including too many measures into the statistical procedure: the "garbage in/garbage out" problem. In developing scoring models,

[70] For more discussion of these sampling issues and other issues related to developing statistical scoring models, see Frederick C. Scherr, "Estimating and Using Failure-Forecasting Functions: Some Problems and Some Proposed Solutions," *Baylor Business Studies*, December 1981.

there is a natural tendency to throw in many ratios and other data and to let the statistical procedure decide what is important. Unfortunately, this tendency can lead to statistical artifacts: measures which are, by chance, important in conjunction with default in the sample, but have no predictive power in the real world.

It is much better to think clearly about the likely causes and correlates of default and to include a limited number of measures representing each of these factors. Clearly, the customer's liquidity, financial leverage, cash flow relative to expenses, variability of cash flow, and asset quality are determinants of survival, and measures should certainly be included to represent these. The customer's age and size are also good representations of the ability to survive. Older and larger firms are less likely to fail. Finally, the stage of the business cycle at the time of failure is important, as more firms fail during recessions than during expansions. Beyond these obvious factors, the firm should include other measures that are believed to be important in association with default in the industries being considered, but only those measures.

Model Development—In this phase, the data are used to develop a statistical scoring model which gives the best results on the data in the samples (results in the world outside of the sample are tested later). To understand how this procedure works, it is useful to analyze an example data set. One is given in Table 6-3.[71] Note that the average liquidity and debt position is as expected: the average current ratio is higher for the nondefaulted group (1.37 versus 0.68 for the defaulted group) and the total debt to total assets ratio is lower (0.56 versus 0.94). But how do you combine these ratios to best differentiate between defaults and nondefaults?

To see how the statistical procedure answers this question, first consider the plot of these data in Figure 6-1. A substantial portion of the distributions of the defaulted and nondefaulted firms are intermingled. This intermingling occurs for debt/assets ratios between about 0.60 and 0.80 and for current ratios between about 0.60 and 1.20.

The effect of this intermingling is made clearer in Figure 6-2, where rough borders are drawn around each of the groups and these borders projected onto the two axises. Note that the ranges of overlap on each ratio (ranges where both N and D occur) are reasonably large relative to the ranges where only defaults or nondefaults occur. This means that rules based on either of these ratios taken individually would do a relatively poor job of distinguishing between high and low default risks in this sample. What is needed is a rule that combines the two ratios to achieve maximum power in differentiating between defaults and nondefaults. Such a rule is portrayed in Figure 6-3, where a new axis has been drawn roughly perpendicular to the range of overlay for the two distributions combined. Note that, on this new axis, the range of overlap is small relative to the ranges where only defaults or nondefaults occur. This is exactly what any of

---

[71] These are actual data from a sample of defaulted and nondefaulted plastic molders, and differs from the data set that would actually be used in formulating a statistical scoring model in only two ways. First, the data set is too small, containing only 10 defaulted and 10 nondefaulted firms. Second, only two measures related to default are included: the current ratio, a measure of liquidity, and total debt/total assets, a measure of financial leverage.

Table 6-3.   Example Data: Defaulted and Nondefaulted Plastic Molders

Case No.	Current Ratio	Total Debt/ Total Assets	Group Designator
Defaulted Group:			
1	1.15	0.72	1
2	0.48	0.60	1
3	0.38	0.73	1
4	0.89	0.98	1
5	0.55	1.06	1
6	0.78	0.88	1
7	0.65	0.71	1
8	0.49	1.16	1
9	0.88	1.20	1
10	0.55	1.32	1
Mean	0.68	0.94	
Nondefaulted Group:			
11	2.12	0.50	0
12	1.09	0.62	0
13	1.32	0.27	0
14	1.81	0.49	0
15	0.73	0.61	0
16	2.05	0.40	0
17	0.56	0.85	0
18	1.03	0.73	0
19	1.78	0.29	0
20	1.16	0.80	0
Mean	1.37	0.56	

the statistical procedures used to develop statistical scoring models does: it generates a combination of the measures (a new axis) to achieve the greatest difference between the defaulted and nondefaulted groups. This produces the best possible classification accuracy for the samples. Of course, this is done statistically rather than by a geometric method since geometric methods will not work for more than two measures.

One important choice that must be made in connection with the model's development is the specific statistical procedure that is to be used to generate the model. Several techniques are available. Among these are the linear probability function, multiple discriminant analysis, logit analysis, and probit analysis. Unfortunately, the choice among these methods involves statistical and causal considerations that are well beyond the expertise of the average credit manager. The choice is best left to a statistician.[72]

Once the statistical technique is chosen and executed, it is up to the credit manager and the statistician to interpret the results. These results describe the

[72] A good text on the statistical aspects of the matter is E. I. Altman et. al., *Classification Techniques in Business, Banking and Finance,* JAI Press, 1981. A summary of causal considerations can be found in Frederick C. Scherr, "Causality, Regression, Discriminant Analysis, and Research on Failure," *Akron Business and Economic Review,* Spring 1989.

Figure 6-1. Plot of Data From Table 6-3

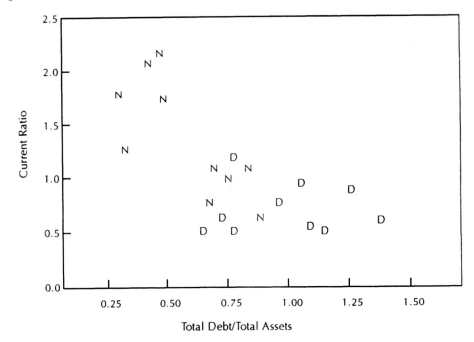

D = Location of a member of defaulted group
N = Location of a member of nondefaulted group

Figure 6-2. Overlaps in the Distributions of Defaults and Nondefaults

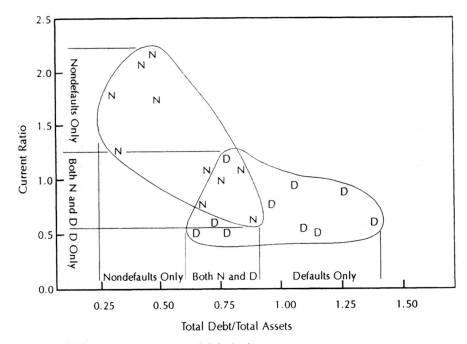

D = Location of a member of defaulted group
N = Location of a member of nondefaulted group

Figure 6-3. A Statistical Scoring Model for the Example Data

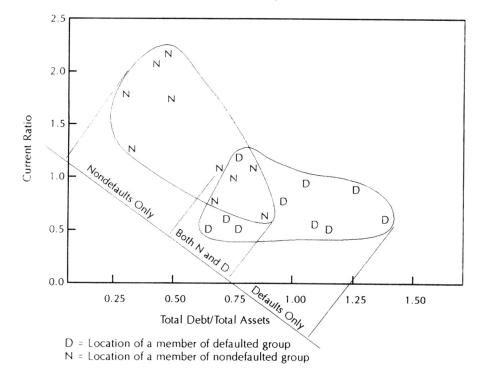

D = Location of a member of defaulted group
N = Location of a member of nondefaulted group

model's ability to identify defaulted and nondefaulted firms in the sample and the importance of various measures in making this determination. In general, an adequate model will identify defaulted and nondefaulted firms with reasonable accuracy and will make sense in terms of the contribution of each measure to credit risk.

As an illustration of this part of the process, the data in Table 6-3 were used with the linear probability function to generate a statistical scoring model, with the group designators set as in this table (defaulted=1, nondefaulted =0).[73] The resulting model is:

Score = 0.3146 – 0.3536 Current Ratio + 0.7332 TD/TA

Note that since defaults are designated as "1," higher scores on this model indicate that the firm is more likely to default. Thus, the coefficients which the statistical procedure estimated for the two ratio measures in the model make sense: a higher current ratio should be associated with a lower probability of default (the negative coefficient on the current ratio variable makes sense), and while a higher

[73] The linear probability model is the simplest of the statistical techniques and is available in Lotus 1-2-3 under "Data" and "Regression." To replicate these statistical results in this subroutine, pull Table 6-3 from the disk accompanying this text and delete the rows separating the two groups. Designate the data in the designator column as the "Y variable" and the ratio data as the "X variables." Then set the "Output Range" below the data and indicate "Go."

Table 6-4.   In-Sample Classification Results for Example Data Using a Linear Probability Function Scoring Model

Prediction Rule: if score > .50, predict default, otherwise predict nondefault.

In-Sample Results:

Case No.	Current Ratio	Total Debt/ Total Assets	Score	Predicted Group
Defaulted Group:				
1	1.15	0.72	0.436	Nondefault
2	0.48	0.60	0.585	Default
3	0.38	0.73	0.715	Default
4	0.89	0.98	0.718	Default
5	0.55	1.06	0.897	Default
6	0.78	0.88	0.684	Default
7	0.65	0.71	0.605	Default
8	0.49	1.16	0.992	Default
9	0.88	1.20	0.883	Default
10	0.55	1.32	1.088	Default
Nondefaulted Group:				
11	2.12	0.50	-0.068	Nondefault
12	1.09	0.62	0.384	Nondefault
13	1.32	0.27	0.046	Nondefault
14	1.81	0.49	0.034	Nondefault
15	0.73	0.61	0.504	Default
16	2.05	0.40	-0.117	Nondefault
17	0.56	0.85	0.740	Default
18	1.03	0.73	0.486	Nondefault
19	1.78	0.29	-0.102	Nondefault
20	1.16	0.80	0.491	Nondefault

Percent Correctly Classified: 17/20 = 85.0%

Hit-or-Miss Matrix:

	Predicted Group Defaulted	Nondefaulted
Defaulted	9	1
Actual Group		
Nondefaulted	2	8

Entries along the upper-left to lower-right diagonal are "hits" (actual and predicted group are the same).

debt ratio should be associated with a higher probability of default (the positive coefficient on the debt ratio makes sense).

Now let us evaluate the accuracy of this formulation in classifying the firms that make up the sample. Because there are equal numbers of defaulted and nondefaulted firms in the sample, the break-even score for this model is 0.50. The model says that firms with scores greater than 0.50 are more likely to be defaults and firms with scores of less than 0.50 are more likely to be nondefaults. Table 6-4 gives the classification results for the sample based on this classification rule and a hit-or-miss matrix portraying these results.

One defaulted firm is incorrectly classified as nondefaulted and two nondefaulted firms are incorrectly classified as defaulted for a correct classification rate of 85.0 percent. This, combined with the fact that the coefficients make sense, is a fairly good statistical result, given that only two aspects of the firms in the samples (liquidity and debt position) are measured. No statistical scoring model will ever be 100 percent accurate, since there are many factors that affect credit risk which simply cannot be quantified accurately or at all, and therefore cannot be used in a statistical scoring model.

Model Validation—Any model's classification accuracy within the sample used in its development inappropriately measures the model's actual ability to predict in the real world because the same data that were used to estimate the model were used in this classification. What is needed is a test of the model outside the data used in its estimation. This process is called model validation.

One way to do model validation is to hold out some data in model development, then apply the developed model to these data and assess the results. This "holdout method" works best when the firm has a lot of data on both defaulted and nondefaulted customers and can, therefore, afford to remove some from the development process.

When there are not enough data to utilize the holdout method, the "U Method" is frequently employed. In this method, small portions of the data (frequently individual cases) are held out and the statistical scoring model reestimated without these data. The held-out data is then classified using the new model. The process is repeated until all the data are held out.

An illustration of the U method is provided in Table 6-5 for our example statistical scoring model. Here, one defaulted and one nondefaulted case were held out sequentially (case number 1 with case number 11, 2 with 12, etc.) and the statistical model reestimated.[74] The reestimated model was then used to classify the two held-out cases. The results show 14 of the 20 cases correctly classified, for a 70.0 percent correct classification rate. This correct classification rate under validation indicates that this approach does a much better job than chance classification, which would correctly classify 50 percent of the customers (since there are equal numbers in each group).

Using Scores from the Statistical Model—When the firm puts the characteristics of a new credit applicant into a statistical scoring system of the type previously developed and computes the score, the raw score is typically an *ordinal measure of default risk* (meaning that serves only to rank firms based on default risk) and can be used to compare one customer to another. In the example model developed above, higher scores indicate higher default risk.

It is usually inappropriate, however, to compare the raw score to a cutoff score, where this cutoff score was developed within the sample, and to make credit decisions on this basis unless an adjustment for differences in default odds is made.

---

[74] One case from each group was held out to keep the sample sizes for the two groups equal; with the two sample sizes equal, the breakeven score remains at 0.50. While sequential pairs were held out, a more rigorous statistical procedure would have held out random pairs.

Table 6-5.   Out-of-Sample Classification Results for Example Data (U Method)

Prediction Rule: If score > .50, predict default, otherwise predict nondefault.

Basic Data				U Method Results				
Case No.	Current Ratio	TD/TA	Group Designator	Intercept	Coeff. of Cur. Ratio	Coeff. of TD/TA	Score	Predicted Group
Defaulted Group:								
1	1.15	0.72	1	0.3674	-0.4142	0.6937	0.3905	Nondefault
2	0.48	0.60	1	0.0916	-0.2482	0.8786	0.4996	Nondefault
3	0.38	0.73	1	0.1538	-0.2799	0.8247	0.6495	Default
4	0.89	0.98	1	0.3582	-0.3647	0.6711	0.6913	Default
5	0.55	1.06	1	0.5459	-0.4353	0.5676	0.9081	Default
6	0.78	0.88	1	0.3281	-0.3755	0.7120	0.6618	Default
7	0.65	0.71	1	0.3612	-0.3891	0.7475	0.6390	Default
8	0.49	1.16	1	0.3456	-0.3558	0.7302	1.0183	Default
9	0.88	1.20	1	0.3583	-0.3812	0.6934	0.8549	Default
10	0.55	1.32	1	0.1953	-0.3049	0.8749	1.1825	Default
Mean	0.68	0.94						
Nondefaulted Group:								
11	2.12	0.50	0	0.3674	-0.4142	0.6937	-0.1639	Nondefault
12	1.09	0.62	0	0.0916	-0.2482	0.8786	0.3658	Nondefault
13	1.32	0.27	0	0.1538	-0.2799	0.8247	0.0070	Nondefault
14	1.81	0.49	0	0.3582	-0.3647	0.6711	0.0269	Nondefault
15	0.73	0.61	0	0.5459	-0.4353	0.5676	0.5744	Default
16	2.05	0.40	0	0.3281	-0.3755	0.7120	-0.1569	Nondefault
17	0.56	0.85	0	0.3612	-0.3891	0.7475	0.7787	Default
18	1.03	0.73	0	0.3456	-0.3558	0.7302	0.5122	Default
19	1.78	0.29	0	0.3583	-0.3812	0.6934	-0.1192	Nondefault
20	1.16	0.80	0	0.1953	-0.3049	0.8749	0.5415	Default
Mean	1.37	0.56						

Percent Correctly Classified: 14/20 = 70.0%

Hit-or-Miss Matrix:

	Predicted Group	
	Defaulted	Nondefaulted
Actual Group Defaulted	8	2
Nondefaulted	4	6

Entries along the upper-left to lower-right diagonal are "hits" (actual and predicted group are the same).

To see why this is so, remember that, because the statistical procedures are controlled by the size of the smallest group, the most cost-efficient data collection procedure is to use equal numbers of defaulted and nondefaulted customers in the samples. But this means that the resulting statistical scoring function assumes equal probabilities of default and nondefault. In reality, however, the probability of failure for the average customer is much lower than the probability of nonfailure. Most customers do not default.

To illustrate this problem and the proper interpretation of the scores from a statistical scoring function, assume that 90 percent of the firms in an industry survive in a particular year, and that 10 percent of them fail. Assume further that data from this industry are used to estimate a statistical scoring system, with equal sample sizes used for defaulted and nondefaulted samples. Given the statistical technique used, assume that the break-even score between the two groups is 2.00, higher scores indicating higher default risk. A new customer comes to the firm and the score for this customer is computed as 2.25. What does this score indicate? It *does not indicate that the customer is more likely to default than not* (the equal-sample size implication). Instead, it indicates that the customer's chance of default is somewhat higher than the average customer, whose score is 2.00 and whose default probability is 10 percent. The credit decision on the new customer should be made with this interpretation in mind.

While most statistical procedures produce only ordinal measures of risk, others can produce scores which are either direct measures of default risk or scores that can be easily transformed into these measures. Models that produce direct measures of risk do so by adjusting the odds of default within the statistical procedure to represent those that occur in the real world. If a model produces a score which is a direct measure of risk, that score corresponds directly to an estimate of the probability of default of the customer. Direct measures of risk can be directly compared to profit margins in making credit decisions (via net present value analysis—see Chapter 3) while ordinal measures cannot.

Using Public-Domain and Commercial Statistical Scoring Models

The prior pages should make clear that developing the firm's own statistical scoring models is a process entailing cost and complication. An alternative is to use a public-domain or commercial statistical scoring model which has been developed by someone else. Doing this, however, requires that the model be examined in detail to determine its value to the firm's credit policy. This section discusses six aspects of these models and how these aspects should be evaluated: (1) the definition of default used, (2) the selection of the sample, (3) the age of the data, (4) the selection of the risk measures, (5) the model's development and validation, and (6) the interpretation of the model's scores. As a running example, we use the best-known of the public-domain models: Altman's Z score.[75]

Background on Altman's Z Score—The sample consisted of 66 manufacturers (33 defaulted and 33 nondefaulted). All firms were medium-sized (assets between $1 and $25 million). Default was defined as filing for bankruptcy under Chapter X between 1946 and 1965. Nondefaults were matched with defaults by industry, size, and time of the financial statement. Twenty-two financial ratios

---

[75] See E. I. Altman, "Financial Ratios, Discriminant Analysis and the Prediction of Corporate Bankruptcy," *Journal of Finance*, September 1968, pp. 589-609.

were chosen as measures of risk. The choice was based on: (1) popularity in the literature and (2) relevance to the study.

Data were collected on these ratios one year prior to bankruptcy. Multiple discriminant analysis was the statistical technique used. The best statistical model, and the one now presented in many popular financial analysis programs, was:

$$Z \text{ score} = 0.012X_1 + 0.014X_2 + 0.033X_3 + 0.006X_4 + 0.999X_5$$

Where:

X_1 = Net Working Capital/Total Assets (as a percent)
X_2 = Retained Earnings/Total Assets (as a percent)
X_3 = EBIT/Total Assets (as a percent)
X_4 = Market Value of Equity/Book Value of Debt (as a percent)
X_5 = Sales/Total Assets (as a decimal)

In this model, lower Z scores indicate higher bankruptcy risk. All five variables have correctly-signed coefficients. All firms with scores of less than 1.81 were in the bankrupt portion of the sample and all firms with scores greater than 2.99 in the nonbankrupt portion of the sample. Scores between 1.81 and 2.99 included both bankrupts and nonbankrupts. The Z score correctly predicted bankruptcy and nonbankruptcy 95 percent of the time within the 66-firm sample used in its development.

Two model validation methods were used: the U method and holdout samples of bankrupts and nonbankrupts. In the U method, 93.5 percent of firms were correctly classified. In the holdout samples, 83.5 percent were correctly classified. Both these proportions are much greater than would be expected by chance.

Definition of Default—In examining the relevance of any statistical scoring model for trade credit management, it is very important to consider how default was defined in generating the sample of defaulted firms. Firms may "default" in several senses: they may default in payments to trade creditors, they may file for bankruptcy, they may default in payments to preferred stockholders, and so forth. These various definitions of default are not completely interchangeable (though they do tend to occur together). A firm may default in one sense but not in another. For example, it may fail to pay preferred shareholders but not declare bankruptcy.

From a trade credit standpoint, default to trade creditors is the most relevant type of default. From this standpoint, there are two problems with the definition of default used in developing the Z score (where default was defined as the filing of a Chapter X petition during the following year). First, such an event would certainly result in default to trade creditors, but so might other events (such as filing a Chapter XI reorganization petition). Further, there are many circumstances where default to trade creditors occurs without any bankruptcy petition being filed. That is, from a trade credit standpoint the definition of default as a Chapter X filing is insufficiently stringent. There may be firms in the nonbankrupt sample that have defaulted to trade creditors but not filed Chapter X. This decreases the ability of the statistical scoring model to describe defaults to trade creditors. Second, as discussed in Chapter 3, a year is a longer time horizon than is required for most trade credit decisions. A trade creditor may grant credit early in a year, collect, and be done with the debtor before the debtor defaults to others. The use of a year's time horizon in developing the Z score tends to make customers look riskier than they actually are from a trade credit standpoint.

Sample Selection—The selection of the sample will determine the domain over which a statistical scoring model is most relevant. Statistical scoring models are most accurate for the types of firms used in their construction. If the sample is limited to one sort of firm, the resulting model is most accurate for that type of firm. Default in other types of firms may be determined by other factors, or the same factors weighted differently. Also, sample selection may be used to control for circumstances that may influence default but that the model's developers do not choose to consider. If this is done, the resulting model cannot incorporate the influence of these factors, and will be less accurate in predicting default when these factors are important.

Since the Z Score was developed using a sample of medium sized manufacturing firms, it will likely be most accurate when assessing the risk of firms with that profile. It will be less accurate in assessing the risk of other types of firms (for example, retailers) if there are differences in the factors which cause default between medium-sized manufacturers and firms of these other types. Also, the Z score was developed using bankrupt and nonbankrupt samples which were matched in (1) size, (2) industry (within manufacturing), and (3) the time (the year) of the financial statement from which the ratios were computed.

This matching was intended to control for differences in default risk that are determined by these three factors. However, use of this matching procedure means that the Z score is insensitive to these factors in estimating default risk. Larger firms, for example, are generally less likely to default, and defaults are greater for all firms at some times of the economic cycle than at others, but the Z score does not allow for such differences.

Age of the Data—If the factors which cause default or the importance of these factors change over time, statistical scoring systems which were developed using recent data are likely to be the most accurate in predicting future default. The data used in developing the Z score are quite old, dating from 1947 through 1965.

Selection of Risk Measures—Good prediction within the sample data can always be achieved by using a large number of risk measures. The danger is "garbage in/garbage out"—the resulting scoring system may contain data artifacts, and will not predict well outside the sample. Given that the sample size is 66, the use of 22 variables used in formulating the Z score is not a particularly large number, though it would have been better if explicit criteria based on a statement of the developer's view of the causes of default had been used in selection.

Model Development and Validation—Selection of the statistical technique which is most appropriate for the data, proper execution of this technique, and proper validation of the model lead to a statistical scoring system which is most likely to be accurate in its predictions. Because of causality considerations, multiple discriminant analysis (used in developing the Z score) would probably not be used today as the statistical system. Logit analysis would probably be selected. However, the validation techniques used in testing the Z score are among the best and most strenuous available, then or now. While the age of the data and the circumscribed sample may limit the Z score's current predictive ability, its validation procedures showed its accuracy at the time of its development.

Interpreting the Model's Scores—Z scores, like the scores produced by the prior numerical example, are ordinal measures of risk. A higher Z score indicates a lower credit risk. However, it cannot be said that customers with a Z score less than 1.81 (the range for which all the firms in the original sample were bankrupt) will almost certainly go bankrupt within one year. All that can be said is that these customers are more likely to go bankrupt in the next year than the average firm.

Summary—Using a public-domain statistical scoring system or purchasing a statistical scoring system from a commercial supplier avoids the substantial cost and effort required to develop a statistical scoring system in-house. However, all public-domain and commercial systems are developed with a general clientele in mind, and are unlikely to be quite as fitting to the firm's circumstances as a system developed to meet the firm's particular needs. In assessing any public-domain or commercial statistical system, the credit policy-maker needs to be aware of the features of the system that influence its accuracy and the proper interpretation of the scores it produces. Among the features that should be understood is the definition of default used to identify defaulted firms in sample selection; the types and sizes of firms in the samples that were used to develop the system; the age of the data; how the risk measures were selected and how many were selected; how the model was developed and validated; and how the model's risk scores relate to default probability. Only by understanding these features can the model's accuracy and value be examined.

Should You Use a Statistical Scoring System in Your Credit Department?— Like expert systems, the primary advantages of employing statistical scoring systems are savings in analysis time, reductions in the required expertise of the analyst, the potential for reduced errors in decision-making, and increased consistency in decisions. Statistical scoring systems also have the advantage of deriving their scores from the data itself, avoiding reliance on the opinion of a particular credit manager or group of managers.

However, statistical scoring systems have disadvantages relative to both judgmental procedures and expert systems. Similar to expert systems developed with the aid of expert system software, statistical scoring systems which are developed in-house entail substantial up-front development costs. To avoid these costs, the credit manager may elect to use a public-domain or commercial system, but these systems are unlikely to be as advantageous as one designed using the firm's own data and for the firm's own industries.

Also, the scores that a statistical scoring system produces are less complete representations of creditworthiness than the scores or decisions produced by a well-designed expert system. Recall that by granting credit to customers, firms incur at least two major types of costs: accounts receivable carrying costs and bad debt expense. Expert systems can incorporate the expert's opinion regarding both of these types of costs (and other factors, such as product profitability) on credit-granting decisions. However, statistical scoring systems only score default risk, and thus only relate to bad debt expense. Without additional analysis, the scores that a statistical scoring system produces do not say anything about the time the customer might take to pay (if payment is received) except to the extent that payment time is correlated with the chance of default. If a statistical scoring system is intended to produce a simple credit-decision rule (for example, deny credit to any customer with a Z score of less than 1.81), such a rule will ignore all important aspects of the customer except default risk.

Finally, one problem that statistical scoring systems share with expert systems is a lack of common sense, that is, the inability to pick out special factors that make the customer obviously creditworthy or not creditworthy. Because of these disadvantages, statistical scoring systems (like expert systems) are a useful device in simplifying credit-granting decisions only when sales volume (and consequently the cost of error in decision-making) is relatively low. However, if the statistical scoring system produces a direct measure of default risk, this measure may be useful in other applications, such as providing the estimate of default probability required for a present value analysis of the credit-granting decision.

Summary of the Policy Implications in this Chapter

Both expert and statistical scoring systems attempt to aid credit analysts in their credit-granting decisions by integrating information on the credit applicant via a mechanical process. In expert systems, this process mimics the options of a particular expert credit analyst. In statistical scoring systems, the process is derived from the statistical characteristics of a sample of defaulted and nondefaulted firms.

One way to use these systems is to employ the scores or decisions they produce to directly make credit-granting decisions. In this application, the scores or decisions of the system tell the analyst whether credit is to be granted. In deciding whether the firm wants to use one of these systems in this way, their reductions in analysis cost and other advantages must be weighed against the costs of developing and installing the systems. When these systems are developed in-house, development and installation costs can be quite large. However, the more that is spent on system development, the more accurate and appropriate will be the resulting system. Though no system of this sort has the common sense to deal with all the particular circumstances that would make the decision obvious to an experienced credit manager, simpler systems make errors more frequently. The upshot is that, unless a large amount of time and effort is spent on system development, these systems are best employed when order sizes are small. Firms whose customer base have this characteristic would do well to consider the adoption of an expert or statistical scoring system.

Another use of expert and statistical scoring systems is as an aid to the experienced credit manager in traditional credit analysis. In this role, the system acts to summarize some part of the information about the customer into a single score. While these systems are useful in this regard, they can add to the required analysis time unless they are executed automatically as part of the firm's credit analysis software.

In making credit policy, perhaps the most important point to remember is that these systems are not panaceas for the difficulties inherent in making credit-granting decisions. Spending a lot of time and money to develop and install them will, in some situations, have important benefits to the firm, but in other situations the money is ill-spent. Only by understanding how these systems are developed and what they actually do can the credit manager appropriately evaluate their use.

Case for Discussion and Analysis

The Case of the Suspicious Scoring System

Matthew Jones was credit manager for Bonzo's Boat Supplies, a firm selling boat equipment and nautical paraphernalia to wholesalers and harbor side retailers. Bonzo's gross sales were $200 million per year, and its receivables balance averaged $30 million. The staff of Mr. Jones' credit department included three credit analysts and one clerical employee.

In addition to administering the department, Mr. Jones handled credit and collections on the firm's 10 largest and most risky "marginal accounts." All remaining customers, large and small, high and low risk, were handled by the credit analysts. These analysts were generally hired directly from college and had no credit experience, though they were energetic and enthusiastic. Of the three credit analysts currently in the department, one had been with the firm for three years. The other two had been hired a year ago.

Mr. Jones was considering updating the financial analysis package that his credit analysts used to evaluate credit applicants. The current system was based on an old spreadsheet template, originally intended only to calculate customers' financial ratios but since modified to provide some graphical trend analysis. He was evaluating several alternative packages, all of which would run on the firm's desktop computer systems.

Because of the limited experience of his credit analysts, Mr. Jones intended to pick a system that contained either an expert or statistical scoring system. Once this system was in place, he wanted to make two modifications to the department's credit procedures. First, he wanted to use the scoring system to make credit decisions quickly on low-volume customers. In this application, credit decisions on customers whose expected sales volume was below a particular dollar amount would be made mechanically using the scoring system. Second, he wanted to use the scoring system to monitor the risk/return decisions that were being made by the credit analysts. For this purpose, he intended to identify customers whose scores indicated high risk and whose exposures were above a particular dollar amount. He would then discuss these accounts with the analysts handling them on a regular basis.

In reviewing the literature from software vendors describing several credit analysis packages, he found that some contained scoring routines based on expert systems while others utilized statistical scoring systems. Some of the software packages included expert systems which had been produced by the system's developers, typically point-scoring systems of various types. Others were intended to help the credit manager develop his or her own expert system. Some of the software that incorporated statistical scoring models used Altman's Z score, while others presented commercially-developed proprietary scoring models.

One of the packages had many useful features for analyzing financial position, presenting industry data for comparisons, viewing financial data graphically, and so forth. The scoring system presented in this package was the "diGriz Hyperscore," a commercially-developed statistical scoring system. Since the scoring system in the financial analysis package was to be a basis for credit policy, Mr. Jones very carefully inspected the information booklet the software vendor had provided.

This information indicated that the scoring system was developed by statistically comparing a sample of 50 firms that had defaulted to trade creditors with a sample of 50 that had not. The samples consisted of several types of firms (manufacturers, wholesalers, and retailers). This broad sample was selected, in the developer's words, to "...make the diGriz Hyperscore useful in evaluating any credit applicant, regardless of the applicant's business line." Data on all firms in both samples were less than three years old, and the Hyperscore subroutine was to be updated periodically (at a cost to the user) to include analysis of more recent data as it became available. The information further indicated that the Hyperscore "...uses information on the applicant's liquidity, cash flow, debt position, and profitability to assess creditworthiness." However, no formula for computing the Hyperscore was given. Instead, "...the actual scoring formula is confidential and contained within the program."

With regard to forecasting accuracy, the Hyperscore "...was 98 percent correct in classifying the 100 firms used in its development." The instruction booklet also indicated that "All Hyperscores greater than 1.00 were defaulted firms. When you use the Hyperscore, you can use this simple rule for determining who is creditworthy and who is not."

Suggestions for Analysis

1. Evaluate the diGriz Hyperscore statistical scoring system based on the facts given in the case. Is this an attractive scoring system for Mr. Jones to use in formulating credit policy?

2. Assume that, for cost reasons, Mr. Jones does not think it is appropriate to either develop an expert system based on expert system software or to develop a statistical scoring system in-house. What alternatives are available which will meet the needs of the firm?

7 Terms of Sale and Collection Policy

Most of this chapter is devoted to the analysis of terms of sale. Terms of sale decisions are unusual in that, unlike decisions regarding credit investigation, credit granting, and credit limits, terms of sale decisions must usually be made for *all* buyers of a particular product or service taken together, rather than on each customer individually. Terms of sale have a broad impact on the firm's costs and revenues. Therefore, changes in terms of sale should be considered carefully and not be made too frequently. However, it was probably true that many firms have been more cautious than necessary in changing terms of sale, even when circumstances were such that a change would be of advantage. There is some evidence that this attitude is shifting, and that firms are more willing to consider changes in terms of sale when these are warranted.[75] This chapter presents methods by which the effects of such changes can be evaluated.

Legal Aspects of Terms of Sale Policy

Under U.S. antitrust statutes, the seller must offer the same price to all customers buying a particular product or service. While this restriction might seem irrelevant to credit policy decisions, courts correctly have interpreted "price" to include "terms of sale."[76] To see why terms of sale are equivalent to price, consider a product which costs one dollar per unit and for which payment is required in 60 days. From a present value standpoint, if the required rate of return is 12 percent per year, the unit price that would make these terms equivalent to cash terms (the "cash equivalent price") is:

$$\text{Present Value} = \$1.00(1/1.12^{60/360}) = \$0.981.$$

---

[75] See "How Credit Managers are Changing Terms & Discounts to Improve Their Corporations' Cash Flow," *IOMA's Report in Managing Credit, Receivables & Collections*, June 1995, pp. 1, 14-15.

[76] A review of the antitrust statutes and their implications for terms of sale and other credit decisions can be found in Charles L. Gahala, *Credit Management: Principles and Practices*, NACM, 1996, pp. 70-72.

Suppose the terms are changed so that payment is instead required in 120 days. The cash equivalent price is then:

$$\text{Present Value} = \$1.00(1/1.12^{120/360}) = \$0.963$$

These calculations show that changing the terms from 60 days to 120 days is equivalent to reducing the price by \$0.018 per unit (= \$0.981–\$0.963), and the courts have interpreted the antitrust statutes in this way. Therefore, under these statutes, the selling firm cannot grant different terms of sale to different customers. The terms of sale must be the same for all customers buying the same product or service.

There are two practical exceptions to these statutes. First, the firm can require cash in advance or similar restrictive terms from customers who are not creditworthy. Second, the firm can "meet competition in good faith," giving longer terms to customers who are getting these terms from competitors who sell them the same product or service. However, to meet competition legally, the firm must be ready to show (in court if necessary) that there was reason to believe that another seller of the same product or service was giving the customer these less restrictive terms. In such a case, a seller may meet these longer terms to the customers receiving them from competitors without granting other customers the same terms.

It is fair to say that these legal principles are very poorly understood by some credit professionals. The author was once asked: "Does this mean I can't give a good customer an additional 30 days to pay if it needs it?" The answer is, *this is not legal unless others selling the same product to the customer have already done so.* Sadly, much of this poor understanding is the result of poor legal advice. Some corporate attorneys are not familiar with how the antitrust statutes apply to terms of sale. Also, there has been an unfortunate tendency to ignore the equal-terms aspects of the antitrust statutes under the idea that the firm is unlikely to be caught. It is true that detection and prosecution are unlikely, but sellers have been prosecuted and have lost under these statutes. The penalties are large. The firm that ignores the statutes in its terms of sale decisions does so at its own peril.

Evaluating Terms of Sale Changes

Principles of Analyzing Changes in Terms of Sale—Because of this antitrust situation, terms of sale changes generally affect all the customers who buy the product. To analyze these effects, a choice must be made between using present value or income statement (profitability) analysis to measure the benefits and costs of the policy change. In most cases the simpler profitability analysis is sufficient for analyzing terms of sale policy.[77] Changing terms of sale policy will typically affect sales volume, cost of sales, bad debt expense, and accounts receivable

---

[77] Situations where this technique is inadequate and where the more complicated present value approach must be employed will be discussed later in the chapter.

carrying costs. It may also affect collection and administration costs and cash discount expense. When using the profitability approach, the task is to estimate the effects of the change in terms of sale on each of these benefits and costs and compute the net effect on the firm's earnings.

This chapter analyzes a change in the firm's terms of sale by comparing the results of a proposed change to the results that would be expected if the firm continued its current policy. However, it should be understood that these proposed terms may not be the best set of terms that the firm could potentially offer. Ideally, it would be best if the firm could simply determine and adopt an optimum set of terms. Unfortunately, the difficulties in reliably estimating all of the cost and revenues that determine this optimum make finding these optimal terms impossible in a practice. Instead, it makes more sense for firms to evaluate incremental changes in terms, undertaking those that seem advantageous and evaluating the results after these terms are instituted.

A firm's terms of sale generally consist of three numbers: the cash discount percent, the cash discount date, and the net date. For example, for terms of 2 percent 10 days net 30 days the numbers are 2, 10, and 30; for net 60 day terms, the numbers are 0, 0, and 60. Changing terms of sale involves changing one or more of these three numbers. Loosening terms of sale involves granting a greater cash discount, a longer discount period, and/or a longer net date. Tightening terms of sale involves the opposite changes.

Estimating Sales Effects—When analyzing terms of sale changes, the prior experience of the firm and its knowledge of its markets will generally be sufficient to make reasonably reliable estimates of the effects of the change on the firm's costs. However, in the analysis of most terms changes, the most important factor influencing earnings is also the most difficult to estimate: the effect of the terms of sale change on sales volume. This effect has two parts: (1) the effect of the change on purchases by new customers and (2) the effect of the change on purchases by currently existing customers.

Loosened terms attract new customers. These are customers for whom the additional time to pay represents a particularly attractive feature, that is, firms that for one reason or another need more time to pay than the firm's current terms allow. There are a certain number of these customers for any change in terms. For example, suppose that the firm offering terms of net 30 days changes its terms to net 60 days. It will pick up sales volumes from those customers who are willing to live with 60 days but not with 30. If it extends terms to 90 days, it will pick up not only those customers who found 60 days attractive but also those customers who will not purchase unless 90 days is granted.

The uncertainty regarding sales volumes from these new customers occurs because, unless the selling firm has performed a very thorough survey of its markets, it does not know before the terms change exactly how many of these terms-sensitive customers exist or how much they will buy. Barring exact knowledge of the market on a customer-by-customer basis, there will always be substantial uncertainty about the increment to sales volume that will be obtained from these customers.

It should be noted that customers who find more time to pay a valuable feature are generally those of higher-than-average credit risk. They have a higher expected default rate and higher credit administration expenses. They find longer terms attractive because they are short of cash and need financing. Tightening credit terms results in lost sales volume from these customers just as loosening gains it.

With respect to customers who currently purchase from the firm, there will be some initial shift in market share due to a loosening of terms, just as there would be if price were lowered. Whether this increased market share persists depends on the response of competitors and the brand loyalty of customers. If competitors match the loosening and customers are not brand loyal (that is, they do not stay with the seller in the same volumes after the competition matches terms), no permanent increase in market share and in sales volume from existing customers will result. If competitors do not match the change, or if customers tend to keep purchasing in the same volumes after the change is matched, permanent market share gains can be achieved. Opposite effects occur if terms are tightened.

The uncertainty with respect to sale volumes coming from current customers results from uncertainty about both competitors' response to the term change and about brand loyalty. While the firm will have some idea of what competitors are likely to do based on responses to prior changes in price and/or terms, this reaction is never sure: will the competition match the change or not? Similarly, because of uncertainty about the brand loyalty of customers, even if competitors match the terms change, there is always substantial doubt as to what eventual market shares will result.

To summarize, estimates of the effects of a terms of sale change on sales volume involve significant uncertainty. This is true whether terms are being loosened (where the intent is generally to gain sales volume) or tightened (where the intent is generally to reduce credit costs). Any complete analysis of a proposed change in the firm's terms of sale needs to address this uncertainty.

An Example Analysis—To illustrate the calculations required to analyze the effects of a change in terms of sale, let us tackle a relatively complex example problem, involving both a change of the net date and the addition of a cash discount. The firm expects sales of a product for the upcoming year to be $150 million if no change in terms is instituted. Terms of sale are currently net 30 days, and the marginal costs of producing products for sale are 75 percent of sales. On average, customers pay in 40 days. One percent of customers typically default in each year. Collection and administrative expenses for current customers total $50,000. The firm's cost of capital is 12 percent.

The firm is considering changing the terms of sale on this product to 2 percent 10 days, net 60 days. If this change is instituted, the firm expects that it will obtain a permanent increase in sales to existing customers of 4 percent, resulting in yearly sales to existing customers of $156 million (= $150 million x 1.04). It also expects to obtain sales of $5 million per year from new customers. It expects that 60 percent of existing customers will pay in 10 days and take the cash discount, the remaining 40 percent paying in 70 days (the same 10 days beyond net terms as in current collections). New customers are expected to be worse off financially than existing customers. It is expected that only 10 percent of the new customers will pay in 10 days and take the discount, the remaining 90 percent paying in an average of 90 days. The expected default rate on these new customers is 5 percent (that is, the firm expects that one in 20 of the new customers will default during the year). Because of their poorer financial position, these new customers are expected to require more collection and administration expense per customer than do current customers; a cost of $10,000 per year is estimated. It is not expected that the change in terms will affect the collection and administration costs for existing customers.

A profitability analysis of this terms of sale change is presented in Table 7-1. There are some calculations in this table that are not obvious, so it is useful to review this table line by line. We will do this for the figures in the "Proposed" columns, which are the more complex of the two sets of calculations. Sales to current customers plus sales to new customers total $161 million, and the costs of these sales are $120,750,000, since these costs are 75 percent of sales. The cash discount is 2 percent of sales. Sixty percent of current customers are expected to take this cash discount, so expected discount expense for current customers is $1.872 million (= $156 million x 0.02 x 0.60). A similar calculation gives discount expense for the new customers of $10,000. Total discount expense is then $1.882 million.

The expected days to pay will be a weighted average of two payment times: 10 days if the customer takes the discount and a longer time if the customer does not. For current customers, it is expected that 60 percent will take the discount and 40 percent will not, paying instead in 70 days. Therefore, their average time to pay will be 34 days (0.60 x 10 days + 0.40 x 70 days). The average exposure to current customers under the new terms will then be $156 million times 34/360 or $14.733 million. Similar calculations give an average payment time of 82 days for new customers and an expected exposure of $1.139 million, so the total accounts receivable balance is expected to be $15.872 million. At a required rate of return (the firm's cost of capital) of 12 percent per year, the yearly cost of carrying this accounts receivable balance will be $1.905 million ($15.872 million x 12 percent).

Turning now to bad debt expense, if 1 percent of current customers default and recoveries are trivial, then the firm will lose, on average, 1 percent of its

Table 7-1. Analysis of Example Terms of Sale Change

(All figures in rounded thousands)

	Present Policy		Proposed Policy	
Sales:				
To Existing Customers	$150,000		$156,000	
To New Customers	$0		$5,000	
Total Sales		$150,000		$161,000
Cost of Sales		$112,500		$120,750
Cash Discount Expense:				
Cash Discount Percent	0%		2%	
Fraction of Current Customers Taking Discount			60%	
Discount Expense, Current Customers	$0		$1,872	
Fraction of New Customers Taking Discount			10%	
Discount Expense, New Customers	$0		$10	
Total Expected Cash Discount Expense		$0		$1,882
Accounts Receivable Carrying Costs:				
Expected Days to Pay, Current Customers	40		34	
Expected A/R Balance, Current Customers	$16,667		$14,733	
Expected Days to Pay, New Customers			82	
Expected A/R Balance, New Customers	$0		$1,139	
Total Expected A/R	$16,667		$15,872	
Cost of Capital	12.0%		12.0%	
Expected A/R Carrying Cost		$2,000		$1,905
Bad Debt Expense:				
Default Rate, Current Customers	1.00%		1.00%	
Expected Bad Debt Expense, Current Customers	$167		$147	
Default Rate, New Customers			5.00%	
Expected Bad Debt Expense, New Customers	$0		$57	
Total Expected Bad Debt Expense		$167		$204
Collection and Administration Costs:				
Expected Costs for Current Customers	$50		$50	
Expected Costs for New Customers	$0		$10	
Total Expected Collection and Administration Costs:		50		$60
Earnings Before Other Costs		$35,283		$36,199
Gain in Earnings from Terms of Sale Change				$916

exposure as bad debt, or $147,000 ($14.733 million x 0.01). Since $57,000 is expected to be lost in bad debts from new customers (= $1.139 million x 0.05), total expected bad debt expense is $204,000. Netting the estimates of cost of sales, cash discount expense, accounts receivable carrying costs, bad debt expense, and collection and administration costs against sales results in expected earnings before other expenses of $36.199 million if the proposed policy is adopted. Since these earnings are only $35.283 million under the present policy, this analysis suggests that earnings are expected to be $916,000 higher if the proposed policy is adopted.

Sensitivity Analysis of Risk—The prior analysis is incomplete in that the uncertainties inherent in the estimates of the revenues and costs from the terms change have not yet been taken into account. As previously discussed, major among these is uncertainty about the change in the volume of sales that the selling firm will yield from this policy change. However, in this particular example problem the firm may also be quite uncertain about the fraction of its current customers that may take the discount, particularly if it does not offer cash discount terms to similar customers buying other product lines. To address questions such as these, the seller can use the same techniques of "sensitivity analysis" that were presented in Chapter 3.

Let us first employ "optimistic-pessimistic-realistic" analysis and evaluate "pessimistic" assumptions regarding the increment to sales volume that the change produces. If competitors match the change in terms of sale and current customers are not brand loyal, there may be no permanent increase in sales to current customers resulting from the change in terms. Also, sales to new customers depends on the number of new customers that value the increase in time to pay sufficiently to buy from the firm, and it is difficult to assess this with great accuracy. Let us assume that the minimum figure for sales to new customers is $3 million. Table 7-2 presents this "pessimistic" analysis, in which the increase in sales to current customers is zero and in which sales to new customers are only $3 million. In this case, the expected increment to profit is negative: a loss of $857,000 occurs relative to the current terms of sale.

Additional analysis of the example is clearly necessary, since there appears to be some downside risk inherent in the proposed change. The "pessimistic" figures are calculated on the basis of unexpectedly low sales to both current and new customers. While this may happen, the probability that *both* sales estimates are much too high is fairly small. Single-parameter sensitivity analysis investigates what would happen if one estimate is inaccurate but the others are correct. A single-parameter sensitivity analysis of sales volume to current customers, sales volume to new customers, and of the fraction of current customers taking the discount is presented in Table 7-3.

This table suggests that the downside risk may not be as serious as might be anticipated based on the "pessimistic" analysis. If sales to new customers are $5 million (the "realistic" estimate), there is a gain in earnings as long as sales to current customers increase by at least $2 million (which is 40 percent of the "realistic" estimate of sales to these customers). If sales to current customers increase by $6 million (the "realistic" figure), there is a gain in earnings as long as sales to new customers are at least $1 million (which is 20 percent of the "realistic" estimate of sales to these customers). Also, uncertainty in the percentage of current firms that will take the discount does not affect the decision: gains are positive for all values of this parameter. To summarize, the accuracy of the sales estimate does influence this decision. If either or both estimates are far too high, the proposed change in terms could reduce earnings rather than increase them. The selling firm needs to consider very carefully the estimates of these two figures. If there is reasonable confidence in them, the change in terms should be undertaken.

Table 7-2.   Analysis of Example Terms of Sale Change: "Pessimistic" Estimates of Sales

(All figures in rounded thousands)

	Present Policy		Proposed Policy	
Sales:				
To Existing Customers	$150,000		$150,000	
To New Customers	$0		$3,000	
Total Sales		$150,000		$153,000
Cost of Sales		$112,500		$114,750
Cash Discount Expense:				
Cash Discount Percent	0%		2%	
Fraction of Current Customers Taking Discount			60%	
Discount Expense, Current Customers	$0		$1,800	
Fraction of New Customers Taking Discount			10%	
Discount Expense, New Customers	$0		$6	
Total Expected Cash Discount Expense		$0		$1,806
Accounts Receivable Carrying Costs:				
Expected Days to Pay, Current Customers	40		34	
Expected A/R Balance, Current Customers	$16,667		$14,167	
Expected Days to Pay, New Customers			82	
Expected A/R Balance, New Customers	$0		$683	
Total Expected A/R Balance	$16,667		$14,850	
Cost of Capital	12.0%		12.0%	
Expected A/R Carrying Cost		$2,000		$1,782
Bad Debt Expense:				
Default Rate, Current Customers	1.00%		1.00%	
Expected Bad Debt Expense, Current Customers	$167		$142	
Default Rate, New Customers			5.00%	
Expected Bad Debt Expense, New Customers	$0		$34	
Total Expected Bad Debt Expense		$167		$176
Collection and Administration Costs:				
Expected Costs for Current Customers	$50		$50	
Expected Costs for New Customers	$0		$10	
Total Expected Collection and Administration Costs:		$50		$60
Earnings Before Other Costs		$35,283		$34,426
Gain in Earnings from Terms of Sale Change				($857)

Effects of Product Profitability—Changes in terms of sale affect sales volume, costs of sales, and credit costs. Looser terms are intended to increase sales with some increase in credit costs; tighter terms are intended to reduce credit costs with some decrease in sales. When product profitability is greater (that is, when costs of sales are a lower fraction of sales), the profit gains before credit costs from loosening terms are greater, and loosening terms is more likely to be advantageous. Similarly, when product profitability is lower, looser terms are less likely to be advantageous, and tighter terms may in fact produce higher earnings.

Note that the prior analysis includes the effects of terms changes on sales and on cost of sales. This assumes that the credit department is evaluated on a profitability basis. However, if the credit department is evaluated on the basis of credit costs, the analysis should include only those costs in analyzing terms changes. To illustrate this, return to our example analysis under the "realistic" conditions (Table 7-1). If the credit department is evaluated on a credit cost basis and cash discount expense is included within these costs, the total of these costs is the appropriate decision statistic. For the present policy, these costs total $2.217 million (= $0 + $2000,000 + $167,000 + $50,000), while for the proposed policy they total $4.051 million. Therefore, the change in terms would be rejected if the department is evaluated on a credit cost basis.

Limitations of Profitability Analysis in Evaluating Terms of Sale Changes— Profitability analysis of terms of sale changes is relatively easy to execute and interpret. However, there are some circumstances in which the profitability analysis approach to this decision does not capture all the important aspects of the situation. When this occurs, substantial modification of profitability analysis is needed, and the method loses its advantage of simplicity; the more cumbersome net present value approach is usually warranted. Some of these circumstances are:[78]

1. Sales volumes are expected to grow substantially. The approach that profitability analysis uses to account for the time value of money in accounts receivable investment assumes that sales do not grow. When sales volumes are expected to grow substantially, and particularly when the different terms of sale policies are expected to influence that growth, profitability analysis may not accurately assess the advantageousness of different terms of sale policies.

Table 7-3. Sensitivity Analysis of Terms of Sale Change

Sales to Current Customers	Earnings Advantage of Proposed Terms	Sales to New Customers	Earnings Advantage of Proposed Terms	Percent of Current Customers Taking Cash Discount	Earnings Advantage of Proposed Terms
$150,000	($439)	$0	($131)	0%	$760
$151,000	($213)	$1,000	$79	10%	$786
$152,000	$13	$2,000	$288	20%	$812
$153,000	$239	$3,000	$497	30%	$838
$154,000	$464	$4,000	$706	40%	$864
$155,000	$690	$5,000	$916*	50%	$890
$156,000	$916*	$6,000	$1,125	60%	$916*
$157,000	$1,141	$7,000	$1,334	70%	$942
$158,000	$1,367	$8,000	$1,544	80%	$968
$159,000	$1,593	$9,000	$1,753	90%	$994
$160,000	$1,819	$10,000	$1,962	100%	$1,020

Note: an asterisk (*) next to a figure indicates that this estimate of the parameter is the "realistic" estimate.

---

[78] More discussion of each of these aspects and a presentation of the net present value approach to the analysis of terms of sale changes can be found in Frederick C. Scherr, *Modern Working Capital: Text and Cases,* Prentice Hall, 1989, pp. 159-175.

2. The terms of sale change affects the timing of capital expenditures. Terms of sale affect the firm's sales volume. Sales volume, relative to current plant capacity, determines the timing of necessary plant expansions. A change in terms of sale will therefore affect the timing and, perhaps, the amount of capital expenditures. For example, a terms change which increases sales volume can hasten a plant expansion. If the timing and amount of capital expenditures are affected, so are depreciation schedules and tax bills. Profitability analysis does not incorporate these effects.

3. The terms of sale change substantially affects the level of the firm's inventory. Terms of sale affect sales volumes. Lower sales volumes require lower inventory, and higher sales volumes require higher inventory. Changes in inventory are not included in profitability analysis.

Terms with EDI and Electronic Payments

In the standard documentation and payment process, the seller sends an invoice by mail to the customer, and the customer matches the invoice with a purchase order and keys information from the invoice into its computer system. Its system then generates a check which is sent to the seller's bank. The seller's bank sends the payment information to the seller, at the same time processing the check for payment through the banking system. The seller keys the check's information into its own computer system, where application of the cash removes the invoice from the seller's accounts receivable. The bank advises the seller when the check has cleared, at which time the funds are available for the seller's use.

Electronic data interchange (EDI) is intended to replace the mailing and keying of documents in this process. Electronic payments are intended to replace the mailing and clearing of checks. The two are usually considered as a package, though they can be adopted independently. While EDI and electronic payments technology has been available for some years, it has not yet swept away the standard procedures. However, there are some gains to be made from going electronic, and the credit policymaker will need to consider the electronic alternative if it has not yet been adopted by the selling firm. Adopting this procedure usually entails some modification of the firm's terms of sale.

To understand why the adoption of EDI and electronic payments usually affects terms of sale, it is necessary to understand the benefits the selling firm receives from adopting these technologies. Among these benefits are:

1. Reduced data entry costs. The firm does not have to rekey data on incoming checks. These data are received in electronic form.

2. Reduced postal costs. These occur since the invoice is transmitted electronically rather than sent through the mail.

3. Reduced accounts receivable carrying costs due to reduced float. Since the payments are received electronically in spendable funds, mail float and clearing float on incoming checks are eliminated. Money is collected more quickly, reducing accounts receivable balances.

Customers also receive benefits in the form of reduced data entry costs (since invoices are received electronically) and reduction in check-writing and mailing costs. However, there are also some major disadvantages to customers if these electronic procedures are adopted. First, the customer gives up its cash more quickly, since the mail and clearing floats on its checks are eliminated. Second, cost reductions from reduced data entry costs depend on the buyer's level of computerization. Smaller customers, who tend to use fewer computer applications, are benefited less. Finally, there are start-up costs for the customer when installing these electronic systems.

The net result is that customers tend to benefit less than sellers by the institution of EDI and electronic payment systems. To compensate customers, and to retain sales, sellers have frequently coupled the transition to EDI and electronic payments with some lengthening of their terms of sale.

One straightforward approach is to simply lengthen the firm's cash discount and net periods by the average length of the mail and clearing floats. For example, if the firm's terms are currently net 30 days, the average mail float on an incoming check is two days, and the average clearing float is one day, extending terms to 33 days neutralizes the float effects of requiring electronic payments. Unfortunately, this approach is not sufficient from the standpoint of many customers, particularly those whose floats were longer than average or for whom the costs of conversion to an electronic regime are particularly high. To maintain the same level of sales to these customers, the firm will have to extend terms beyond those that neutralize average float. However, at some point the increased costs of extending terms outweigh the benefits of instituting an electronic system. Determination of this point can be made by using profitability analysis. Suppose that a seller can save $150,000 per year in data entry and mailing costs by going to an electronic system. The firm's terms are net 30 days, customers pay in an average of 47 days, that average including three days of mail and clearing float. The firm's sales are $65 million per year, 1.5 percent of customers default in a year (so bad debt expense will be 1.5 percent of exposure), and the firm's cost of capital is 12.5 percent per year. Analysis of the effects of several new terms on the firm's costs is presented in Table 7-4, under the assumption that customers continue to pay 14 days beyond terms. Any effect of terms changes on sales and costs of sales is not included in this analysis because the intent of this strategy is to reduce costs while keeping sales constant.

In this example, the seller can make net cost reductions if terms of net 35 days or less and electronic payments are instituted, but not if terms of net 40 are required. That is, if customers are willing to purchase the same sale volumes from the seller with five additional days, paying electronically, the seller will be able to reduce costs. However, the same is not true if 10 additional days are required. In

Table 7-4. Cost Effects of Instituting EDI and Electronic Payments for Several Terms of Sale

(all dollar values in rounded thousands)

	Present policy	EDI but no terms change	EDI plus 3 days	EDI plus 5 days	EDI plus 10 days
Terms (days)	30	30	33	35	40
Mail and Clearing Float (days)	3	0	0	0	0
Expected Slowness (days)	14	14	14	14	14
Accounts Receivable Carrying Costs:					
Expected Days to Pay	47	44	47	49	54
Expected A/R Balance	$8,486	$7,944	$8,486	$8,847	$9,750
Cost of Capital	12.5%	12.5%	12.5%	12.5%	12.5%
Expected A/R Carrying Cost	$1,061	$993	$1,061	$1,106	$1,219
Bad Debt Expense:					
Default Rate	1.5%	1.5%	1.5%	1.5%	1.5%
Expected Bad Debt Expense	$127	$119	$127	$133	$146
Savings in Data Entry and Mailing	$0	$150	$150	$150	$150
Total of these Costs	$1,188	$962	$1,038	$1,089	$1,215
Gain in Costs from Terms of Sale Change		$226	$150	$99	($27)

that case, the reductions in data entry and mailing costs are outweighed by the increases in accounts receivable and bad debt costs. Of course, these conclusions are particular to the parameters of this particular problem.

Once the firm determines whether there is a set of terms that will result in the same sales volume but produce lower yearly costs, the yearly cost savings from instituting these terms is compared to the initial cost to the seller of instituting the EDI and electronic payment system. This initial cost will be composed of the cost of changing the seller's procedures to this system, and will include programming, software, and other costs. Comparison of the yearly savings to this initial cost will determine whether the institution of the electronic system is worthwhile.

Cash Discounts and Creditworthiness

In the example analyzed in Table 7-1, the cash discount served several functions. First, it accelerated the payments of some customers (60 percent of the existing customers and 10 percent of the new customers) relative to when payments would have been made without the discount. The reduction in exposures reduced accounts receivable carrying costs and bad debt expense. Also, the cash discount attracted purchases from firms that found the cash discount an attractive feature, which increased sales volume.

However, these effects on carrying costs, bad debt costs, and sales volumes do not tell the whole story regarding cash discounts. Cash discounts can be used as a means of assessing the creditworthiness of customers. In this function, cash discounts serve to reduce credit investigation expenses and/or to signal the financial circumstances of customers when credit information is incomplete.[79]

Principles—To see how cash discounts can perform this function, consider the very high cost of funds that is implicit in a typical cash discount. Suppose, for example, that the seller offers terms of 2 percent 10, net 30. The cost of skipping the discount and paying in 30 days is:[80]

$$r = \text{discount}/(1 - \text{discount}) = .02/(1 - .02) = 0.0204$$

This 2.04 percent cost is for the 20-day difference between paying in 10 days and paying in 30 days. To get the yearly rate, we need to compound this rate for the number of 20-day periods in a year:

$$r_{comp} = [(1+r)^{\text{number of periods}}] - 1 = [1+.0204)^{360/20}] - 1 = 43.84 \text{ percent per year}$$

This is a very high effective rate of interest. Most customers who are in good financial condition can borrow at much lower rates, take the discount, and save on the interest differential between the borrowing and this cost. Customers in poorer financial conditions, however, are less likely to have borrowings available, and thus are more likely to skip the discount in order to provide themselves with financing. Therefore, skipping or not skipping the discount is a powerful indicator of a customer's true financial condition. The cash discount is also a very good way of monitoring existing customers regarding changes in their financial condition. A customer who has been discounting but starts paying beyond the discount is a customer whose financial position has deteriorated.

The Effective Cost of the Cash Discount and Stretching—The effective interest rate declines with the time beyond the discount period that the customer takes to pay. This is one of the areas where terms of sale policy, credit-granting policy, and collections policy interact. If the creditor does not require that net payments be made relatively quickly after the net date, the effective interest rate can decline such that the cash discount is useless as an indicator of creditworthiness. For example, suppose that the customer is allowed to stretch to 75 days if the discount is skipped. This is a 65-day difference from paying a discount, so the yearly effective rate is:

$$r_{comp} = [1+.0204)^{360/65}] - 1 = 11.84 \text{ percent per year}$$

This rate is lower than the rate at which many customers in good financial condition can borrow. If the seller allows this degree of slow payment, the value of the cash discount as an indicator of financial condition is reduced. The relationship between effective cost and time to pay at net for 2 percent 10 net 30

---

[79] For more on how cash discounts function in this way, see Janet K. Smith, "Trade Credit and Information Asymmetry," *Journal of Finance*, September 1987, pp. 863-872.

[80] The two formulas that follow give the yearly interest rate which is inherent in a cash discount. More on these formulas and their use can be found in any modern textbook on working capital management, including Frederick C. Scherr, *Modern Working Capital: Text and Cases*, Prentice Hall, 1989, pp. 398-399.

Table 7-5.   Relationship Between Time to Pay at Net and Effective Yearly Cost of Skipping the Discount for 2% 10 Net 30 Terms

Days to Pay	Effective Yearly Interest Rate
30	43.84%
45	23.09%
60	15.65%
75	11.83%
90	9.51%
105	7.95%
120	6.83%
135	5.99%
150	5.33%

terms is portrayed in Table 7-5. Similar profiles showing declining effective interest rate and with time to pay apply for all discount terms.

Analysis of Cash Discounts for Evaluating Creditworthiness—When the firm institutes a cash discount for the purpose of signaling customers' financial condition, the tradeoff is between the cost of the cash discount and the reductions in carrying cost and bad debt expenses that result. Taking or not taking of the cash discount by the buyer enables the selling firm to identify firms that are high credit risks and to withdraw or limit credit to these firms. Though sales volumes are affected to some extent by any change in terms, this is not the primary intent of this cash discount strategy, and the firm might adopt a set of cash discount terms which are expected to leave total sales relatively unaffected. For example, the firm could institute a cash discount but reduce the time required to pay at net.

Table 7-6 presents an analysis of this type of terms of sale change. It is assumed that the change in terms, from net 60 days to 2 percent 10 net 30, will produce the same sales volumes ($50 million). Cost of sales is 80 percent of sales and the firm's cost of capital is 10 percent per year. Under the present terms of net 60 days, customers are expected to pay in 75 days. Two percent of customers are expected to default, and credit and administrative costs are $100,000. If the discount terms are adopted, 80 percent of the firm's customers are expected to take the discount, paying in 10 days, and the remainder to pay in 45 days. Because the firm is better able to detect which customers are in poor financial condition, only 1 percent of customers are expected to default under this policy, and credit and administration costs are reduced to $75,000.

In this example, the cash discount strategy produces savings in expected accounts receivable carrying, bad debt, and administration expenses which are greater than the expected discount expense. This results in an increase in expected earnings of $215,000. Sensitivity analysis can be used to assess the relationship between this advantage and the estimates of various parameters (the fraction of

Table 7-6. Analysis of Example of Cash Discount Terms to Aid in Evaluating Credit Worthiness

(all figures in rounded thousands)

Terms	Present Policy Net 60		Proposed Policy 2% 10 Net 30	
Sales		$50,000		$50,000
Cost of Sales		$40,000		$40,000
Cash Discount Expense:				
Cash Discount Percent	0%		2%	
Fraction of Customers Taking Discount			80%	
Expected Cash Discount Expense		$0		$800
Accounts Receivable Carrying Costs:				
Expected Days to Pay	75		17	
Expected A/R Balance	$10,417		$2,361	
Cost of Capital	10.0%		10.0%	
Expected A/R Carrying Cost		$1,042		$236
Bad Debt Expense:				
Default Rate	2.00%		1.00%	
Expected Bad Debt Expense		$208		$24
Collection and Administration Costs		100		$75
Earnings Before Other Costs		$8,650		$8,865
Gain in Earnings from Terms of Sale Change				$215

customers taking the discount, the default rate under the proposed policy, and so forth). While in this case a gain is expected, in other cases insufficient reductions in other credit costs relative to discount expense will result, and the cash discount policy will not be of advantage.

In summary, another way to use cash discount policy is to employ the discount as an indicator of the customer's financial situation. If the net date is enforced, firms taking the cash discount are likely to be relatively more creditworthy than firms that do not. Credit policy can reflect this, reducing the costs of bad debt, collection, and credit administration. A cash discount strategy for this purpose is likely to be particularly useful in industries where, for one reason or another, credit data are difficult to get and creditworthiness is difficult to assess. However, the adoption of a cash discount can be a relatively expensive way to identify these customers. Additional credit investigation can achieve the same goal, frequently at a lesser expense. The use of cash discounts for this purpose needs to be weighed against other methods of achieving the same result.

Collection Policy

The aim of collections is to obtain funds from past-due customers. Many strategies and tactics are available for this purpose: collection letters, telephone calls, collection visits, and so forth. Systematic follow-up is important for effective collections. The credit policymaker should be aware of the various collection mechanisms and follow-up systems that are available, and there are many good references detailing these procedures.[81]

Collection decisions are generally made by credit analysts customer-by-customer based on their assessment of the most effective strategy in dealing with that particular customer. From a policy standpoint, the credit manager needs to guide the credit analyst in understanding the basic tradeoffs inherent in the collection choices that the analyst makes.

These basic tradeoffs concern carrying costs, bad debt expense, collection costs, and profits from future sales. The longer a receivable is outstanding, the greater is the accounts receivable carrying cost that the seller bears. Also, the longer a receivable is outstanding, the less likely it is that the customer will eventually pay--that is, the more likely the receivable is to become a bad debt. Aggressive collections which result in quicker payment reduce accounts receivable carrying and bad debt expenses but are more costly in terms of the opportunity costs of the collector's time and the out-of-pocket costs for postage, telephone calls, etc. Further, aggressive collection techniques can alienate customers, who will then be less likely to buy in the future. Lenient collections are less costly to execute and alienate fewer customers, but also result in higher accounts receivable and bad debt expenses. For product lines where product profitability (price/cost margins) is higher, lost future sales are more important, and a lenient collection policy is more appropriate.

Unfortunately, beyond educating credit analysts in these tradeoffs, the collection techniques available, and the value of systematic follow-up, as well as monitoring collectors to ensure that these principles are applied, there is relatively little the credit manager can do to enhance collection efforts. This is so because of the interpersonal nature of communications between the collector and the debtor, and the implications of this for alienation. Some debtors become disillusioned with the seller at the mildest of collection efforts, while others are more thick-skinned. Since an alienated customer is far less likely to purchase in the future, it is up to the collector to find the right level and type of collection effort that will balance collection costs, accounts receivable carrying, and bad debt expenses, and the probability of obtaining future sales.

Summary of the Policy Implications in this Chapter

It is often advantageous to make many sorts of credit decisions on a customer-by-customer basis so that the characteristics of each particular customer and that customer's relationship with the seller can be considered in the decision. While appropriate for collection and other decisions, setting terms of sale on a customer-by-customer basis is generally illegal under U.S. antitrust laws. Terms of

---

[81] For example, see *Principles of Business Collections: A Professional Handbook*, NACM, 1992.

sale decisions are one of the few types of credit decisions that must be made based on their effects on all customers of a product taken together.

Because of difficulties in estimating the many parameters that are necessary to determine the optimal set of terms, practical determination of such an optimum is not feasible. Instead, the effects of a set of proposed terms are evaluated against the alternative of continuing with present terms. Changes in terms will typically affect sales volume, cost of sales, and many credit-related costs. The net effect of a terms of sale change on the product's earnings can be calculated via profitability analysis, with sensitivity analysis of the expected increment to sales used to assess the influence of uncertainties in the estimation of revenue figures. However, the profitability analysis technique is somewhat limited in the circumstances it can address, and the credit manager needs to be aware of these so as to apply the technique only in its proper context.

While traditional methods of transmitting information and cash are still used by most firms, electronic transmittals are becoming more common. Adopting an electronic transmittal system typically gives more benefits to the seller than to the buyer. To compensate buyers, sellers may lengthen their terms of sale when electronic transmittals are instituted. However, the costs of lengthened terms of sale must be compared to the benefits of an electronic regime. If customers require a substantial extension, adopting an electronic transmittal system may not be advantageous.

Terms of sale decisions concern the setting of the seller's cash discount amount, cash discount date, and net date. Analysis of these decisions typically centers on tradeoffs between credit costs and profits on sales. However, cash discounts can be used in another way: to detect the customer's true financial condition. As long as net terms are enforced, the yearly cost of foregoing most cash discounts is quite high. Customers who are in good financial shape are better off borrowing and taking the discount. Firms in poorer financial condition cannot borrow at reasonable interest rates, and are more likely to find foregoing the discount attractive. Taking or not taking the cash discount is an important signal of creditworthiness.

Unlike terms of sale policy, collection decisions can be and generally are made on a customer-by-customer basis. Indeed, it is the interpersonal nature of collection policy that makes the specifics of this credit policy (what collection instruments to use and when to use them) relatively difficult to establish. Collectors must weigh the effects of collection aggressiveness on accounts receivable carrying costs, bad debt costs, collection costs, and the probability that the customer will return to the firm for future purchases. Each customer reacts differently to collection techniques, and only by knowing individual customers can these tradeoffs be properly made. No one set of collection policies is appropriate for every customer.

Case for Discussion and Analysis

The Case of the Tenuous Terms

Acme Industries, Inc., was faced with a dilemma. Acme's terms of sale were net 30 days. However, Acme's management knew there were potential customers that were not purchasing from Acme because they were getting longer terms from other suppliers of similar products. Acme knew it could meet these terms to these customers if it chose to do so under the "meeting competition in good faith" provisions of the antitrust statutes and gain sales volume by this maneuver. The question was whether longer terms should be granted and to whom they should be granted.

Acme had identified a group of potential customers that was receiving net 60 days from competitors, and had estimated that granting net 60 days to this group would result in sales to them of $4 million per year. These customers were, on average, of very high default risk, and it was expected that about 1 in 10 would default. Those who did not default were expected to pay in 75 days. Yearly credit administration and collection expenses for the group were expected to be $50,000. Given that Acme's cost of sales was 85 percent of sales and that its cost of capital was 13 percent, it had already been calculated that extending 60-day terms to these firms would be profitable. The calculations are given in Table 7-1C.

While granting 60-day terms to these new customers but leaving terms to current customers at 30 days made some sense, Acme's managers were concerned with the effect of the differential in terms on purchases by its existing customer base. If current customers learned that the firm was giving better terms to others, some current customers might be angry and take their business elsewhere, which would wipe out the gains from sales to the new customer group. Consequently, Acme was considering another strategy: granting 60 days to all of Acme's cus-

---

Table 7-1C. Acme's Analysis of Granting 60-Day Terms to New Customers Only

(all figures in rounded thousands)

Sales to New Customers		$4,000
Cost of Sales to New Customers		$3,400
Accounts Receivable Carrying Costs:		
Expected Days to Pay	75	
Expected A/R Balance	$833	
Cost of Capital	13.0%	
Expected A/R Carrying Cost		$108
Bad Debt Expense:		
Default Rate	10.00%	
Expected Bad Debt Expense		$83
Collection and Administration Costs		$50
Gain in Earnings		$358

tomers, including current customers. Although Acme's competitors would almost certainly match the new terms, Acme's managers felt they could expect an increase in sales of $1 million from current customers if terms were changed.

If net 30 day terms were continued, sales to current customers were expected to be $75 million for the upcoming year. Current customers paid in an average of 42 days, and 1.50 percent of these customers defaulted in a year. Credit administration and collection costs for these customers were $150,000 per year and were not expected to increase if terms were changed.

Suggestions for Analysis

1. Based on the facts of the case and assuming that the current customers will pay in 72 days if granted 60-day terms, analyze the expected effects on the firm's earnings of granting 60-day terms to all of Acme's customers.

2. Your calculations in response to question one should show that this change in terms is not expected to be advantageous. However, this analysis is based on sales of $4 million to new customers, which is Acme's estimate for the group of firms it has identified. In fact, more patronage may be gained. Using sensitivity analysis, calculate the volume of sales to new customers that would be sufficient to generate an earnings gain for Acme, assuming that 60-day terms are granted to all customers.

8 Monitoring Credit Performance

Credit policy and customers' response to this policy together affect many of the selling firm's major revenues and costs. Customers' response to credit policy may change over time as economic and competitive conditions change. This chapter discusses the monitoring of revenues and costs which are affected by credit policy. One major purpose of this monitoring is to gauge the effectiveness of credit policy and its implementation. A second is to detect changes in customers' responses to this policy so that policy can be adjusted to these new responses.

Principles of Monitoring Credit Performance

If the credit department is evaluated on a profitability basis, the credit manager should monitor the things that are affected by the firm's credit policy and that affect profitability. As discussed in prior chapters, these are sales volume, costs of sales, discount expense, credit investigation expense, accounts receivable carrying costs, bad debt expense, and collection and administration expense.[82] The credit manager needs to: (1) accurately measure each of these; (2) compare the measures to what the firm intended to achieve; and (3) adjust policy or its implementation accordingly. Monitoring credit performance encompasses the first two of these three. Policy formulation and adjustment are discussed elsewhere in this book.

Unfortunately, difficulties arise in accurately measuring outcomes with respect to some of the costs that are influenced by credit policy. While sales volume, cost of sales, credit investigation expense, and collection and administration expenses are accurately measured by their dollar values, it is more difficult to accurately measure discount expense, accounts receivable carrying costs, and bad debt expense. The next three sections of this chapter are devoted to these measurement

---

[82] In firms where the credit department is evaluated solely on the basis of its effects on credit costs, sales volume and cost of sales would not be monitored, since the effects of credit decisions on sales volume are not deemed to be the direct concern of the credit department.

difficulties. This is followed by discussion of budgeting, which is the process by which the firm sets its intended goals.

Measuring Discount Expense

If the firm offers a cash discount, it expects that some fraction of customers will take this discount, and the firm utilizes this fraction to balance the cost and revenue effects of its terms of sale policy (see Chapter 7). The fraction of customers actually taking the cash discount must be measured to see if this is according to expectations. If it is not, or if this fraction has changed over time, the firm may want to reconsider its terms of sale decision.

However, the cash discount expense that appears on the selling firm's income statements is expressed in dollars, not as a fraction of payments made. The dollar amount of cash discounts taken depends on this fraction but also the time pattern and volume of the firm's sales. To find the fraction, the firm must disentangle it from the effects of sales volume and the time pattern of sales.

This would seem a simple task which could be readily addressed by dividing the discount expense recorded in a period by the sales recorded in the same period. Unfortunately, when sales vary over time due to seasonality, growth, or other factors, this simple procedure can produce misleading results. These misleading results are produced because, for accounting purposes, both sales volumes and discount expense are recorded in the periods in which they occur, even though some of the discount expense results from sales which occurred in prior periods.[83]

A numerical example is provided in Table 8-1. In this table, sales are $10 million per month for the months of November through March, they dip in the second quarter, and reach a seasonal peak in September. There are two panels in this table, representing two sets of terms and collection rates. In Panel A, the terms are 2 percent 10 net 30, 50 percent of customers pay in 10 days, and the remaining 50 percent pay in 30 days.

The monthly collections in dollars in Panel A are constructed using these collection rates. There are three sources of collections in this panel. The first is collections from the current month at discount, which represent two-thirds of the customers who pay the current month's sales (those who purchase in the first 20 days of the month) in 10 days and take the 2 percent cash discount. For example, since 50 percent of customers discount, the cash collections from these customers in January are $3.27 million ($10 million in sales for January times 50 percent of the customers who discount times 2/3 times 0.98).

The second source of collections comes from the customers who pay at discount but purchased in the last 10 days of the prior month, so that their collections are received in the current month. Since 50 percent of customers discount, for January these collections are $1.63 million ($10 million in sales for December

Table 8-1. Calculation of Percent of Customers Taking Discount Based on Discount Expense as a Percent of Quarter's Sales (30-day months, even sales throughout the month; all dollar figures in rounded millions)

	Prior Year		Current Year											
Month	Nov.	Dec.	Jan.	Feb.	March	April	May	June	July	Aug.	Sept.	Oct.	Nov.	Dec.
Sales	$10.00	$10.00	$10.00	$10.00	$10.00	$7.00	$5.00	$7.00	$10.00	$15.00	$20.00	$15.00	$10.00	$10.00
Panel A			First Quarter			Second Quarter			Third Quarter			Fourth Quarter		

Terms: 2% 10 Days, Net 30 Days
Collections: 50% in 10 days (discount), 50% in 30 days (net)

	Jan.	Feb.	March	April	May	June	July	Aug.	Sept.	Oct.	Nov.	Dec.
Collections from the Current Month (at Disc.)	$3.27	$3.27	$3.27	$2.29	$1.63	$2.29	$3.27	$4.90	$6.53	$4.90	$3.27	$3.27
Collections from the Prior Month at Discount	$1.63	$1.63	$1.63	$1.63	$1.14	$0.82	$1.14	$1.63	$2.45	$3.27	$2.45	$1.63
Collections from the Prior Month at Net	$5.00	$5.00	$5.00	$5.00	$3.50	$2.50	$3.50	$5.00	$7.50	$10.00	$7.50	$5.00
Discount Expense from Sales in Prior Month	$0.033	$0.033	$0.033	$0.033	$0.023	$0.017	$0.023	$0.033	$0.050	$0.067	$0.050	$0.033
Discount Expense from Sales in Current Month	$0.067	$0.067	$0.067	$0.047	$0.033	$0.047	$0.067	$0.100	$0.133	$0.100	$0.067	$0.067
Month's Total Discount Expense	$0.100	$0.100	$0.100	$0.080	$0.057	$0.063	$0.090	$0.133	$0.183	$0.167	$0.117	$0.100
Discount Expense for Quarter			$0.300			$0.200			$0.407			$0.383		
Sales for Quarter			$30.00			$19.00			$45.00			$35.00		
Discount Expense as a Percent of Sales			1.0000%			1.0526%			0.9037%			1.0952%		
Implied Percent Taking the Discount			50.00%			52.63%			45.19%			54.76%		

| Panel B | First Quarter | | | Second Quarter | | | Third Quarter | | | Fourth Quarter | | |

Terms: 2% 30 Days, Net 60 Days
Collections: 50% in 30 days (discount), 50% in 60 days (net)

	Jan.	Feb.	March	April	May	June	July	Aug.	Sept.	Oct.	Nov.	Dec.
Collections from First Prior Month (at Disc.)	$4.90	$4.90	$4.90	$4.90	$3.43	$2.45	$3.43	$4.90	$7.35	$9.80	$7.35	$4.90
Collections from Second Prior Month (at Net)	$5.00	$5.00	$5.00	$5.00	$5.00	$3.50	$2.50	$3.50	$5.00	$7.50	$10.00	$7.50
Discount Expense for the Month	$0.100	$0.100	$0.100	$0.100	$0.070	$0.050	$0.070	$0.100	$0.150	$0.200	$0.150	$0.100
Discount Expense for Quarter			$0.300			$0.220			$0.320			$0.450		
Sales for Quarter			$30.00			$19.00			$45.00			$35.00		
Discount Expense as a Percent of Sales			1.0000%			1.1579%			0.7111%			1.2857%		
Implied Percent Taking the Discount			50.00%			57.89%			35.56%			64.29%		

times 50 percent times 1/3 times 0.98). The third source of collections comes from the 50 percent of customers who pay at net, and thus pay in the month following the sale. Since December's sales were $10 million and 50 percent of customers pay at net, in January these collections total $5 million.

Cash discount expense is the difference between the face amount of an invoice and the amount paid when the cash discount is deducted. In January, two-thirds of 50 percent of the current month's sales are paid at discount during the month, for a discount expense from current month's sales of $0.067 million (10 million times 2/3 times 50 percent times 0.02). One-third of 50 percent of the prior month's sales are also paid at discount during the current month, for a discount expense in January of $0.033 million ($10 million times 1/3 times 50 percent times 0.02). Therefore, total discount expense for January is $0.100 million (= $0.067 million plus $0.033 million).

All collection figures and discount expenses in both panels are constructed similarly, using the assumed terms of sale and collection rates (in Panel B, the terms of sale are 2 percent 30 net 60, and 50 percent of customers pay at discount while 50 percent pay at net). Summing the discount expense for the months of the quarter gives the total quarterly discount expense. Dividing this by the quarter's sales gives discount expense as a fraction of sales. For the first quarter in Panel A, discount expense is $0.300 million and sales for the quarter are $30 million, so discount expense is 1.0000 percent of sales.

The fraction of customers taking the discount that is implied by this figure is calculated by dividing discount expense as a fraction of sales by the cash discount. For example, for Panel A during the first quarter, the discount expense is 1.000 percent of sales and the cash discount is 2 percent, so the implied fraction of customers taking the discount is 50.00 percent. This particular figure is exactly correct; as previously discussed, the dollar collections in this panel were, in fact, constructed using exactly this figure.

However, in the other quarters, where sales are not the same in each month, this method produces implied percents of customers taking the discount *which is not correct*. In the third and fourth quarters of Panel A, these figures are off by about 5 percentage points, a 10 percent error since the correct figure is exactly 50 percent. It is very important to note that these differences from 50 percent *are not, in fact, due to fluctuations in customer payments* since the collection dollar figures all use the same collection rates.

What is happening instead is a mismatch between the discount expense in dollars incurred in the quarter and the quarter's sales. At the end of each quarter, there are receivables outstanding which will be paid at discount, but these payments will be received in the next quarter and will be recorded as discount expense in that quarter according to standard accounting conventions. However, the fraction of the discount expense attributable to these receivables depends on sales volume in *the period in which the sale originated*, not sales in the period in which the payment is received.

The larger is the cash discount percent, the longer are discount terms, and the larger the fluctuations in sales over time (from seasonality or from growth), the greater will be the distortion in the fraction of customers taking the discount. In Panel B of Table 8-1, the same sales figures are used but the discount terms are longer, so larger dollar discount expenses slip from one quarter to the next. The distortions in the implied percent of customers taking the discount are consequently larger, reaching 15 percentage points in each of the last two quarters. These are 30 percent errors, since the actual fraction of the receivables collected at discount is always 50 percent.

Thus, calculating the percent of customers taking the discount using standard accounting data contains a basic, and frequently large, measurement error when sales fluctuate over time. When a measurement error of this sort occurs, the credit manager cannot tell whether the difference from expectations is caused by inaccurate estimates of the effects of credit policy, changing customer payment patterns, or distortions due to the measurement error. Attempts to address this measurement problem can be made by changing the period over which data are collected, for example by using six months of sales and collections (a procedure we will discuss in the following section). However, changing the averaging period does not address the basic problem, which is that part of the discount expense is matched to sales in a future period, not in the period in which the sales were made. The solution is to match the discount expenses to their period of origin, a procedure which is portrayed in Table 8-2.

Panel A of this table contains the same sales and dollar collection figures as Panel A of Table 8-1. However, in Table 8-2, the discount expenses relating to a particular month's sales are accumulated from the various months in which they occur and matched to the sales volume from the month in which the discount originated. For example, of the $0.080 million in cash discounts taken in April, $0.047 million results from collection of sales made in April and $0.033 million results from collections of sales made in March. Of the discount expense in May, $0.023 million is from sales made in April and $0.033 million is from sales made in May. Therefore, total discounts related to April's sales are $0.070 million: $0.047 million taken in April and $0.023 million taken in May. Discount expense for April as a percent of April's sales is then $0.070 million divided by $7 million (April's sales volume), or 1.000 percent, which is the correct figure, since this is the number used in construction of the dollar collections.

Looking across the "Discount Expense as a Percent of Month's Sales" line in Panel A, all figures are correct despite the seasonality in sales; *a measurement error is not introduced* in this procedure by fluctuating sales volumes. The average discount expense as a percent of sales for each quarter is this same 1.000 percent,[84] and the implied percent of customers taking the discount for the quarter is correct at 50.00 percent.

---

[84] A weighted average based on sales volume in each month of the quarter could also be used here.

Table 8-2. Calculation of Percent of Customers Taking Discount Based on Discount Expense as a Percent of Sales in Month of Sale (30-day months, even sales throughout the month; all dollar figures in rounded millions)

Month	Prior Year Nov.	Prior Year Dec.	Current Year Jan.	Feb.	March	April	May	June	July	Aug.	Sept.	Oct.	Nov.	Dec.
Sales	$10.00	$10.00	$10.00	$10.00	$10.00	$7.00	$5.00	$7.00	$10.00	$15.00	$20.00	$15.00	$10.00	$10.00
			First Quarter			Second Quarter			Third Quarter			Fourth Quarter		

Panel A: Same Collection Rates Throughout
Terms: 2% 10 Days, Net 30 Days
Collections: 50% in 10 days (discount), 50% in 30 days (net)

	Jan.	Feb.	March	April	May	June	July	Aug.	Sept.	Oct.	Nov.	Dec.
Collections from the Current Month (at Disc.)	$3.27	$3.27	$3.27	$2.29	$1.63	$2.29	$3.27	$4.90	$6.53	$4.90	$3.27	$3.27
Collections from the Prior Month at Discount	$1.63	$1.63	$1.63	$1.63	$1.14	$0.82	$1.14	$1.63	$2.45	$3.27	$2.45	$1.63
Collections from the Prior Month at Net	$5.00	$5.00	$5.00	$5.00	$3.50	$2.50	$3.50	$5.00	$7.50	$10.00	$7.50	$5.00
Discount Expense from Sales in Prior Month	$0.033	$0.033	$0.033	$0.033	$0.023	$0.017	$0.023	$0.033	$0.050	$0.067	$0.050	$0.033
Discount Expense from Sales in Current Month	$0.067	$0.067	$0.067	$0.047	$0.033	$0.047	$0.067	$0.100	$0.133	$0.100	$0.067	$0.067
Month's Total Discount Expense	$0.100	$0.100	$0.100	$0.080	$0.057	$0.063	$0.090	$0.133	$0.183	$0.167	$0.117	$0.100
Total Discount Expense for Month's Sales	$0.100	$0.100	$0.100	$0.070	$0.050	$0.070	$0.100	$0.150	$0.200	$0.150	$0.100	
Discount Expense as Percent of Month's Sales	1.000%	1.000%	1.000%	1.000%	1.000%	1.000%	1.000%	1.000%	1.000%	1.000%	1.000%	
Average of Monthly Discount Expense/Sales			1.000%			1.000%			1.000%		1.000%	
Implied Percent Taking the Discount			50.00%			50.00%			50.00%			

Panel B: Changing Collection Rates
Terms: 2% 10 Days, Net 30 Days
Collections:
First Quarter: 50% in 10 days, 50% in 30 days
Third Quarter: 35% in 10 days, 65% in 30 days

	Jan.	Feb.	March	April	May	June	July	Aug.	Sept.	Oct.	Nov.	Dec.
Collections from the Current Month (at Disc.)	$3.27	$3.27	$3.27	$2.29	$1.63	$2.29	$2.29	$3.43	$4.57	$3.43	$2.29	$2.29
Collections from the Prior Month at Discount	$1.63	$1.63	$1.63	$1.63	$1.14	$0.82	$0.80	$1.14	$1.72	$2.29	$1.72	$1.14
Collections from the Prior Month at Net	$5.00	$5.00	$5.00	$5.00	$3.50	$2.50	$4.55	$6.50	$9.75	$13.00	$9.75	$6.50
Discount Expense from Sales in Prior Month	$0.033	$0.033	$0.033	$0.033	$0.023	$0.017	$0.023	$0.023	$0.035	$0.047	$0.035	$0.023
Discount Expense from Sales in Current Month	$0.067	$0.067	$0.067	$0.047	$0.033	$0.047	$0.047	$0.070	$0.093	$0.070	$0.047	$0.047
Month's Total Discount Expense	$0.100	$0.100	$0.100	$0.080	$0.057	$0.063	$0.070	$0.093	$0.128	$0.117	$0.082	$0.070
Total Discount Expense for Month's Sales	$0.100	$0.100	$0.100	$0.070	$0.050	$0.070	$0.070	$0.105	$0.140	$0.105	$0.070	$0.070
Discount Expense as Percent of Month's Sales	1.000%		1.000%	1.000%		1.000%	0.700%		0.700%	0.700%	0.700%	
Average of Monthly Discount Expense/Sales			1.000%			1.000%			0.700%		0.700%	
Implied Percent Taking the Discount			50.00%			50.00%			35.00%			

To illustrate that this procedure accurately captures changes in payments when these occur, in Panel B of Table 8-2 the same sales figures and terms are used but the collection rates are changed from those in Panel A for all sales made after June. In the new collection rates, only 35 percent of customers discount, the balance paying at net. The correct cash discount expense as a percent of the month's sales is 0.700 percent (= 0.35 times 0.02). This calculation procedure correctly captures this figure without measurement error, and correctly obtains the 35 percent figure for the percent of customers discounting in the third quarter.

There are two disadvantages to this procedure of matching the discount expense to its month of origin in computing the percent of customers taking the cash discount. First, the discount expense as a percent of the month's sales cannot be computed for the most recent month because not all cash discounts relevant to that month's sales have been taken yet. This is why there are no discount expense figures in the December column of Table 8-2. Second, to make this calculation, discount expense must be identified with its month of origin. This requires that the firm keep records of how much discount expense was taken at various times during a month if discounts from more than one month's sales are taken. For example, in Table 8-2, discounts taken during the first 10 days of the following month relate to the prior month's sales, while discounts taken in the last 20 days of the month relate to the current month's sales. To make this distinction, the firm must keep records of how much discount expense was taken in each day of the month. However, when sales vary over time, these disadvantages would seem a small price to pay for the elimination of measurement error in monitoring an important aspect of credit policy.

Measuring Collection Rates: DSO

Accounts receivable carrying costs are the product of the receivables balance times the firm's cost of capital. Receivables balance, in turn, depends on sales volumes and collection rates. Collection rates are typically measured by Days Sales Outstanding (DSO), which is intended to represent the weighted average time the firm takes to collect an invoice, with the weighting based on invoice dollar size. Unfortunately, like the computation of the fraction of customers taking the discount, there are substantial measurement problems in calculating a DSO statistic that is an accurate representation of this weighted average.

Traditional DSO Defined—Traditional DSO is calculated as the period-ending accounts receivable balance (or an average balance over several periods) divided by average monthly sales, times 30 days per month. Sales are usually averaged over the prior three months, though shorter or longer averaging periods are also used. As an example, if the accounts receivable balance is $14 million and average monthly sales are $10 million, then traditional DSO is:

$$DSO = (\text{Accounts Receivable Balance/Average Monthly Sales})(30 \text{ days per month})$$
$$= (\$14,000,000/\$10,000,000)30 = 42.00 \text{ days}$$

Traditional DSO has two major virtues. First, it is very simple to calculate. Second, because no figures except those from standard accounting statements are required, DSO figures on competitors can be calculated for comparison purposes, or can be obtained from commercial sources which use these statements, such as Dun & Bradstreet's *Key Business Ratios* or Robert Morris Associates' *Annual Statement Studies*. Set against these advantages are three measurement errors which are inherent in using traditional DSO for monitoring purposes: (1) distortions due to the averaging of sales figures, (2) differences in terms and conditions among receivables, and (3) problems in measuring the time-pattern of collections within the month.

Distortions Due to the Averaging of Sales Figures[85]—Like the calculation of discount expense as a percent of sales using accounting data, traditional DSO produces substantial measurement errors when sales fluctuate over time due to seasonality or growth. A numerical example is provided in Table 8-3. In this example, the firm experiences a seasonal sales pattern. Sales are flat at $10 million per month from October through January, peak at $20 million in March, and reach a minimum of $5 million in May, recovering in June.

In Table 8-3, the firm makes 10 percent of sales for cash, collects 60 percent of sales in the month following the sale, and collects the balance in the second month following the sale. The receivables balances in this table are all constructed using these collection rates. The correct average collection time is therefore always 36.0 days (= .10(0) + .6(30) + .3(60)) and, since no change in actual collection rates occurs in the example, any variations in DSO are measurement errors.

In this Table, DSOs are calculated in the standard way for averaging periods for sales of two, three, and four months. For example, the 39.6 day figure representing the DSO for February using a two-month sales averaging period is $16.5 million (the total receivables balance at the end of February) divided by $12.5 million (average sales for January and February) times 30 days.

Notice in this table that *although the average invoice is always collected in 36.0 days, DSOs vary* from 18.0 days to 49.1 days. The average error in DSO relative to the correct figure (the average measurement error) varies from 4.0 days for the two-month sales averaging period to 8.4 days for a four-month sales averaging period. For this particular example problem, the two-month averaging period produces the lowest measurement error, but this averaging period will not necessarily produce the lowest error for other time patterns of sales. Further, even for the two-month averaging period, DSOs vary from 30.0 to 42.0 days, a sufficient fluctuation that an actual difference from expected collection rates may not be detected.

To assess whether these errors are important, we need to understand how important accuracy is in measuring DSO. Because accounts receivable carrying costs are a large part of total credit-related costs, small differences from expected

[85] Much of the discussion in this section and in the later section on variance analysis also appears in *Principles of Business Collections: A Professional Handbook*, NACM, 1992, Chapter 6, and in the April 1992 issue of the Credit Research Foundation's *Staff Report*. This problem with traditional DSO was originally described in W.G. Lewellen and R.W. Johnson, "A Better Way to Monitor Accounts Receivble," *Harvard Business Review*, May-June 1972, pp. 101-109.

Table 8-3. Traditional DSO with Fluctuating Sales Volume

Collection Rates Used to Construct Receivables Balances:

Cash Sales	10%
Collected in First Month	60%
Collected in Second Month	30%

Correct DSO: 36.0 Days

Month:	Oct.	Nov.	Dec.	Jan.	Feb.	March	April	May	June	Average Error
Sales (Millions)	$10	$10	$10	$10	$15	$20	$10	$5	$10	
Receivables Balances:										
Outstanding From Current Month				$9.0	$13.5	$18.0	$9.0	$4.5	$9.0	
Outstanding From Prior Month				$3.0	$3.0	$4.5	$6.0	$3.0	$1.5	
Outstanding From Two Months Ago $0.0				$0.0	$0.0	$0.0	$0.0	$0.0	$0.0	
Total Receivables				$12.0	$16.5	$22.5	$15.0	$7.5	$10.5	
Traditional DSOs Calculated for Various Sales Averaging Periods:										
Using Average of Last Two Months' Sales				36.0	39.6	38.6	30.0	30.0	42.0	4.0
Using Average of Last Three Months' Sales				36.0	42.4	45.0	30.0	19.3	37.8	6.7
Using Average of Last Four Months' Sales				36.0	44.0	49.1	32.7	18.0	28.0	8.4

turnover can affect these costs enormously, and thus small differences in turnover have important implications for credit policy choice. While the seasonality in sales in Table 8-3 is large, it is clear from this table that traditional DSO results in so much measurement error that it is not an advantageous monitoring device when sales change over time.

The problem with traditional DSO is a difficulty in averaging—receivables from various periods are compared to average sales. As with discount expense, the solution is to measure collection rates with ratios which do not require averaging. Sales Weighted Days Sales Outstanding (SWDSO) performs this function.

The calculation SWDSO is best illustrated by example, and is performed in Table 8-4, using the same sales volumes and collection rates as in Table 8-3, except that collection rates change in April.

To obtain SWDSO, the first step is to calculate the Ratios of Receivables Outstanding (RROs). These are simply the receivables balances outstanding from each month divided by sales from that month. For example, the ratio of receivables outstanding for January for the first prior month is 30 percent and is calculated as follows: the receivables balance outstanding in January from the prior month (December) is $3.0 million. Sales in December were $10.0 million, so 30 percent of these sales are outstanding. Once the RROs at a month-end are computed, they are summed and multiplied by 30 days per month to get the SWDSO for that month-end. For example, in Table 8-4 the sum of the RROs for January is 1.20, which times 30 days, gives an SWDSO of 36.0 for January.

The SWDSO always gives the true days to pay with no error due to averaging. The SWDSO correctly measures, at 36.0 days, the average collection rate during January, February, and March. When the collection rates change in April, so does the SWDSO, to the new correct figure of 39.0 days $(= .10(0) + .50(30) + .40(60))$. Unlike the traditional DSO, the SWDSO is not vulnerable to changes in sales over time: it does not induce any measurement error in assessing receivables turnover.

Differences in Terms and Conditions Among Receivables—All times to pay figures are computed using accounts receivable balances and sales figures. However, these data may be composed of sales and receivables among which the seller has very different expectations about collections. Receivables resulting from products may be sold under different terms and market conditions will have different expected collection rates.

The difficulty that this causes in monitoring collections occurs when the mix of collection rates changes over time. When the mix changes, it is hard to disentangle changes in overall time to pay caused by this changing mix from those caused by changes in collection rates. For example, suppose that the firm sells some products on which collections are expected in 15 days and others on which collections are expected in 45 days. If time to pay increases from 32.0 days to 35.0 days, this could indicate that collections were slower than previously, or it could

Table 8-4.   Calculation of Sales Weighted Days Sales Outstanding

Collection Rates Used to Construct Receivables Balances:

Cash Sales	10%	10%
Collected in First Month	60%	50%
Collected in Second Month	30%	40%
Correct DSO:	36.0 days	39.0 days

Month:	Oct.	Nov.	Dec.	Jan.	Feb.	March	April	May	June
Sales (Millions)	$10	$10	$10	$10	$15	$20	$10	$5	$10
Receivables Balances:									
Outstanding From Current Month			$9.0	$9.0	$13.5	$18.0	$9.0	$4.5	$9.0
Outstanding From Prior Month			$3.0	$3.0	$3.0	$4.5	$8.0	$4.0	$2.0
Outstanding From Two Months Ago			$0.0	$0.0	$0.0	$0.0	$0.0	$0.0	$0.0
Total Receivables			$12.0	$12.0	$16.5	$22.5	$17.0	$8.5	$11.0
Ratios of Receivables Outstanding:									
Current Month				90%	90%	90%	90%	90%	90%
First Prior Month				30%	30%	30%	40%	40%	40%
Second Prior Month				00%	00%	00%	00%	00%	00%
Sum of Ratios of Receivables Outstanding				1.20	1.20	1.20	1.30	1.30	1.30
SWDSO (days)				36.0	36.0	36.0	39.0	39.0	39.0

mean that proportionately more sales were made to customers whose payments were expected in 45 days relative to those whose payments were expected in 15 days.

Therefore, when the mix of terms and conditions has the potential to change over time, it is not generally advantageous to monitor collection rates by a single time to pay number. Instead, it is best to compute separate time to pay figures, each representing collection rates on a particular set of receivables. The sets of receivables are determined by differences in expected collection rates. In the prior example, the credit manager would compute one time-to-pay figure for those customers who are expected to pay in 15 days and one for those customers who are expected to pay in 45 days. This way, changes in the mix do not confound the monitoring process.

Problems in Measuring the Time-Pattern of Collections Within the Month—Traditional DSO and SWDSO are computed using receivables balances at the end of a particular period, usually a month. This procedure results in a relatively simple calculation process, but may mask differences in collection patterns within the month because both DSO and SWDSO essentially assume that collections occur evenly throughout the month. When they do not, DSO and SWDSO are misleading representations of actual collection rates.

Consider Table 8-5. In this example, the firm collects all of its receivables in the month following the sale. Sales occur evenly during the month, were $10,000 for the prior month, and are $15,000 for the current month. Collections are

Table 8-5.   Illustrations of Different Collection Rates Within the Month

(all receivables are collected in the month following the sale)

Proportion Collected:	A	B	C
First 10 Days of the Month	80.0%	33.3%	10.0%
Second 10 Days of the Month	10.0%	33.3%	10.0%
Last 10 Days of the Month	10.0%	33.3%	80.0%
Beginning Receivables:	$10,000	$10,000	$10,000
Sales (all on credit):	$15,000	$15,000	$15,000
Collections:			
First 10 Days of the Month	$8,000	$3,333	$1,000
Second 10 Days of the Month	$1,000	$3,333	$1,000
Last 10 Days of the Month	$1,000	$3,333	$8,000
Total Collections	$10,000	$10,000	$10,000
Ending Receivables	$15,000	$15,000	$15,000
DSO (Days; two months' avg. sales)	36.00	36.00	36.00
RROs:			
First Prior Month	1.000	1.000	1.000
Sum of RROs	1.000	1.000	1.000
SWDSO	30.00	30.00	30.00

Table 8-6.   Illustration of Average Days to Collect (ADC)

Age of Receivables in Days at Collection	Dollar Amount of Receivables Collected	Days Times Amount
20	$9,377	$187,540
22	$9,783	$215,226
25	$466	$11,650
30	$242	$7,260
35	$5,794	$202,790
37	$3,125	$115,625
39	$2,384	$92,976
40	$5,419	$216,760
42	$9,596	$403,032
44	$4,815	$211,860
48	$4,645	$222,960
50	$55	$2,750
52	$6,208	$322,816
55	$6,169	$339,295
58	$7,530	$436,740
60	$5,964	$357,840
61	$3,854	$235,094
65	$5,488	$356,720
80	$543	$43,440
Totals	$91,457	$3,982,374
ADC		43.54 Days

illustrated for three sets of collection rates. In set A, the firm makes 80 percent of its collections in the first 10 days of the month; in set B, collections occur evenly throughout the month; and in set C, the firm makes 80 percent of its collections in the last 10 days of the month. DSO is computed by averaging sales for two months and is 36.00 days (= ($15,000/($10,000 + $15,000)/2)30) regardless of the collection pattern within the month. Likewise, the SWDSO is 30.00 days regardless of the collection pattern.

These three collection patterns are clearly very different, despite their equivalence in DSO and SWDSO. Therefore, firms which suspect that their collection rates are not even throughout the month need a monitoring tool which is sensitive to these differences. One such tool is Average Days to Collection (ADC). ADC is the dollar-weighted-average time from the point a receivable comes on the books until it is collected. Calculation of ADC is not as simple as for DSO and SWDSO. To calculate ADC for the period being analyzed (typically a month), data on daily collections and the ages of receivables paid by these collections must first be retrieved from the firm's database of customer payments received. An example is given in the first two columns of Table 8-6.

Once these data are collected, the age of the receivable at collection in days is multiplied times the dollar amount of receivables collected for each age at collection. These numbers appear in the third column of Table 8-6. This column is

Table 8-7.   Calculation of Average Days to Collect for Collection Rates in Table 8-5

Collection Day	Amount Collected	Average Age of Receivable Collected (days)	Amount Times Age
Example A			
10	$8,000	25	$200,000
20	$1,000	35	$35,000
30	$1,000	45	$45,000
Totals	$10,000		$280,000
Average Days to Collect			28.00
Example B			
10	$3,333	25	$83,333
20	$3,333	35	$116,667
30	$3,333	45	$150,000
Totals	$10,000		$350,000
Average Days to Collect			35.00
Example C			
10	$1,000	25	$25,000
20	$1,000	35	$35,000
30	$8,000	45	$360,000
Totals	$10,000		$420,000
Average Days to Collect			42.00

then summed up and the total divided by the total amount collected to get the dollar-weighted ADC, in this case 43.54 days (= $3,982,374/$91,457). Table 8-7 shows how the ADC differentiates among the three sets of collection rates in Table 8-5. In Table 8-7, for example purposes, it is assumed that all collections are made on the 10th, 20th, and 30th days of the month, and that these collections are evenly spread over the firm's receivables, all of which are 1-30 days old at the beginning of the collection month. (Thus, the average age of a receivable collected on the 10th day of next month is 25 days (= 10+15), etc.). Under these assumptions, the "A" set of collection rates produces an ADC of 28.00 days, "B" produces an ADC of 35.00 days, and "C" produces an ADC of 42.00 days. We see that ADC captures differences in collection rates that occur within the period whereas DSO and SWDSO do not.

Unfortunately, ADC cannot be used as the sole device in receivables monitoring, but must be used in combination with DSO and SWDSO. This is so because, while ADC measures receivables *collected*, firms are also concerned with receivables that *remain outstanding*. To see this, suppose that the firm's ADC from one month to the next is steady at 35.0, but that SWDSO increases from 38.0 to 45.0. These figures indicate that, while the collections *that were received* were made in the same time as last month, the average receivable *remaining on the books* got older, and is therefore less collectible in the future. Divergences like this between ADC and DSO provide important signals that ADC alone will not give.

To summarize the monitoring of receivables turnover, traditional DSO is simple to calculate and is a particularly useful figure when the seller's receivables turnover is being compared to that of other firms. However, when sales volumes change over time, traditional DSO produces measurement errors that make it less effective as a monitoring device. SWDSO, though more complicated to calculate, does not suffer from these measurement problems. When collection rates vary over the month, neither DSO nor SWDSO will capture this variation, and monitoring of ADC is also required.

Measuring Bad Debt Expense

There are two major problems associated with measuring bad debt expenses and comparing them to the firm's expectations. The first is a matching problem similar to that which occurs for discount expense and receivables turnover. The second has to do with the infrequent nature of bad debt losses.[86]

In the prior sections, it is illustrated that when sales vary over time, making accurate measurements requires that cash discount expense and accounts receivable balances be compared to sales volume in the period which the discount or receivable originated. The same is true for bad debt expense, but the difference in timing is greater since firms usually exhaust all reasonable collection efforts before a bad debt is recognized, and this process takes many months.

The problem and its solution are illustrated in Table 8-8 under the assumption that the time between a sale and the recognition of a bad debt arising from this sale is six months. For variety, this table uses a pattern of growing sales volume rather than the seasonal sales patterns used in prior examples. In this table, when bad debt expense is compared to sales in the quarter in which the bad debt is *recognized*, the quarterly average bad debt figures for the last two quarters are about 1.2 percent of sales. However, if bad debt expenses are compared to sales in the month in which the bad debt *originated* (July's bad debts to January's sales, etc.), bad debt expenses are about 1.5 percent of sales. Similar distortions can occur if sales are seasonal rather than growing.

The bad debt expenses in Table 8-8 are also intended to illustrate the second problem in monitoring bad debt: the relatively infrequent occurrence of defaults. In four of the six months, July to December, the firm recognized no bad debt expenses at all, while in the other two months these expenses were large. This realistic pattern occurs even for very large firms and is caused by the empirical fact that most firms' dollar bad debt expenses are centered in a relatively few large defaults. To deal with this, the credit manager must average the ratio relating bad debt and sales over several months. Averages over a quarter are used in Table 8-8.

---

[86] More discussion of both of these problems in monitoring bad debt can be found in Frederick C. Scherr, *Modern Working Capital: Text and Cases,* Prentice Hall, 1989, pp. 267-270.

Table 8-8. Measuring Bad Debt Expense

(all dollar figures in rounded thousands)

Sales for First Six Months of the Year:

Month	Jan.	Feb.	March	April	May	June
Sales	$10,000	$10,500	$11,000	$11,500	$12,000	$12,500

Analysis of Bad Debt Expense for the Second Six Months of the Year:

Month	July	Aug.	Sept.	Oct.	Nov.	Dec.
Sales	$13,000	$13,500	$14,000	$14,500	$15,000	$15,500
Bad Debts Recognized	$0	$0	$500	$0	$550	$0
Bad Debts/Current Month's Sales	0.00%	0.00%	3.57%	0.00%	3.67%	0.00%
Average of Bad Debt/Current Month's Sales for Quarter			1.19%			1.22%
Bad Debts/Sales Six Months Ago	0.00%	0.00%	4.55%	0.00%	4.58%	0.00%
Average of Bad Debt/Sales Six Months Ago for Quarter			1.52%			1.53%

This required averaging, combined with the long lead time between the granting of credit and the eventual recognition of resulting bad debts, means that it will be months between the time a firm estimates the effects of credit policy on bad debts and when the effects of this policy can be observed. This long lag is in contrast to the effects of credit policy on discount expense and receivables turnover, which can be observed shortly after the event. Unlike turnover and cash discount expense, the delay in observing the effects of a credit policy change on bad debts or in detecting changes in customers' default rates makes the effects of credit policy on bad debt expense a particularly difficult policy aspect to manage.

Comparing Performance to Budgets

It is usually useful to express budgetary targets in the same terms that are used in estimating the effects of credit policy. Therefore, for sales volume, credit investigation, and collection and administration expenses, these budgetary goals will generally be expressed as dollar targets; for discount expense, as the percentage of the customers taking the discount; for accounts receivable carrying cost, as DSO or one of its variants; and for bad debt expense, losses as a fraction of sales.[87]

Principles for Setting the Budgetary Targets—Once it is decided how the outcomes of credit policy will be measured, the process of setting budgetary targets for these measures can begin. The credit manager, along with other executives of the firm, will have important input into this process. Four principles are important in setting these targets.

As long as the credit department is evaluated on the basis of profitability, the first principle of budgeting is that the goals for sales, credit investigation expense, collection and administration expense, accounts receivable turnover, discount expense, and bad debt expense should reflect the tradeoffs inherent in making and implementing credit policy. A realistic budget for one of these cannot be formulated without reference to the others. For example, a lower budget target for credit investigation expense cannot be set without recognizing that this generally means a higher budget for bad debts. Another example is that higher sales can be budgeted, but achieving this goal generally necessitates slower turnover, higher bad debt, and higher administration and collection costs as credit is granted to increasingly marginal accounts. Failure to recognize these tradeoffs results in budgetary goals which are contradictory or not achievable.[88]

The second principle of budgeting is that budgets should be set to reflect differences in circumstances, particularly differences in the relationship between a product or service's price and the cost of making the product or service. For products where this margin is wider, the seller can afford to bear higher credit-related costs.

---

[87] While the cost of sales was mentioned earlier as something affected by credit policy, it is not generally necessary to monitor this cost separately because, in analyzing credit decisions, it is usually a fixed percent of sales volume. Monitoring sales volume also monitors costs of sales.

[88] When budgets are set for credit departments that are evaluated solely based on credit costs, and consequently are not penalized for lost sales, the interactions between credit costs and sales need not be taken into account. However, in this circumstance, it should be noted that restrictive budgets for credit costs can be achieved simply by stringent credit-granting and collection decisions.

Budgets for sales, receivables turnover, bad debt expense, and credit and administration costs should therefore be higher. However, in higher-margin situations the budget for credit investigation expense should be lower, reflecting the fact that a greater fraction of customers represents profitable sales, and less investigation is therefore required to distinguish profitable from unprofitable sales (see Chapter 2).

Exactly how much higher and exactly what the budgeted figures should be is not a question which is easily answered. Except for terms of sale decisions, credit decision-making is usually best done at the level of the individual customer. There is no straightforward way to scale up these customer-level decisions into budgets for the firm as a whole or for particular product lines. The best that can be done is to examine past budgets and budgetary results, to talk with credit analysts about the decisions they are making, and to adjust budgets accordingly. For example, if the credit manager finds that analysts are enforcing very restrictive credit policies on profitable customers because of unwarranted concerns about collection rates, it is time to rethink goals for collection rates.

The third principle of budgeting is that deviations *either above or below* any budgetary target are generally disadvantageous. The budgets represent the credit policy-maker's *best current assessment of the appropriate tradeoffs* among the revenues and costs that are affected by credit policy. If one set of costs or revenues is not as expected, the best tradeoff among the various revenues and costs may not be achieved. The only exception to the all-deviation-is-disadvantageous rule is when *all* deviations from expectations are in a direction which unambiguously produces higher profits, that is, when sales are higher than budgeted and all indicators of credit costs are lower than budgeted.

The fourth and final rule of budgeting is that small deviations from budgets may not indicate inappropriate results. In the real world, there are always random events that occur and can affect sales, turnover, bad debts, and so forth. As examples, the purchasing agent of a major customer gets sick, and the replacement employee orders from someone else; the mail is slower than usual, delaying important receipts; a key person at a marginal customer quits to go elsewhere, and the customer fails as a result. However, the effects of random events of these sorts tend to even out over time, and are likely to be reversed in a future period. It is the overall performance of the credit department relative to budgets over a reasonable period of time that indicates the true effectiveness of credit management policies.[89]

Factors Which Can Cause Differences From Budgets—While small and temporary deviations from budgetary targets may be the result of random events, large and permanent deviations are signals that something unexpected has occurred. It is then up to the credit manager to investigate, assess why the budget target was not met, and take the necessary action.

---

[89] Separating out random variations in performance from those caused by controllable factors can be done statistically using the "control limits" technique. For a discussion of this, see *Principles of Business Collections: A Professional Handbook,* NACM, 1992, Chapter 6, and Frederick C. Scherr, *Modern Working Capital Management: Text and Cases,* Prentice Hall, 1989, pp. 260-262.

There are four common results of this investigation, and each result requires that the credit manager take a different action. First, the difference from budget may have been caused by an inaccurate estimate of customer response (sales, collections, etc.) to credit policy. For example, a credit-granting and collection policy intended to produce one set of collection rates may in fact produce another. This can occur whether credit policy has been changed or simply been continued. Whenever policy is revised, estimates of customer response to such revision are always uncertain, and results are not always as expected. Even the continuation of existing policy does not guarantee customer response, since customers' purchase and payment patterns can and do change over time.

Second, the difference from budget may be caused by a policy implementation problem within the credit department. Once credit policy and budgetary goals are set, analysts must be educated about what the policies are and how they relate to the goals. Credit analysts may fail to achieve these goals because they do not understand them. Credit policy and budgetary goals are not easy messages to communicate, and are frequently misunderstood, resulting in decisions with regard to credit-granting, collections, etc., that are not in line with policy. Third, credit analysts may not achieve goals, even when these goals are realistic, simply because they do not have the personal capability necessary for doing so. Additional training and/or redeployment of personnel is called for in this case.

Finally, the budgetary goals simply may not be realistic. It is not unknown for firms to set goals of sales and costs which simply cannot be achieved, given the tradeoffs inherent in credit management. When it is clear that this has occurred, budgetary goals must be revised.

Variance Analysis of Accounts Receivable Balances

While turnover ratios like DSO and SWDSO are useful indicators of collection rates, it is frequently helpful for the credit manager to know how these collection rates are related to accounts receivable balances. Unfortunately, these balances are affected by both collections and sales volumes. When both sales and collection rates vary from expectations, the credit manager must separate the effects on the total receivables balance of differences from expected sales and of differences from expected collections. This separation can be performed by using "variance analysis," a system developed by cost accountants for separating the effects of multiple factors on the difference between a budgeted and an actual balance.[90]

Variance analysis does this by computing a hypothetical accounts receivable balance that would occur for *actual sales* but *budgeted rates of collection*. The difference between this hypothetical balance and the *budgeted* receivables balance is due to differences from expected *sales*; the difference between this hypothetical bal-

---

[90] More discussion of the application of variance analysis to accounts receivable balances can be found in G.W. Gallinger and A. J. Ifflander, "Monitoring Accounts Receivable Using Variance analysis," *Financial Management*, Winter 1986, pp. 69-76, and J. A. Gentry and J. M. De la Garza, "A Generalized Model for Monitoring Accounts Receivable," *Financial Management*, Winter 1985, pp. 28-38.

ance and the *actual* receivables balance is due to differences from expected *collection rates*. By this method, the total difference between the budgeted and actual accounts receivable figures is partitioned into sales and collection rate effects.

While the variance analysis procedure sounds complicated, a numerical example will show that it is not. Assume that it is early April, that the quarter has just ended, and that the credit manager is evaluating collection rates for the past quarter. Quarterly budgets were made in early January. At that time, it was known that December's sales had been $10 million, and it was expected that sales for January would be $10 million, February would be $15 million, and March would be $20 million. It was expected based on credit policy that 5 percent of sales would be for cash, that 50 percent of sales would be collected in the month following the sale, 35 percent would be collected in the second month following the sale, and that the remaining 10 percent would be collected in the third month following the sale. (Therefore, expected RROs were 0.95 for the month of the sale (1.0 minus 5 percent collected), 0.45 for the month following the sale (1.0 minus collections of 5 percent and 50 percent), 0.10 for the second month following the sale, and 0.00 for the third month following the sale. Since the sum of these RROs is 1.50, the expected SWDSO was 45.0 days.) Based on these expectations, the expected accounts receivable balance for the end of March was $26.75 million. See Table 8-9, columns 1-3, for the calculation of this balance.

At the end of March, the actual accounts receivable balance is $35.80 million, or $9.05 million greater than the expected balance. Of this $35.80 million, $24.00 million was outstanding from March, $9.46 million was outstanding from February, $2.04 million was outstanding from January, and $0.30 million was outstanding from December. However, sales had been greater than budgeted; January's sales were $12 million, February's were $22 million, and March's were $25 million. The actual SWDSO was 47.7 days (see column 6 of Table 8-9). The question is how much of the difference between the actual receivables balance and the expected balance is due to the larger volume of sales and how much is due to differences from expected collection rates.

To answer this, the credit manager first constructs the balances that would have occurred, given budgeted RROs and actual sales. This appears in column 7 of Table 8-9. Each figure in this column is computed by multiplying the *budgeted* RRO for the month times that month's *actual* sales. (For example, the $23.75 figure for March is 0.95, the budgeted RRO, times March's actual sales of $25 million.) Summing these gives a balance of $34.85 million, which is the balance that *would have occurred, given actual sales*, if collection rates had been as budgeted. The difference between this and the actual receivable balance is called the collection variance, and is $950,000. The remaining $8.10 million difference between the budgeted and actual receivables balance is due to greater-than-expected sales.

The credit manager may now gain further insight into costs by partitioning the collection variance further, into its months of origin. This decomposition

Table 8-9.   Variance Analysis of Accounts Receivable Balances

(all currency figures in millions of dollars)

Column:	1	2	3	4	5	6	7	8
Month	Budgeted Sales	Budgeted RRO, end March	Budgeted Balance from Month	Actual Sales	Actual Balance from Month	Actual RRO, end March	Balances with Actual Sales and Budgeted RROs	Collection Variance by Month
March	$20.00	0.95	$19.00	$25.00	$24.00	0.96	$23.75	$0.25
February	$15.00	0.45	$6.75	$22.00	$9.46	0.43	$9.90	($0.44)
January	$10.00	0.10	$1.00	$12.00	$2.04	0.17	$1.20	$0.84
December	$10.00	0.00	$0.00	$10.00	$0.30	0.03	$0.00	$0.30
Totals	$55.00	1.50	$26.75	$69.00	$35.80	1.59	$34.85	$0.95
Sales Variance				$14.00				
SWDSOs		45.0 days				47.7 days		

appears in column 8. Figures are calculated by subtracting the receivables balances, given actual sales and budgeted collection rates, (column 7) from the actual receivables balances (column 5). Positive figures indicate the amounts by which collections of sales from that month were lower than expected. Negative figures indicate the amounts by which collections were higher than expected. In this example, lower-than-expected collections have occurred on sales made in the current month and the second and third prior months. Higher-than-expected collections have occurred on sales made in the first prior month.

Summary of the Policy Implications in this Chapter

The process of developing measures to budget, making the budget, and comparing the actual results with those budgeted is valuable primarily for its feedback on the formulation of credit policy. By comparing results with expectations, the firm gets important evidence on the effectiveness of its credit policy, and can use this evidence to make future policy decisions.

However, the value of the evidence depends in part on the accuracy of the measures the firm uses to monitor the effects of credit policy. Simple measures of discount expense, accounts receivable turnover, and bad debt expense contain inherent measurement errors that cause these measures to indicate a deviation from expectations when none has, in fact, occurred. Measures of these costs which do not introduce measurement errors are more complicated to calculate. However, the increased accuracy is almost always worth the calculation cost when compared to the results of less efficient credit policy.

Budgets for the revenues and costs that are affected by credit policy are set in accordance with the expected results of such policies. For the profit-oriented credit department, these credit policies include tradeoffs between sales volume and credit costs. Budgetary goals based on these policies are targets for the credit department, and represent the policy makers' current view of the best tradeoff among credit costs and sales. When actual credit costs are lower than budgeted, this is not a positive result unless sales targets are met.

While this chapter views monitoring and budgeting at the level of the credit department, it is often useful to decompose the department's budget to the level of the credit analyst. In this process, each individual credit analyst has his or her own budgetary goals for sales and credit costs. In this way, the performance of individual analysts in executing credit policy can be assessed, and personnel actions taken accordingly.

The monitoring and budgeting process is difficult, and may not be well understood by some credit managers, yet it is vital to effective policy formation and revision. The credit manager who can make the link among monitoring, budgeting, and policy formation will be the manager who makes the most effective credit policy.

Case for Discussion and Analysis

The Case of the Dubious DSO

It was early in July 1995, when George Kaplan, the credit manager of Intergalactic Products, received word that he had won the state's lottery, and would be paid $200,000 per year for the next 20 years. One of his coworkers commented, "That's great, George, and you're only five years from retiring on a company pension. Will you be staying until you get your pension?"

"Stay five years?" replied Kaplan, "I'm not even staying for lunch!" With that, he was off to Tahiti, stopping only to pick up his spare pair of glasses.

Unfortunately, Mr. Kaplan's good fortune and speedy departure left something of a gap in Intergalactic Products' credit department. The senior of the firm's credit analysts, Roger Thornhill, was quickly elevated to credit manager (over lunch that day, in fact), and was faced with the task of presenting the mid-year report on the condition of the firm's receivables and collections to the firm's treasurer. Mr. Kaplan had finished the calculations necessary for the report just before his departure.

Intergalactic Products has two divisions, the Zefod Division and the Prefect Division (the divisions were named for their founders, rather than for the products they sold). Zefod Division's products were sold on terms of 2 percent 10 days, net 30 days, while Prefect Division's products were sold on net 30 day terms. Sales of both divisions were growing rapidly, but Zefod Division's sales growth had been the slower of the two lately. Monthly sales histories for each of the two divisions are presented in Table 8-1C.

Because of the discount terms offered by the Zefod Division, payments were received on their invoices more quickly than those issued by the Prefect Division. The firm's budget target for accounts receivables collections was 30 days as measured by traditional DSO using quarter-ending receivable balances and aver-

Table 8-1C. Intergalactic Products: Sales by Division
(all currency figures in rounded thousands of dollars)

Month	Zefod Division			Prefect Division		
	Month's Sales	Quarter's Sales	Quarterly Growth	Month's Sales	Quarter's Sales	Quarterly Growth
October 1994	$11,000			$5,000		
November 1994	$11,500			$6,000		
December 1994	$12,000	$34,500		$5,500	$16,500	
January 1995	$11,000			$5,750		
February 1995	$11,250			$6,000		
March 1995	$13,975	$36,225	5.0%	$6,400	$18,150	10.0%
April 1995	$12,000			$6,500		
May 1995	$12,500			$6,750		
June 1995	$13,000	$37,500	3.5%	$6,500	$19,750	8.8%

Table 8-2C. Intergalactic Products

Receivables Balances at End of Quarters

	4th Quarter 1994 (12/31/94)		1st Quarter 1995 (3/31/95)		2nd Quarter 1995 (6/30/95)	
	Zefod Division	Prefect Division	Zefod Division	Prefect Division	Zefod Division	Prefect Division
Outstanding From Current Month	$5,200	$5,500	$6,321	$6,400	$6,070	$6,500
Outstanding From Prior Month	$1,750	$3,000	$1,913	$3,120	$2,250	$3,510
Outstanding From Two Months Ago	$500	$1,250	$660	$1,495	$780	$1,820
Total Receivables by Division	$7,450	$9,750	$8,894	$11,015	$9,100	$11,830
Total Receivables for the Firm		$17,200		$19,909		$20,930
Quarterly Sales by Division	$34,500	$16,500	$36,225	$18,150	$37,500	$19,750
Quarterly Sales for Firm		$51,000		$54,375		$57,250
Overall DSO (days)		30.35		32.95		32.90

age monthly sales for the quarter. This was an aggregate target in that this DSO was computed by summing receivables and sales for both divisions. Mr. Kaplan's calculations of DSOs for the past three quarters are presented in Table 8-2C.

These figures were reviewed by the treasurer and the credit manager on a quarterly basis. The treasurer was able to give Mr. Thornhill some insight into their interpretation. "We hit the 30-day DSO at the end of the fourth quarter for last year," the treasurer had said. "For the first quarter of this year, DSO was a little high at about 33 days, but George and I agreed this was probably due to the higher sales growth by the Prefect Division, which we didn't expect. I see that DSO for the second quarter is also 33 days, so I'd have to say we are basically on target."

Suggestions for Analysis

1. Discuss the two problems inherent in Intergalactic's method of measuring accounts relievable turnover, given the firm's structure and time pattern of sales.

2. Compute SWDSOs for the Zefod Division and for the Prefect Division at the end of each of the three quarters. What do these SWDSO figures tell you about collection patterns? Is the relatively more rapid growth of the Prefect Division the explanation for the slower collections? Have collection rates stabilized between the first and second quarters of 1995?

9 Credit Strategy

Prior chapters discussed various aspects of credit policy and how various policies should be evaluated. One thing that has not yet been discussed is *credit strategy*. Strategy consists of the broad overall concepts that drive policy-making.

Three aspects of strategy are discussed in this chapter. The first of these is *competitive strategy*, which is the general means by which a firm attempts to achieve superior performance, therefore enhancing the wealth of its owners. The second is *outsourcing strategy*, which concerns what necessary functions the firm should perform itself and what should be contracted to outside vendors. The third is *credit strategy for smaller firms*, which deals with the ways that smaller firms can incorporate the special circumstances they face into their credit policies.

Introduction to Competitive Strategy

Through competitive strategy, the firm seeks *sustainable competitive advantage*.[91] Sustainable competitive advantage is the means by which the firm tries to make profits beyond those routinely made by other firms in its industry. Policies for the functional units of the firm (manufacturing, sales, credit, etc.) are to flow from the firm's decisions on its competitive strategy. There are four steps in deciding on and implementing a competitive strategy: analysis of the industry, formulation of the competitive strategy, structuring the firm to achieve this strategy, and performance evaluation.

Analysis of Industry—In this step, the current structure of the industry is assessed, including the characteristics of competitors. Included among these characteristics are what products or services each competitor provides, how these products differ among competitors, what market shares each competitor holds,

---

[91] Many of the modern concepts of competitive strategy are credited to Michael E. Porter. The following discussion draws heavily on these concepts. More information can be found in Porter's texts, *Competitive Strategy*, Macmillian, 1980, and *The Competitive Advantage of Nations*, The Free Press, 1990.

and the strengths and weaknesses of each competitor. An important aspect of this assessment is the analysis of the *five forces that affect industry profitability*:

1. **The threat of substitutes.** The easier it is for other products to substitute for the products that the industry produces, the less ability the firms in the industry have to raise prices, and the lower is their profitability.

2. **The threat of new entrants.** When barriers to entering an industry are low (for example when name recognition is not required to sell products or when the amount of capital necessary to establish a firm is not large), firms not currently in an industry can enter it easily. The threat of such entry makes it difficult for the firms currently in the industry to raise prices, because they know that if they do, new firms will enter to sell at a lower price.

3. **The bargaining power of suppliers.** In some industries, only a few firms supply critical goods to the industry. In such cases, suppliers will tend to set their own prices high, and firms in the industry will be left with thin margins.

4. **The bargaining power of buyers.** Similarly, in some industries there are many firms competing for only a few customers. When this occurs, customers call the tune and the industry's selling prices tend to be low.

5. **Rivalry among competitors.** In some industries, whether they are composed of few firms or many, there is heavy price competition, which tends to drive down industry price level. In others, there is little price competition and prices tend to stay high.

Formulation of Competitive Strategy—Analyzing the industry will give the firm insight into what opportunities it has for making profits beyond those of competitors. There are generally two strategies which lead to these higher-than-average profits: *differentiation* and *cost leadership*.[92] In a differentiation strategy, the firm tries to provide a product that is different from existing products in features which customers consider important. By providing valuable features, the firm can charge a higher price and can obtain a larger margin, as long as it can keep down the cost of providing these features. (In terms of the five forces, since the product is different from that of the competition, the threat of substitute products is lower, so price can be higher.) These features may include the product's style, performance, reliability, or the credit terms under which the product is sold. Since any feature of a product or service can be copied by the competition if enough cost and effort are expended, it is important for the firm with a differentiation strategy to continuously seek new mechanisms for differentiation so as to sustain its advantage and stay ahead of its imitators.

If the firm's strategy is, instead, cost leadership, the firm tries to make extraordinary profits, not by charging a higher price, but by finding ways to provide an acceptable product at a lower production cost. This involves examining the product to find and remove superfluous features, finding new and more efficient methods of manufacture, designing products with lower manufacturing costs in mind,

---

[92] There is another dimension to competitive strategy: whether the firm focuses on a particular market segment or attempts to sell to the entire market. However, this dimension is not very relevant for formulating credit policy and, consequently, is not discussed here.

and similar tactics. Firms that use cost leadership study the production processes and costs of the competition, as well as their own, and find many ways to improve upon efficiency, which leads to lower costs.

It should be stressed that, like differentiation, cost leadership is a long-term strategy, not a temporary response to the firm's problems. Cost leadership is not a matter of realizing that the firm's costs are too high, doing a burst of cost cutting, and returning to the prior ways of doing business. Firms that successfully utilize cost leadership strategies make them an endemic part of their corporate culture. They stay ahead of the competition (which can copy any particular cost reduction) by making cost decreases an ongoing effort. They continuously search for things that will reduce cost and implement these strategies. They may make investments if these lead to lower costs. By this process, they are always ahead on costs and superior on margin.

Structuring the Firm to Achieve the Strategy—Once the competitive strategy is decided upon, it is up to the managers of the firm to make the changes in structure that are necessary to implement this strategy. They may adopt new policies, close or open plants, or change lines of authority and responsibility. The important point is that, once the firm decides to go in a particular strategic direction, this has implications for all of the firm's policies, and these policies need to be reevaluated to be in accord with the competitive strategy.

Performance Evaluation—This monitoring and adjustment step provides the firm the opportunity to judge whether its policy has been effective. The firm can then make any needed adjustments. Continuous monitoring of industry structure, on which strategy is based, is an important part of this process. Changes in this structure can occur quickly, including the emergence of new substitutes for the industry's products, changes in the behavior of competitors, etc. Each of these changes may require adjustments in strategy.

Credit Policy When the Competitive Strategy is Differentiation

Markets consist of customers with somewhat varying needs. That is, customers vary in the values they put on the various attributes of a product. Differentiation strategies try to find those attributes that most customers (or some large group of customers) value highly, and make the product distinct from the competition on those attributes. All differentiation is costly. The differentiator will have to spend money in order to enhance the aspects of the product that customers value. The key is to find attributes that customers value more than they cost to produce. The differentiator is always looking for aspects of the product that have these characteristics.

Under some circumstances, credit policy can provide a basis for differentiation.[93] That is, making the firm's credit policy different from those of the compe-

---

[93] Some additional discussion of the use of credit as a differentiator can be found in Lynn Tylczak, *Credit and Sales: The Winning Team*, NACM, 1994, pp. 2-3 and 7-8.

tition can be one of the ways in which the firm differentiates. This strategy has been used very effectively in the consumer credit sector. In this sector, there are many customers with poor credit histories who want goods but cannot pay cash. Rent-to-own firms like Colortyme provide appliances to such customers, and firms like Fingerhut sell them consumer products. Customers pay a somewhat higher price for the goods, but are granted credit they otherwise will not receive.

There are several requirements for trade credit policy to be an effective differentiator. The first requirement is that there be some relatively large set of customers for whom the availability of credit is extremely important. One group of potential customers that fits this profile are those firms that are small and/or young. For many reasons (including their higher default risk), many small and young firms find it very difficult to obtain financing from banks and other financial institutions. They are frequently starved for funds or have to pay more for funds. Consequently, when a large portion of the seller's market is composed of small and/or young firms, credit policy has the potential to provide one element of the firm's differentiation strategy. Differentiation based on credit can be granting longer terms than the competition, granting credit where the competition refuses to do so, or granting more credit than the competition.

The second requirement for credit to be an effective differentiator is that the seller must be able to provide this service at a cost that is lower than the value the customer receives. That is, the increment to margin before credit costs that results from using credit policy as a differentiator must be greater than the increase in credit costs. To determine this, a profitability analysis can be performed in the same way that a change in terms of sale was evaluated in Chapter 7. In this analysis, estimated effects on sales volume, cost of sales, and so forth are netted against estimated changes in credit costs. However, in this analysis care must be taken so that the intent of differentiation is not primarily to raise *sales volume in units* (as is typical in analysis of changes in terms of sale when terms are loosened) but instead to enable the firm to *raise the price per unit* sold. That is, the estimate of the increment to dollar sales will largely be based on a price change rather than a volume change.

The third requirement is that the firm's credit policy should be relatively difficult to copy. Unless the seller has some innate advantage over trade competitors in granting credit (such as a lower cost of capital), this is probably the most difficult requirement to fulfill. Individually, changes in terms of sale, amount of credit granted, and similar strategies, can be copied quite readily by competitors. To stay ahead, the seller must develop a *core competency* in credit management, investing in training and in personnel and innovating so that competitors are always a step behind it in credit-granting.

The fourth and final requirement is that the aspects of credit policy that are used as differentiators must be communicable to the customer. It is ineffective to invest in making a product different in some aspect if the customer cannot be told about this aspect. For differentiation based on credit to be effective, credit policy must be such that differences from those of competitors can be readily communicated to customers. Otherwise, there is no effective way for the sales force to promote these differences to potential buyers.

To summarize, when the firm chooses a competitive strategy of differentiation, credit policy should be considered (along with all other aspects of the product or service) as one means by which differentiation can be achieved. In markets where customers particularly value credit, differentiation via credit policy can be cost-effective. However, it is impossible to specify exactly how the firm should adjust its credit policy to most effectively provide this differentiation. In some circumstances, longer terms will be the best differentiator. In others, granting credit (perhaps on a secured basis) where others do not will be best. Regardless of the tool used, it is up to the credit manager to find effective ways to provide this differentiation and to innovate credit policy to stay ahead of imitators.

In other markets, the characteristics of customers or of competitors will be such that credit policy will not be an effective differentiating aspect in a differentiation strategy. When this is true, credit should be treated just as any other aspect of a product, where this aspect is not a basis for differentiation. These aspects are managed in such a way as to provide an acceptable and competitive level of value to the customer, but no more.

Credit Policy When the Competitive Strategy is Cost Leadership

When the seller's chosen competitive strategy is cost leadership, the firm seeks to control the critical drivers of each of its costs, and to reduce costs continuously, primarily via innovation. Remember that the costs affected by credit policy are credit investigation expense, discount expense, accounts receivable carrying cost, bad debt expense, and collection and administration expense. Pursuing a cost leadership strategy means that part of the job of the credit manager is to continuously examine the firm's policies to seek better ways of performing the tasks of credit management so as to reduce these costs.

Credit Investigation Expense—Innovation and cost reduction in this area can come from the choice of sources of credit information. The information revolution has provided new sources of credit information and new ways to obtain this information. The credit manager needs to evaluate these new information sources, seeking procedures that allow the credit analysts to assess creditworthiness at reduced time and cost while producing acceptable results.

While innovation is the primary means of reducing costs in a cost leadership strategy, current policies need to be reexamined frequently to see that they are cost-efficient. For example, we saw in Chapter 2 that the amount of time and money best spent on credit investigation is governed by exposure. But should this exposure figure be determined by the exposure that would result if the current order is approved (the current exposure) or by the exposure that would result if the salesperson's expectations about increased future orders come to pass (the potential exposure)?

There are advantages to each approach. Using the lower current exposure saves credit investigation costs, since salespeople's expectations about sales volumes frequently do not occur, so the higher level of credit investigation is often unnecessary. However, investigating based on potential exposures can avoid delays in shipment if future orders will require additional investigation. In a cost leadership strategy, where cost is always a concern, the credit manager will be more inclined to adopt the current exposure as a policy guideline.

Discount Expense—We saw in Chapter 7 that discount expense can serve two functions: reducing accounts receivable carrying costs and indicating creditworthiness when credit information is lacking. In a cost leadership strategy, the credit manager is very concerned about the tradeoffs involved in the first of these, and would seek the minimum discount that would do the job. While employing a cash discount as an indicator of creditworthiness can be useful, granting a discount (typically of 1 or 2 percent of sales volume) to all customers just to identify high risks may not make sense from a cost standpoint. In a cost leadership strategy, the credit manager will examine the discount policy very closely and will seek an alternative policy to identify high credit risks at lower cost.

Bad Debt Expense, Accounts Receivable Carrying Costs, and Administration and Collection Costs—These are largely determined by the firm's credit-granting policy. If the firm has adopted a cost leadership strategy, it may seem that credit granting should be restrictive, but this is not the case since such a policy will result in lower sales. Instead, the credit manager is charged with formulating credit-granting policies which will reduce the sum of these costs but produce much the same level of sales volume. The firm may use security devices to reduce bad debts, adopt innovative collection techniques, or find other ways of doing business to reduce these costs.

It should be stressed that employing a cost leadership strategy is not the same as using only credit costs to judge credit department performance. It is true that, in both, lower costs are the aim. However, there are important differences between these systems. A cost leadership strategy seeks a *permanent* lowering of *all* costs, primarily by means of innovation. These innovations are intended to produce cost reductions without affecting the attributes of the product, and thus without reducing sales volume. Judging credit department performance by costs, on the other hand, is oriented toward short-term cost reductions by any means, with less regard for the effects on sales.

In summary, when the firm's strategy is cost leadership, credit (like any other part of the firm) is seen as a potential source of cost advantage. However, cost leadership does not imply a conservative credit-granting policy. Instead, cost reductions in credit management come primarily from creativity in the design of credit policies. The creative reexamination of these policies with an eye to costs is a continuous and ongoing process.

Outsourcing Credit Functions

There are several functions which must be performed in order for the firm to produce and sell its products and services. The products must be made, they must be sold, credit must be granted to the buyer to finance the purchase, and the receivable must be collected. Outsourcing strategies concern which of these necessary functions should be performed in-house and which should be farmed out to outside vendors.[94]

While there has been much recent discussion of outsourcing as a new and innovative strategy in the business press, many routine business decisions are really outsourcing decisions under other names. All make-or-buy decisions are actually outsourcing decisions: should we make this item in-house or buy it ready made from someone else? What is relatively new in outsourcing is the consideration of whether functions which are traditionally done within the firm would, in fact, be better done outside it.

Basics of Outsourcing Credit Functions—In credit management, the traditional functions are: (1) making credit-granting decisions; (2) performing routine collections; (3) financing the accounts receivable; and (4) bearing the credit risk (that is, taking the loss if the customer defaults). Each of these functions entails costs to the firm. While many firms, particularly larger ones, have chosen to perform most of these functions in-house and bear these costs, there are alternatives to this strategy. From a profitability standpoint, whether it is advantageous or not for the firm to bear these costs depends on whether it has a comparative advantage in bearing the costs itself. (That is, whether it can do the job more cheaply than an outsider.) If not, it may be advantageous to consider contracting out the bearing of the cost to an outside agent.

Table 9-1 relates these traditional credit functions to some of the financial institutions that serve as outsourcing alternatives. This table is useful for thinking about the effects of outsourcing credit functions on the firm's costs. In it, decisions in which the firm bears most of the costs are near the top of the table, and the number of costs the firm bears decreases as one progresses down the table. Let us examine this table in more detail.

If the firm does not use any outsources, it performs all the functions and bears all costs, financing the receivable from its usual package of financing sources. Using *credit insurance* passes part of the default costs to the credit insurance company in return for the insurance premium (only part is passed because such ar-

[94] More discussion of outsourcing decisions for credit can be found in "A Broad Look at Credit Policy," CRF *Staff Report*, October 1992, and in S. L. Mian and C. W. Smith Jr., "Accounts Receivable Management: Theory and Evidence," *Journal of Finance*, March 1992, pp. 169-200.

Table 9-1.   Outsourcing Institutions for Traditional Credit Functions

Institution	Who makes the credit granting decisions?	Who performs routine collections?	Who finances the accounts receivable?	Who bears the credit risk?
None Used	Firm	Firm	Firm's General Credit	Firm
Credit Insurance	Firm	Firm	Firm's General Credit	Firm and Insurer
Accounts Receivable Secured Debt	Firm	Firm	Firm's Secured Debt	Firm
Recourse Maturity Factoring	Firm	Factor	Firm's General Credit	Firm
Recourse Advance Factoring	Firm	Factor	Factor	Firm
Non-Recourse Maturity Factoring	Factor	Factor	Firm's General Credit	Factor
Non-Recourse Advance Factoring	Factor	Factor	Factor	Factor

Source: Abstracted from S. L. Mian and C. W. Smith Jr., "Accounts Receivable Management: Theory and Evidence," *Journal of Finance*, March 1992, pp. 169-200.

rangements involve deductibles and co-payments). Financing investments in receivables via *accounts receivable secured debt* alters the financing cost of receivables investments, but the other costs are still borne by the firm. In *factoring*, the factor generally performs the collection function and bears those costs. Which party bears the costs of credit granting and of default depends on whether the factoring arrangement is *recourse factoring* or *non-recourse factoring*. When it is recourse, the firm bears the costs; when it is non-recourse, the factor bears them. With *maturity factoring*, the factor advances no funds, and the firm bears the cost of carrying the receivable until payment is received from the factor. With *advance factoring*, the factor advances most of the value of the invoice, less a product quality hold back and a factoring charge, and the firm is released from most receivables financing costs. Thus, the first line on the table (where no outsourcing is used) is the antithesis of the last (non-recourse advance factoring). For the first case, all credit costs are borne by the seller, and for the last case, virtually all credit costs are passed to the outside contractor.

To best manage outsourcing strategy, the firm needs to carefully consider which of the costs it can best bear and which may be less burdensome to have borne by others. Of course, the basis for this decision should be the comparative advantage to the firm of alternative strategies in terms of costs and other factors. The advantage of keeping a particular function in-house versus outsourcing it will depend on the characteristics of the costs involved and the firm's own circumstances. Let us consider each of the traditional credit functions in turn.

Outsourcing the Credit-Granting Decision—The question of who makes the credit-granting decision involves some relatively deep issues. Since the decision as to whom credit is granted, along with the amount and speed of collection effort, ultimately determines the level of bad debt expense, when the firm outsources the credit-granting decision, it must also outsource collections and the responsibility for bad debts. Adopting non-recourse factoring does both of these, and has been very popular in retail credit where the acceptance of MasterCard and VISA has supplanted many of the consumer credit programs previously run by individual sellers.[95]

For trade sellers, outsourcing the credit-granting decision, collections, and bad debt expense saves several sorts of costs. First, the firm can dispense with much of the staff it uses for credit analysis and collection since non-recourse factoring arrangements typically require that the seller factor most or all or its accounts receivable.[96] Along with salary costs, the out-of-pocket costs of credit analysis and collection are also saved. Finally, bad debt expenses are eliminated. For this, the factor charges a fee, often about 1.0 to 1.5 percent of the sale. This fee ex-

---

[95] While popular in retail credit, making purchases by credit cards issued to firms themselves has not yet made much headway in trade transactions, though such cards entail substantial paperwork savings. The reason appears to be that trade credit departments can administer credit more cheaply than the cost of these credit card systems. For discussion, see F. R. Bleakly, "When Corporate Purchasing Goes Plastic," *Wall Street Journal*, June 14, 1995, pp. B1 and B9.

[96] While factoring deals can be made for individual customers or groups of customers, factors usually insist on first right of refusal with respect to any potential sale. This keeps sellers from retaining low-risk accounts while passing high-risk accounts on to the factor. If the factor refuses credit, the firm can still grant credit itself. Note that while certain salary expenses are saved by factoring, some additional clerical and other expenses are required to keep records of dealings with the factor.

cludes interest expense if the seller wishes to finance via the receivable, and will vary from seller to seller, depending on the default risk of the seller's customers and other considerations.

There are three elements which determine whether non-recourse factoring is an advantageous arrangement. First and most obviously, the factor's fee needs to be compared with the cost of the firm's credit operations that will be saved if factoring is undertaken. This comparison can be made on a straight dollar-for-dollar basis, with the lowest cost solution being preferred.

Second, for sellers who for one reason or another have difficulty raising funds from outside lenders or investors, the availability of borrowing via the advance aspect of factoring has value. This borrowing may be used in one of three ways. First, it may replace more costly borrowing so the firm can save on interest expense. Second, it may expand on the total amount of available borrowing, enabling the firm to undertake valuable projects. Finally, it may by used as reserve borrowing to tide the firm over times of cash flow difficulties. It is relatively easy to assign a dollar saving to the factoring arrangement if the borrowing is used in the first way, but it is more difficult to assign a value to the savings if the second or third uses are important.[97]

The third element which determines whether non-recourse factoring is of advantage to the firm is the effect of this policy on the firm's sales volume. This is important because comparing the factor's fee to the firm's credit costs does not necessarily hold credit-granting policy constant. Customers who may be acceptable credit risks to the seller, based on the comparison of the seller's margin on sales to credit costs, may not be acceptable risks to the factor. This is so because the factor's fee is generally much smaller than the margin between the sellers' unit price and its unit cost of production. Consequently, the factor has less room to accept bad debt and other expenses in granting credit. The potential difference in credit policy can be important when the firm makes a substantial fraction of its sales to high-risk customers. If the factor declines to approve credit to these accounts, the firm may still elect to grant credit to them, and the factor will attempt to collect, though the firm is responsible for any bad debt (that is, the factoring is with recourse). However, making such credit decisions regarding high risk customers requires that some permanent credit staff be retained, reducing the cost benefits in staffing that come from factoring.

Let us perform an example analysis of the effects on expected profits from the adoption of a non-recourse maturity factoring arrangement.[98] A firm currently utilizes no outsourcing. Sales are $200 million per year, terms are net 30 days, and average collections are made in 45 days. Bad debts average 4.00 percent of receivables balance.[99] The firm's cost of capital is 12 percent per year, and costs of

---

[97] It is also vital to note the potentially detrimental effects of factoring on the borrowing availability and costs of other funding sources. When the firm factors, a valuable asset (accounts receivable) is no longer available to other creditors. Costs of borrowing from these sources many go up and availability may go down. These disadvantages must be netted against any savings.

[98] Actual factoring arrangements are negotiated individually, and are frequently both secret and relatively complex. The simplified arrangement presented here is not necessarily typical.

[99] Since receivables turn over eight times per year, this corresponds to a bad debt expense of 0.50 percent of sales.

Table 9-2. Analysis of Example Factoring Arrangement

(All figures in rounded thousands)

	Present Policy		Factoring Arrangement	
Sales		$200,000		$200,000
Cost of Sales		$160,000		$160,000
Accounts Receivable Carrying Costs:				
Expected Days to Pay	45		30	
Expected A/R Balance	$25,000		$16,667	
Cost of Capital	12.0%		12.0%	
Expected A/R Carrying Cost		$3,000		$2,000
Expected Bad Debt Expense:				
Exposure	$25,000		$833	
Default Rate	4.00%		35.00%	
Expected Bad Debt Expense		$1,000		$292
Collection and Administration Costs		$300		$100
Factor's Fee				
Fee as a Percent of Sales			1.25%	
Fee in Dollars		$0		$2,500
Earnings Before Other Costs		$35,700		$35,108
Gain in Earnings From Factoring Arrangement				($592)

sales are 80 percent of sales. Expenses for investigation, collection, and administration expenses are $300,000 per year, including salaries and all out-of-pocket costs.

A proposal has been received from a factor. The factor's fee will be 1.25 percent of sales. In this proposal, the factor will remit all invoices for all sales in 30 days. The factor will bear all bad debts for those receivables factored on a non-recourse basis. It is estimated that $190 million of the sales will be on this basis. The remaining $10 million in sales will be made on a recourse basis. These sales involve high credit risk, and it is expected that bad debts will average 35 percent of receivables balances from these customers.[100] If the factoring arrangement is undertaken, it is expected that investigation, collection, and administration costs will be reduced to $100,000 per year. This proposal is for maturity factoring only, so the factoring arrangement will have no effect on the selling firm's cost or availability of debt.

A profitability analysis of the factor's proposal relative to the firm's current policy is given in Table 9-2. The calculations are the same as those in the profitability analyses presented in prior chapters, except for bad debt. Without the factor, the firm is exposed to bad debt expense on all of its receivables. The expected bad debt expense is its receivables balance of $25 million times the default rate of 4 percent for an expected bad debt of $1 million. With the factor, the exposure to bad debt is only on the receivables factored with recourse, which

---

[100] With a 30-day turnover, this corresponds to a bad debt expense of 35/12 = 2.92 percent of sales to these customers.

total about $833,000 (= $10 million in sales divided by turnover of 12 times per year). With a 35 percent default rate on these receivables only, the expected bad debt expense is approximately $292,000.

In this example, the factoring arrangement reduces earnings by about $592,000, and is not advantageous. It is important to note that this example is for maturity factoring, and consequently no gains have been included due to the financing effects of factoring. If this were instead advance factoring, dollar figures representing any such gains would be included in the analysis.

Outsourcing Routine Collections—Routine collections are those where the special expertise of a collection agency (in skip tracing, filing suit, attaching assets, etc.) is not required. Using any sort of factoring outsources these collections to the factor; maturity factoring with recourse affects only this aspect of credit management. Factors possess great expertise in collections, and can do them very efficiently, in some cases resulting in factoring fees that are lower than the firm's collection expenses. A straightforward cost comparison is sufficient to detect such situations.

Outsourcing the Financing of Receivables—While advance factoring moves the financing of the receivable asset from the seller to the outsource, this result can also be achieved by the use of accounts receivable secured debt. To utilize this mechanism, large firms can issue special classes of debt secured by their receivables assets. Smaller firms can grant a general lien or a lien against specific receivables to a financial institution such as a bank. The bank will then allow the firm to borrow up to a certain fraction (often 80 percent) of the receivables balance. The more liquid and creditworthy are the receivables, the larger this fraction. As receivables are paid, new receivables are pledged to keep the borrowing available.

As with advance factoring, using accounts receivable secured debt can increase the amount the firm can borrow, allow borrowing when none was previously available, or reduce the cost of borrowing. However, these advantages must be weighed against two disadvantages: (1) the detrimental effects of pledging a valuable asset on the firm's other borrowings and (2) the clerical costs involved in using accounts receivable secured debt.

With regard to the clerical costs, the advantage to the lender that lends against accounts receivable is that the high quality of the receivables asset means the losses in default are reduced. But to assure the lender of this quality on a continuing basis, a steady flow of information is required between the borrower and the lender. This information advises the lender of which accounts receivable have been paid and what new receivables have been generated, including identification of the customers from whom the receivables are due and the amounts of these receivables. The cost that this continuous accumulation and transmission of information entails for the seller depends on the sophistication of the seller's accounts receivable system. Some systems can generate these data quickly and cheaply while others cannot. Also, there may be other costs in addition to these

Table 9-3.   Analysis of Example Accounts Receivable Secured Debt Arrangement

	Current Borrowing Arrangement	Secured Borrowing Arrangement
Amount of Available Borrowing	$150,000	$240,000
Increase in Available Borrowing		$90,000
Expected Rate of Earnings on Increase		15%
Expected Earnings From Increased Availability		$13,500
Interest rate	10.00%	9.00%
Interest Cost	$15,000	$21,600
Application Fee		$1,000
Increase in Clerical Costs		$2,500
Yearly Costs Net of Increase in Earnings	$15,000	$11,600
Expected Increase in Earnings From Secured Arrangement		$3,400

clerical expenses; some banks charge a fixed yearly fee for administering these borrowings, regardless of the amount borrowed.

Let us analyze an example in the use of accounts receivable secured debt. A firm currently borrows under an unsecured line from its bank. The expected interest rate on this line for next year is 10 percent, and the firm expects to borrow an average of $150,000, the maximum that the bank will allow. The firm has approached the bank with the proposition of pledging its accounts receivable, on which the average balance is $300,000. The bank advises that it will lend up to 80 percent of the value of the accounts receivable, at an expected interest rate of 9 percent. The bank will also require a $1,000 application and administration fee. If the loan against receivables is made, the unsecured credit line will be withdrawn. The firm expects to borrow the maximum amount on the receivables loan and to earn 15 percent on its investment of the additional funding. It expects that the clerical costs of furnishing the bank with reports on its receivables will be $2,500 per year.

Analysis is provided in Table 9-3. The amount to be borrowed under the accounts receivable secured financing is $240,000 (= 80 percent of $300,000). This is a $90,000 increase in borrowing, and the firm expects to earn 15 percent on this money, increasing earnings by $13,500. The net effect on earnings is calculated as the sum of the interest, application, and clerical costs of each borrowing arrangement, net of this increase in earnings. Since this net effect reduces costs by $3,400, the secured borrowing is advantageous. (However, it should be noted that this analysis ignores any effects of the secured arrangement on borrowings from sources other than the bank.)

Outsourcing the Bearing of Credit Risk—Both non-recourse factoring and the use of credit insurance will pass part of the default risk to an outside party.[101]

---

[101] The discussion here is oriented toward the use of credit insurance in connection with domestic sales. Credit insurance is also available for export sales. In addition to default risk, export credit insurance also covers losses from other risks associated with exporting, such as a change in a country's political policies which inhibits customers within that country from making payments to creditors in other countries.

However, when using credit insurance (unlike non-recourse factoring), the seller retains the collection functions and a good part of the credit-granting decision.

To see why the use of credit insurance covers only part of the bad debt loss and why the seller retains only part of the credit-granting decision, it is important to understand roughly how credit insurance works.[102] Credit insurance for domestic sales may cover the entire receivables portfolio or only selected accounts. However, how much of the actual bad debt expense is insured depends on the specifics of the coverage and largely determines the premium that will be charged for the coverage. Insurers view some level of bad debt expense as a normal and expected cost of doing business, and bad debt insurance is seen by them as protecting against the kind of *catastrophic* unexpected loss that can topple the creditor as well as the debtor.[103] (Insurers can bear these large losses better than some firms because they have large portfolios and are diversified among various lines of business.) When the insurance is structured so that its deductible represents expected losses, premiums are fairly low, sometimes as low as 0.1 percent of sales. Policies with lower deductibles have higher premiums, sometimes 1.25 percent of sales or more.[104] That is, to get reasonable premium levels, firms are required to retain part of their bad debt expense even if they are insured.

The reason why the selling firm retains only part of the credit-granting decision relates to what happens after the insurance contract is signed. Once the contract is in place, it would not be wise for the insurer to allow the seller to grant unrestrained credit, because some sellers might grant credit to very risky accounts, increasing the default risk in the receivables portfolio beyond that for which premiums were determined. To counter this potential problem, the insurance policy will specify the maximum amounts of credit to be granted to customers of various levels of default risk. The seller may make credit granting decisions but must adhere to these guidelines. If it does, the insurance company will pay the firm a prespecified percent (frequently 90 percent) of the bad debt loss in excess of the cumulative yearly deductible within 60 days of the loss over the one-year life of the typical contract.

When analyzing the desirability of credit insurance, besides its effects on bad debt loss, it is also necessary to understand its relationship to accounts receivable secured borrowing. In accounts receivable secured borrowing, the fraction of the accounts receivable balance that the bank is willing to advance and the interest rate charged depend on the quality of the receivables asset. By purchasing credit insurance, the quality of this asset is enhanced, and better terms on secured borrowings can result.

Analysis of the advantageousness of credit insurance centers on its effects on costs: its premium costs, the deductible bad debt that remains uncovered, the

---

[102] Good discussions of the basics of credit insurance can be found in C. Carey, "Enter the Brave New World of Business Insurance," *Business Credit*, February 1993, pp. 38-39, and A. Starchild, "Insurance Can Minimize Your Bad Debt Losses," *Business Credit*, March 1993, p. 22.

[103] This possibility is called the "domino effect" and is also discussed in Chapter 5.

[104] It should be noted that there is a small tax timing advantage in paying the premiums rather than incurring the bad debt expense because the premiums are immediately deductible while the bad debts are not deductible for tax purposes until they are actually realized.

Table 9-4.   Analysis of Effects of Credit Insurance on Accounts Receivable Secured Debt

(all dollar figures in rounded thousands)

	Current Borrowing Arrangement	Borrowing Arrangement with Credit Insurance
Sales	$120,000	$120,000
Receivables Balance	$15,000	$15,000
Advance Fraction	80%	90%
Amount of Available Borrowing	$12,000	$13,500
Increase in Available Borrowing		$1,500
Expected Rate of Earnings on Increase		16%
Expected Earnings from Increased Availability		$240
Interest Rate	12.00%	11.50%
Interest Cost	$1,440	$1,553
Insurance Cost, Percent of Sales		0.50%
Insurance Cost, Dollars		$600
Yearly Costs Net of Increase in Earnings	$1,440	$1,913
Expected Increase in Earnings from Credit Insurance		($473)

fraction of the bad debt covered in excess of the deductible, its effect on borrowing costs and availability, its effects on sales volumes to marginal customers, and the risk reduction that its catastrophic coverage provides. While the dollar value of most of these can be estimated relatively easily, the merit of the last is more difficult to estimate. The value of the catastrophic coverage depends on the types and costs of the difficulties the firm would experience if large defaults occur. It is hard to assign a dollar value to these difficulties before the fact.

Table 9-4 presents an analysis of an example which centers on the effects of credit insurance on secured borrowings. In the example, the firm has been offered credit insurance coverage for bad debt expenses beyond their expected level. Sales are $120 million per year. This coverage will not result in the firm making any additional sales to marginal accounts, and will cost 0.5 percent of sales. By undertaking this coverage, the firm will be able to increase its borrowings from 80 percent of its accounts receivable balance of $15 million to 90 percent of this balance. The firm expects the additional funding to return 16 percent per year. The insurance will also enable the firm to reduce the interest rate of these borrowings from 12.0 percent per year to 11.5 percent per year.

Since the coverage is deductible at the level of expected bad debt expense, no reduction in expected bad debt expense is shown in this analysis. For this example, the gains from changes in the firm's accounts receivable secured borrowings are not sufficient to make the use of credit insurance advantageous.

Combining More Than One Outsource—While the prior discussion has usually dealt with each of the outsourcing institutions independently, there is no reason why they cannot be used in combination to partition the traditional credit functions in ways the firm finds attractive. The combination of credit insurance with accounts receivable secured debt in the prior example is one possibility, but other strategies can also be used. For example, the firm wishing to retain its credit-granting decisions (partly, at least) while outsourcing collections, financing, and risk bearing could combine recourse advance factoring with credit insurance. Strategies like these are evaluated as with single outsourcings: their costs and benefits are compared with those of performing these functions in-house.

Summary of Outsourcing—Credit policy questions are usually phrased in terms of *how*. *How* should credit granting decisions be made? *How* should receivables be collected? *How* should receivables financing cost be controlled? *How* should we address credit risk? The questions are formed in this way because most trade credit granting is done such that the selling firm bears all the costs of credit granting.

Outsourcing considerations suggest that the credit policy maker back up a step and ask *whether* it is in the interests of the selling firm to bear these costs *at all*. It is only in the case where the selling firm can bear these costs more advantageously than can an outside contractor that it makes sense for the firm to bear them.

Credit Strategies for Smaller Firms[105]

Small and large firms are different in a number of real and important ways. In this section, we consider the impact of two of these differences on the most major of the firm's credit strategies: credit investigation decisions, credit-granting decisions, and terms of sale decisions.

The first difference is that small firms are at a disadvantage in using credit management strategies which require the firm to commit to spending fixed costs of one sort or another to reduce credit-related costs. They are at this disadvantage because many credit-related costs (such as accounts receivable carrying costs and bad debt expense) are proportional to sales volume. Smaller firms have smaller sales volumes. Therefore, they will find strategies which entail fixed costs of less advantage than would larger firms.

A chief example of this problem is in the hiring of full-time expert credit personnel. An expert credit manager enhances profitability by accurately assessing credit costs and comparing them to profit margins. However, the salary of such a manager represents a fixed cost to the firm. For sales volumes below a certain level, it is more advantageous to make credit decisions less expertly and to bear the additional credit-related costs. Small firms which have sales volume below this level, and who consequently cannot economically hire an experienced full-time credit manager, need to find cost-effective ways of making credit decisions with less-experienced or part-time credit personnel. Contributing to this problem is the fact that most small business owners are far more knowledgeable about

---

[105] See Frederick C. Scherr, "Credit Management Strategies for Small Firms," *Journal of Small Business Strategy*, Fall 1995, for a more extensive discussion of this topic.

the production and marketing sides of the business than they are in finance, and consequently can provide little guidance to employees on credit matters.

The second difference between larger and smaller firms is that smaller firms have less access to financing from capital markets and financial institutions. This affects credit strategy in two ways. First, the smaller firm is more reliant on its internal cash flows and cash reserves to provide financing for expansion and to tide it over during periods of poor financial performance. It will be more averse to credit policies which put these cash flows at risk than will larger firms. (That is, smaller firms are more subject to the domino effect than larger firms.) Second, because they have access to fewer and more expensive sources of outside funding, the smaller firm will be more favorably deposed to credit strategies which allow it to gain additional borrowing capacity.

Credit Investigation Decisions—If the small firm elects to perform this function internally, the important questions it faces revolve around the type and amount of credit information that is to be collected. With respect to type, the smaller firm is less likely to have the experienced personnel necessary to integrate various pieces of credit information into an assessment of credit risk. Consequently, the small firm needs to select sources of credit information which require less integration, even if these sources cost a bit more or incorporate the various aspects of creditworthiness in a rougher fashion than would an experienced credit manager. Credit agency ratings and reports have these characteristics, and the smaller firm might choose to rely on these more heavily than a larger firm.

With respect to the amount of information collected, the smaller firm's greater susceptibility to the domino effect makes it more averse to credit risk than larger firms. Consequently, it is in the smaller firm's interest to spend more time and money on credit investigation than a larger firm. That is, the level of exposure necessary to trigger additional credit investigation should be lower for a smaller firm than for a larger firm.

Rather than perform credit investigation within the firm, the small firm can outsource this decision (and all other aspects of credit granting) by utilizing non-recourse factoring. While only a small fraction of smaller firms currently use this outsource, more should probably consider it, since it addresses many aspects of the small firm's special problems. Since the factor's expertise is applied to the receivables from many smaller firms, factoring provides expert decision-making without each firm having to cover the entire fixed cost of the expert.[106] Further, this process outsources the bearing of the credit risk, defeating the domino effect. Finally, factoring allows the firm the option of using maturity factoring as a source of outside funding. This is particularly valuable to the small firm because of its limited sources of funding. Of course, the advantage of non-recourse factoring to the small firm must be compared to its costs, and factoring is not cheap. When performing this cost comparison, the small firm needs to keep in mind

---

[106] Sharing a credit manager with other small firms (co-hiring) also accomplishes this purpose and should be considered.

that there are really two parts of the advance factor's fee: the part that compensates the factor for taking over the credit functions and the part that represents the interest on borrowings. If the firm does not intend to borrow from the factor, only the first part of the fee is relevant for cost comparison purposes.

Credit-Granting Decisions—Once credit investigation has been performed, the credit-granting decision must be made. There is little way to outsource this decision except to use non-recourse factoring. If the decision process is kept within the firm, because of the limited expertise of the credit personnel there are substantial advantages to the smaller firm in utilizing expert systems or using public-domain or commercial statistical scoring models. While these approaches to the credit-granting problem will not generally produce as accurate a decision as an expert credit manager, they are simple to use and do not entail substantial fixed costs.

With respect to the amount of credit granted, the importance of the domino effect argues that smaller firms should assign lower risk-based credit limits than would be granted by larger firms. However, the smaller firm can outsource this problem by obtaining credit insurance, which transfers the credit risk to someone more able to bear it. Because the intent of such an insurance strategy is to avoid the large loss that threatens the selling firm's survival, it is best to obtain a policy that covers only the firm's larger customers. Premiums can be reduced by incorporating a fairly large deductible, since it is the catastrophic loss that is targeted, not everyday losses in smaller amounts.

Terms of Sale Decisions—Because of their limited access to capital markets, terms that bring in cash more quickly are advantageous to smaller firms, even if they must charge a slightly lower price than competitors in order to make sales on these terms. Cash discounts also have more appeal to small firms than large ones for two reasons. First, smaller firms have higher costs of capital due to higher costs of borrowing, resulting in higher costs of carrying accounts receivable. Therefore, they have more to gain by bringing in cash more quickly, which a cash discount accomplishes. Second, the informational function of the cash discount (customers who do not take the cash discount are more likely to be in financial trouble) is more important for the smaller firm than for the large because of the smaller firm's more limited ability to evaluate creditworthiness.

These recommendations for credit strategy are summarized in Table 9-5. In general, smaller firms need to: (1) adopt credit strategies which require less expertise of credit personnel (even if these strategies are somewhat less accurate in producing credit decisions) and (2) find ways to limit or outsource credit risk, which can destroy the smaller firm.

Table 9-5. Suggestions for Credit Strategies for Smaller Firms

Area of Strategy	Suggestions
Credit Investigation	1. Consider using sources of credit information which, in themselves, relate this information to an assessment of credit risk, even if these sources cost a little more and the assessments of credit risk they provide are approximate.
	2. Because credit risk is inordinately important, perform a very extensive credit investigation of all large customers.
	3. Consider non-recourse factoring to outsource credit investigation and credit-granting decisions, to outsource the bearing of credit risk, and to provide financing.
Credit Granting	1. Consider using expert systems, public-domain scoring models, or commercial scoring models to limit the expertise required to make this decision, even though these models are limited in accuracy and domain.
	2. Consider imposing risk-based credit limits or purchasing credit insurance to control the domino effect.
	3. Consider non-recourse factoring to outsource credit investigation and credit-granting decisions, to outsource the bearing of credit risk, and to provide financing.
Terms of Sale	1. Use shorter terms to bring in money faster, even if price must be reduced.
	2. Consider using cash discount terms to bring in money faster and to indicate which customers are in poor financial position.

Summary of the Policy Implications in this Chapter

Strategy gives the general direction from which policy is derived. In this chapter, three aspects of strategy were discussed: competitive strategy, outsourcing strategy, and credit strategy for smaller firms. The first of these, competitive strategy, is about the general means a firm uses to make extraordinary profits. After analyzing its industry, the firm chooses one of two broad strategies: either differentiation or cost leadership. If it chooses differentiation, it makes its products unique in some of the important features that customers value. In some markets, credit can be one of these features. When credit is used as a differentiator, the credit department must adopt policies that make the firm's credit-granting different from and superior to that of its competitors. It is expected that credit costs will be higher than normal, but the firm recoups this by charging a premium price.

However, there are few differentiation strategies that cannot be eventually copied, credit strategies included. Consequently, when credit is used as a differentiator, the credit department must continuously search for new ways to provide superior service and maintain differentiation. If the firm adopts a differentiation strategy but market conditions are not such that credit is a useful differentiator, then the goal of credit policy is to provide an adequate level of credit to support the firm's sales at a reasonable cost.

If the firm's strategy is cost leadership, a quite different view of credit policy is required. In this strategy, the firm attains superior returns by charging the same price as competitors for its products or services but produces these at a lower unit cost. Firms that utilize cost leadership require that all the parts of the firm (the credit department included) are continuously searching for ways to reduce unit costs. It is extremely important that this process of cost reduction be an ongoing and continuous part of the firm's culture: it is by continuous innovation that costs are reduced. The credit department seeks to reduce costs by finding new and more efficient ways to perform credit investigation, to reduce bad debts, and so forth. However, this search must not lead to a deterioration in sales volume. The idea is to produce the same sales volume at a lower credit cost.

One set of strategies that may allow the firm to reduce credit costs are those which involve outsourcing. Traditionally, firms have performed all the important credit functions internally (making credit-granting decisions, performing collections, financing the receivable, and bearing the credit risk), bearing their entire cost. However, there are financial institutions (factors, insurers, and banks) that for various reasons may be better equipped to do these jobs than the firm itself. These institutions may have more expertise than the firm in one area or another, they may have a larger or more diversified receivables portfolio which makes them more able to bear credit risk, or they may enjoy returns to scale advantages due to their larger size.

Some institutional arrangements (such as non-recourse factoring) entail farming out almost all of the credit functions, while others (such as credit insurance) outsource only one of these functions. The firm may choose to use these arrangements separately or in combination to achieve superior results. The challenge in considering these outsourcing alternatives is to identify and compare the benefits and costs of outsourcing a function or functions with those of performing operations within the firm.

Outsourcing strategies are particularly useful for smaller firms. Smaller firms face two problems in formulating their credit strategies that larger firms do not face. First, the smaller size of their receivables portfolios (with consequently lower bad debts and accounts receivable carrying costs) mean that it is less advantageous for them to invest in the development of in-house credit expertise. They need to find methods of making credit decisions that are simpler, even if these decisions are not the best that could be made. Thus, purchasing summarized credit information and employing scoring or expert systems for making decisions has more appeal to them than to the larger firm. Also, outsourcing collection and credit-granting decisions to a factor may make sense for the smaller firm.

Factoring and the use of accounts receivable secured debt also addresses the second problem of small firms that affects their credit strategy: outside sources of funding provide financing to them only at higher cost and under more restrictive terms. This means that small firms must take greater care to safeguard the firm's cash flow and be on the lookout for credit strategies that allow them additional financing. Factors do both of these by bearing the credit risk and advancing funds against receivables. Restrictive credit policies, assignment of risk-based credit limits, and the purchase of credit insurance also act to safeguard the firm's cash flow from catastrophic bad debts.

Unfortunately, strategy is one of the aspects of management that frequently does not get the attention it deserves. In addressing everyday problems, it is easy to neglect the big picture. But without a clear strategy, mediocre results are the best that can be expected. Formation of strategy requires that decision-makers put aside immediate concerns and form a clear notion of the direction that the firm should move, given its circumstances. Innovation and nontraditional thinking is the key: if everyone else is doing it, it cannot be a source of advantage. Instead, management needs to find ways to do things differently—and better.

Case for Discussion and Analysis

The Case of the Financing Factor

Minute Manufacturing was a small firm with $12 million in sales. The firm was organized in a simple fashion: Mr. Minute, the owner, made all strategy and policy decisions. The only other executives (besides Mr. Minute) were the production supervisors. The balance of the firm's staff was clerical or production employees. The firm's accounting and payroll were handled by a local accounting firm.

Credit decisions were made by one of the clerical employees using Dun & Bradstreet reports and commercial trade clearances as sources of information. This employee also performed collections. The firm's credit policy was relatively simple. A D&B report and trade clearance were ordered on all new customers. If the D&B report showed there were no suits against the customer and it had been in business for more than 10 years, and the trade clearance showed it generally paid in less than 90 days, credit was granted for exposures up to $5,000. If orders were such that exposures would be greater than $5,000, the credit file was taken to Mr. Minute for a decision. Mr. Minute almost always approved the requested credit. Expenses for credit reports and trade clearance were $20,000 per year.

This policy resulted in the firm suffering bad debts of about 3 percent of sales and receivables turnover of about 60 days (terms were net 30 days). These figures seemed high to Mr. Minute, and contacts with managers in other firms in his line of business suggested their bad debts were lower and their turnovers were faster. Mr. Minute's areas of expertise were not in finance, but he recognized his limitations and knew the firm's relatively simple credit strategy was likely the problem. He simply did not know enough to make good credit decisions.

Also, the problem in managing credit was symptomatic of other problems he also faced. Minute Manufacturing was growing and had reached a size where it was really too large for him to manage without the aid of other managers. While giving up parts of the management process to professionals was a wrenching process, he felt that something needed to be done in credit and in other areas. Further, he was very worried that a large loss would bankrupt his firm. The firm's receivables of $2 million included 10 customers with balances over $75,000. The rest of the customers had balances of much lower amounts. If any two of the larger customers defaulted, the firm would be in real trouble.

After consulting with his accountant and making some telephone calls, Mr. Minute devised two plans which would address the problem. In the first plan, he would hire a professional credit manager, at a yearly cost of $65,000 including benefits. The clerical employee who currently assisted with credit would be assigned to assist the new credit manager.

Mr. Minute anticipated the credit manager would be able to make decisions that would reduce bad debts to 1.0 percent of sales and receivables turnover to 45 days. (These figures came from conversations with other business owners in the same line of business who employed credit managers.) He knew the credit manager would achieve these figures partly by reducing credit to the riskiest customers, and expected the firm's sales would fall by $500,000 as a result. This reduction would come entirely from sales to smaller customers. He expected the credit manager to achieve these results using the same amount of credit investigation expense the firm currently spent, but spending the money more effectively. He also expected that the out-of-pocket costs of collection would be $10,000, as they currently were. To address the credit risk problem, he intended to take out credit insurance on his 10 largest customers, to whom he sold $6 million per year. His inquiry to a credit insurance firm indicated the cost of insurance would be 0.75 percent of sales to these customers.

The second alternative was to factor the firm's receivables on a non-recourse basis. In this system, the current clerical employee would be reassigned to do the factoring paperwork, but no additional employees would be hired. As with the first plan, he expected that customers representing $500,000 in sales would not be granted credit by the factor, and he saw no advantage in granting them credit on a recourse basis. The factor would handle all credit investigation and collection and would bear all bad debt expenses. For these services, the factor would charge a fee of 2 percent of the firm's sales.

An additional advantage of the factoring arrangement was the financing to be provided: this was to be non-recourse maturity factoring. The factor would advance the firm 90 percent of the value of receivables, the remaining 10 percent being a quality holdback which would be paid to the firm in 45 days. The interest charged on the advance was 12 percent, paid on the amount advanced from the date of the sale to the maturity of the invoice. Mr. Minute expected that he would be able to earn 15 percent with these funds. This new financing arrangement would not affect any of the firm's other borrowings.

Suggestions for Analysis

1. Use profitability analysis to determine the earnings advantage of each of the two plans over the firm's current policies. (Note that the current policy will not be continued in any case because it exposes Minute Manufacturing to unacceptable credit risk.) Use $12 million per year as expected sales under the current policy. Ignore the clerical expense since this is common to all situations. Assume that the firm's costs of sales are 75 percent of sales and that the firm's cost of capital is 13 percent per year. Indicate which of the two plans is most advantageous.

2. Discuss the use of discount terms in combination with credit insurance to address the firm's credit problems. What would be the costs and benefits of this strategy?

Index

S

T

U

V

Z

About the Author

Dr. Frederick C. Scherr holds a B.S. in Industrial Engineering from Rensselaer Polytechnic Institute and an MBA and a Ph.D. from the University of Pittsburgh. He is currently a Professor of Finance at West Virginia University, where he has won awards for his teaching and research. His work experience includes time as an assistant credit manager for a Fortune 500 firm. He has authored numerous articles, including academic works and publications in *Business Credit, Credit Research Digest,* and *Credit and Financial Management Review.* He has taught extensively in NACM's executive education programs. This is his fourth book.

CPSIA information can be obtained
at www.ICGtesting.com
Printed in the USA
FFOW01n1244010717
37387FF